BRITISH AND IRISH AUTHORS

Introductory critical studies

SAMUEL RICHARDSON

This book provides a concise introduction to Richardson, by combining a close reading of *Pamela*, *Clarissa*, and *Sir Charles Grandison* with a discussion of their central themes.

An outsider by birth, education and profession, Richardson found common cause with women in a world that needed change. Employing forms familiar to them, letters and tales of courtship and marriage, he urged his readers to train their powers of reason and morality by debating the issues of his novels. Dr Harris explores Richardson's vision that the relationship between men and women is as politically charged as that between monarch and subject. In *Clarissa* this relationship is imaginatively represented by means of the characters' archetypes – Eve, Lucretia and Queen Elizabeth on the one hand, Satan, Don Juan, Faust and King on the other. In *Grandison*, Richardson shows men what they must be if they wish to marry women like Clarissa, and argues that marriage, then the necessary female destiny, can only thus be made to work to women's advantage.

T0371461

BRITISH AND IRISH AUTHORS
Introductory critical studies

In the same series:

SAMUEL RICHARDSON

JOCELYN HARRIS

Associate Professor in English,
University of Otago

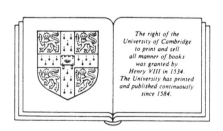

The right of the
University of Cambridge
to print and sell
all manner of books
was granted by
Henry VIII in 1534.
The University has printed
and published continuously
since 1584.

CAMBRIDGE UNIVERSITY PRESS

CAMBRIDGE

NEW YORK   PORT CHESTER

MELBOURNE   SYDNEY

CAMBRIDGE UNIVERSITY PRESS
Cambridge, New York, Melbourne, Madrid, Cape Town, Singapore, São Paulo, Delhi

Cambridge University Press
The Edinburgh Building, Cambridge CB2 8RU, UK

Published in the United States of America by Cambridge University Press, New York

www.cambridge.org
Information on this title: www.cambridge.org/9780521315425

First published 1987
Reprinted 1989
Re-issued in this digitally printed version 2009

A catalogue record for this publication is available from the British Library

Library of Congress Cataloguing in Publication data

Harris, Jocelyn.
Samuel Richardson
(British and Irish authors : introductory critical
studies)
Bibliography.
Includes index.
1. Richardson, Samuel, 1699—1761 — Criticism and
interpretation.   I. Title.   II. Series: British and
Irish authors.
PR3667.H37   1987   823'.6   86—17126

ISBN 978-0-521-30501-3 hardback
ISBN 978-0-521-31542-5 paperback

For John, James, and Lison Harris

Contents

Preface

References are to the first edition *Pamela* edited by T. C. Duncan Eaves and Ben D. Kimpel (Houghton Mifflin, Boston, 1971), a photographic reproduction of the 1801 *Pamela in her Exalted Condition* (Garland, New York and London, 1974), a modernised first edition reprint in one volume of *Clarissa* edited by Angus Ross (Penguin and Viking, Middlesex and New York, 1985), the first edition reprint of *The History of Sir Charles Grandison* in three parts, edited by Jocelyn Harris (Oxford English Novels, London, New York and Toronto, 1972, repr. 1986), *Selected Letters of Samuel Richardson*, edited by John Carroll (Clarendon Press, Oxford, 1964), T. C. Duncan Eaves and Ben D. Kimpel, *Samuel Richardson: A Biography* (Clarendon Press, Oxford, 1971), and John Locke, *Two Treatises of Government*, edited by Peter Laslett (Cambridge University Press, New York, 1960, repr. 1965). Locke references are to section numbers.

It is a pleasure to recollect how many people have helped me during the Richardson years. My most long-standing debts are to Margaret Dalziel, Alan Horsman, Duncan Isles, and the late Geoffrey Tillotson, my most recent to Terence Moore, Claude Rawson, Pat Rogers and Angus Ross. Ian Donaldson, Margaret Anne Doody, Jonathan Lamb, Michael Neill, Ruth Perry, Peter Sabor, and Marijke Rudnik-Smalbraak were true friends who never changed the subject too soon. The University of Otago was generous with its leave, and Susan Ash, Annabel Cooper and Mary Sullivan gave essential aid, at the end. All error, though, is mine.

J. M. H.
Grenoble and Dunedin, 31 December 1985.

A chronology of Samuel Richardson

1689	Born in Derbyshire, the son of a joiner
1701–2	Writes love-letters for neighbourhood girls and moral stories for friends. Educated at Merchant Taylors'?
1706–13	Apprenticed to John Wilde, a notable printer
1718 or	
1719	Sets up own printing house in Fleet Street
1721	Marries his master's daughter; five sons and a daughter will die in infancy, and his wife in 1731
1723	Establishes himself in Salisbury Court, and prospers. Soon printing for Parliament, the Society for the Encouragement of Learning, and the Royal Society; will edit as well as print works by Defoe, L'Estrange, and Sir Thomas Roe
1732	Writes *The Apprentice's Vade Mecum* for the Stationers' Company
1733	Marries again; a son will die in infancy and four daughters survive
1740	*Pamela* I–II published, an immediate success. Richardson revises it for the rest of his life
1741	Publishes *Familiar Letters*, from which *Pamela* had sprung
1742	*Pamela* III–IV
1747	(1 December) *Clarissa* I–II published, amid copious debates
1748	(28 April) *Clarissa* III–IV; correspondents beg for her life (6 December) *Clarissa* V–VII
1749–54	Debates on *Clarissa* and *Tom Jones* slide into the writing of *Sir Charles Grandison*
1750	Publishes *Meditations on the Sacred Books . . . mentioned in Clarissa*
1751	Contributes No. 97 to Johnson's *Rambler*; publishes a volume of 'restorations' to *Clarissa*, which will be incorporated into the later revised editions
1753	Publishes *Sir Charles Grandison*, which he will at once start to revise; fends off an Irish piracy of the work

1755   *A Collection of the Moral and Instructive Sentiments . . .*
          Contained in the Histories of Pamela, Clarissa, and Sir
          Charles Grandison
1761   (4 July) Richardson dies, and is buried in St
          Bride's, Fleet Street

Introduction

In his own day Samuel Richardson was read and admired by all
kinds of people, from the King to a small boy who liked eating
gingernuts. His reputation soon fell precipitously away. A recent
renewal of interest drew attention first to the solidity of his worlds
and to the perceptiveness, which some called confessional, of his
psychological understanding. Later admirers, dissatisfied with this
reduction of his work to document or naive self-exposure, explain
its place in English literature and ideas, or point out how very well
he wrote. Still others apply psychoanalysis, Marxism, feminism,
semiotics, hermeneutic criticism and reader response theories to
Richardson, who is great enough to reward them all. The gap between 'humanists' who recover a deliberate artist and 'subversives'
who discover a modern man need not, however, exist if we can agree
that wherever we turn in the symbolism of the unconscious, the
politics of property or of sex, the subjectivity of reading, the
philosophy of signs, and the meaning of meaning, Richardson has
usually been there first. In the hope of reconciling historical explanation with present-day critical concerns, I shall therefore work
closely from Richardson's own words to explore the ideas that in-
form his novels and the strategies that present them.

Richardson's image as a sober middle-class printer is deceptive,
for the life he gives to radical ideas about hierarchy, power, education and reform demonstrates a considerable awareness of the intellectual and political ferment which had existed since the Civil
War. His father was 'personally beloved' by that unlikely leader
of the last great peasant revolt, the Duke of Monmouth (Carroll,
p. 228), and he himself printed in the 1720s a periodical called *The
True Briton*, which supported the English liberties guaranteed by
the Glorious Revolution of 1688 and attacked the government of
the day for upsetting the balance of power. Richardson wrote
elsewhere that he 'always gave that Preference to the Principles of
LIBERTY, which we hope will for ever be the distinguishing
Characteristic of a *Briton*' (Eaves and Kimpel, pp. 29–35). The
vocabulary, though vague, refers specifically to the traditional hope
of seventeenth-century revolutionaries that England would be

1

relieved of the Norman yoke and restored to its ancient Anglo-Saxon birthright of liberty. This suggests that Richardson was not untouched by the millenarian dreams that his father must have known.

The approaching millennium, it was thought, would reverse the disastrous effect of the Fall and restore a Golden Age of brotherhood, justice and innocence.[1] The means was education, a general dissemination of knowledge which, being at once understood by all reasonable men, would bring about a change of heart and a paradise within. As a printer, Richardson took an essential part in the advancement of learning. For instance, he printed books of science, medicine, travel and the transactions of the Royal Society – that is, the kind of works whose tendency was to reveal truth and restore the purity of the word. The harbinger of the millennium was said to be a growing and general depravity, which Richardson, as well as many others in his time, earnestly believed in. Its warning could be a comet, and its manifestations would be the defeat of avarice and luxury, and the unmasking of Anti-Christ by providential agents. The consequent community of the saints would be marked by a benevolence as universal as the sun's impartial rays, by the disappearance of slavery and hierarchy (especially that created by property and the universities), by the conversion of the Jews, and by the diffusion of peace, tolerance, and understanding throughout a temperate, very English paradise here on earth.

Richardson's own work expresses just these hopes. First *Pamela* sketches the overthrow of wickedness and the return to a prelapsarian state; then *Clarissa* shows goodness confronting avarice, Anti-Christ, hierarchy, and clerical privilege, and finally *Grandison* presents a carefully worked out vision of millennial love, justice and reform. What this means is that Richardson's best work is profoundly political. It sets examples of the new against the old, such as liberal and conservative, Whig and Tory, freedom and hierarchy, woman and man, meritocracy and power, Modern and Ancient, progress and tradition. Related issues like natural and learned genius, vernacular and classical, scriptural and pagan, simple and allusive, plain and baroque, truth and deceit, sincerity and acting, realism and romance recur constantly in his work. They are the necessary contraries by which progression through the debates of reasonable people brings about the general reconciliation so much wished for.

Although to call him feminist is an anachronism, Richardson particularly speaks, in consequence, to feminist concerns. The words of the millennial theorist Mary Astell on marriage and female education seem especially to echo through his novels,[2] and he would have encountered everywhere the assumptions of the 'fair sex debate'. Ultimately, though, I think he drew his ideas directly from the clash of libertarian with authoritarian politics that gave rise to what we now call 'feminism'. Domestic relations, at that time, reflected for political theorists like Filmer and Locke the social relations of the state, while conversely, in the edgy amorous civil warfare of Restoration plays, characters very much like Richardson's bandied about the risky terminology of usurpation, tyranny, slavery, rebellion, liberty and birthright. Many of these themes came into focus in the well-known story of Lucretia's rape and suicide, a fable of individual liberty confronting the state whose political and sexual implications go far to explain Pamela's resistance and Clarissa's death.[3]

Women writers also were quick to complain of men's 'usurpation' of their poetic birthright,[4] and Mary Astell, Lady Chudleigh and Mary Leapor, for instance, demanded in their attacks on domestic Divine Right a balance of powers very much akin to the checks on a constitutional monarchy. 'If absolute Sovereignty be not necessary in a State,' wrote Astell unanswerably, 'how comes it to be so in a Family?'[5] Whenever Richardson wrote of relationships, then, he inevitably wrote of politics.[6]

He was attracted to these large themes because he believed fiction could be nationally important, and (heretical though it may be to say so) Richardson is crucial to his own work. Like Pope in the *Dunciad*, he believed that vice and virtue could readily coalesce into 'one putrid Mass, a Chaos in the Moral and Intellectual World';[7] like the millenarians, he thought that Anti-Christ was to be found, and fought, in the human heart. Here the passions are constantly at war with reason, especially in 'love' relationships; where, he wrote bleakly, men and women are devils to one another, they need no other tempter (*Grandison*, I. 439). His remedy, like theirs, was words, his trust in their power deriving from the apotheosis of reason in his time. To John Locke, the great Modern whose views on the mind's capacity, education and political implications were as axiomatic as the Bible in the eighteenth century, Richardson must have been particularly susceptible, for though formal education had been largely denied him, Locke's *Some Thoughts concerning Education* (1693) explained how to educate oneself, the *Essay concerning Humane Understanding* (1690) demonstrated the development of the reason, and his *Two Treatises of Government* (1690) advised rational men struggling to set up a just society. And if

Richardson shared the belief of the Moderns that progress spread through printing, education, and the dissemination of reasonable words, his own 'mite' to mend the world (Carroll, p. 175) can be seen as the representation of political, moral and educational ideas in his fiction.

Richardson spoke largely to women, because his topics concerned them and himself most nearly. Although awkward with educated men, Richardson saw women as uneducated outsiders like himself, and therefore potentially progressive. A clever woman had no choice but to be a 'natural genius', too. The 'Cause of the Sex' was 'the Cause of Virtue' (Carroll, p. 112), and indeed if women followed Locke's recommendation to educate the young they could reclaim themselves, men, and the world.[8] But who was to educate them? The blank slates of their minds were often said to have suffered a second fall, scored over by the frivolity of their fashionable accomplishments. But if, as Locke said, education rather than innate ideas were crucial in shaping the mind, women's capacities might be restored by reading their favourite novels, once those novels were washed and brought to church.

Richardson reached out to women, who in their idle incarceration read romances, by using love stories as a structure to contain much else. Like Herbert, whom he quotes approvingly for seeking him 'who a Sermon flies' (Carroll, p. 91), Richardson smuggles moral and ethical debate into his tales of 'love and nonsense, men and women' without which he would catch, he said, none but grandmothers (Carroll, pp. 46–7, 221). His important characters are mostly women, heroines who stand for principle under stress: Pamela Andrews defends her 'own self' against assaults from a powerful master; Clarissa Harlowe, having escaped from her persecuting family to a lover who drugs and rapes her, dies to remain herself; Harriet Byron maintains her own life's choice; and Clementina della Porretta weighs love, religion and duty in the face of madness and oppression.

To the characters, stories and techniques of romance and drama he added the lures of letters and realistically observed scenes. After the collapse of Mary Astell's end-of-the-century scheme for a Protestant nunnery where woman who did not wish to marry could pool their resources and live together, those conscious of educational neglect could at least correspond with men more favoured than themselves, as did Astell herself, or Lady Damaris Masham, or the whole circle of women whose correspondence with Richardson intersected excitingly with his fictional worlds. By this important principle, which he called 'accommodation' (Carroll, p. 98), he spoke through young, lively characters, suggested different points of view to pull his readers in, domesticated romance so that it read like their own lives, discussed their own main concerns, courtship and marriage, and enthralled them with letters just like the ones they wrote themselves. The result was fictional realism, his most extraordinary and obvious accomplishment.

Above all, Richardson trained his readers to be 'if not Authors, Carvers' (Carroll, p. 296),[9] who practise their rational gifts in protected, mock encounters of innocence with treachery, as Johnson saw in *Rambler* 4. The idea that every reader is competent to judge, Richardson promoted, for instance, by the novels being typically built upon matters debated by all, so that when he screens himself behind 'the umbrage of the editor's character' (Carroll, p. 42) he forces his 'Sovereign Judges the Readers' to choose and to decide (Carroll, p. 280). In the absence of obvious direction arises a sudden dizzying sense that our decision is vital indeed.[10]

Outside the works, too, Richardson ran what amounted to interpretative schools, prodding, teasing, provoking his friends into the reasoned response that was the Puritan reply to rigid authoritarianism. Increasingly he fused life and fiction, prompting debate over characters and scenes upon which he invited fresh comment to weave back into the book. Out of the consequent proliferation of points of view, each novel challenges readers to find an ideal reading, just as each heroine seeks someone who will understand. 'Many things,' he wrote, 'are thrown out in the several Characters, on purpose to provoke friendly Debate; and perhaps as Trials of the Readers Judgment, Manners, Taste, Capacity.' Something also, he said, must be left for the reader to make out (Carroll, pp. 315, 296). Although many later commentators have triumphantly brandished against him points that he first made, Richardson's novels consequently demonstrate what some think the highest art, the ability to contain their own criticism.

If Richardson encouraged his readers to think independently, they often pushed him to reconsider and rewrite. *Pamela* enlarges upon a situation sketched in his *Familiar Letters*, *Pamela in her Exalted Condition* writes over the top of *Pamela*, *Clarissa* courageously faces the implications of them both, and *Sir Charles Grandison* explores aspects of *Clarissa*. When Johnson accused his friend of terminal vanity[11] he may not have seen how Richardson needed his 'flatterers' to let him know what to say and whether he was saying it. In all his novels and letters Richardson worried away at the triangular relationship of author, work and reader in ways that we are only now beginning to respect. He involved his readers in the composition of his works, suited his books to them, and trained them to comprehend what he wrote. Reading his readers became the necessary habit of a lifetime.

Three major literary events might not have occurred without them: *Pamela*, which raised fiction to the dignity of serious debate, *Clarissa*, which to Johnson was perhaps the finest work in the language,[12] and *Sir Charles Grandison*, so significant a touchstone for writers in the following century that Jane Austen (for instance) drew on it extensively for three of her novels. But the enthusiasm of his audience proved embarrassing. Increasingly confident that they shared in his creativity when his letters and female subjects magnified their own lives, they seized the chance to escape from what Lady Winchilsea had called 'the dull mannage, of a servile house' into the heady complicity of authorship. His physical and psychological particularity, together with the fact that the characters, their own authors, editors and commentators, apparently write themselves into existence, persuaded readers to believe in the actuality of his created worlds. They responded to the letters as if they were addressees, spurned his characters, or fell in love with villains as real to them as their own neighbours. In these ways Richardson's readers became not rational carvers, but upstart novelists shouldering him out of his place. They demanded a continuation for *Pamela*, a happy ending for *Clarissa*, and private messages to be placed in *Grandison*, and made him remark despairingly that 'I have met with more Admirers of Lovelace than of Clarissa', for everyone took measure of a character by their own standard, everyone put himself or herself into the character and judged of it by their own sensations.[13]

His correspondent Lady Echlin thought 'accommodation' mistaken, but Richardson knew it was essential (Carroll, p. 322). It was certainly fatal to his contentment when it forced upon him a deference to his audience that he often groaned under. By his reasoning he had to write for nine out of ten readers who were in 'hanging-sleeves' (Carroll, p. 42) – that is, young, needy and often obtuse. But he could not dare to doubt the typicality of silly little Miss Westcomb, who even after reading *Clarissa* was still fond of rakes.

When readers' responses went awry, he fought to regain control in the private correspondence and the novels, revised, or started all over again. But his difficulties were perhaps inevitable. If words are not just conduits for meaning but signs arbitrarily agreed upon, their sense can be undermined at any time by failures of expression, incomprehension, or stubbornly resistant self-love, so that optimism gives way to the consternation of Babel. Perhaps it is true that works are only completed by their readers, but whenever his contemporaries invaded his work they made it swerve from its own imperatives, and impelled him to modify his text, to explain his explanations.

They also made him revise. Richardson, who could think of a text as unfixed probably because he was a printer, rewrote almost as much as he wrote, and often revised his last novel at the same time as he invented the new one. But since, as he realised, revisions could only do so much, in a strange sense each novel 'corrects' its predecessor. His anxiety often made him simplify before and after publication, but having once abandoned the closure of didacticism for the openness of fiction, he found he had granted his readers a freedom inadmissible in instruction. Once his design depended upon character, story and figure, in short, upon imaginative art, it instantly became ambiguous, and capable of as many readings as readers. After years of struggle to control them individually through correspondence or more generally by revision and rewriting, he eventually resorted to exhortation in his Indexes to *Clarissa* and *Grandison* and the *Collection of Moral and Instructive Sentiments* garnered from the three books. Just before his death, he felt he had written to little purpose (Carroll, p. 340).

To watch his career is, however, to witness a printer creating himself as author, for reader consultation and response, painful as they were, induced in Richardson constructive dissatisfaction. An autodidact in this above all else, he was persistent enough and humble enough to learn from failure as well as success, and embarked at the end of his writing life upon ambitious new experiments in *Grandison* with a lightness of touch and prodigality of invention which were remarkable, given that he was so tired and ill. Samuel Johnson was right to assure his friend, 'You, Sir, have beyond all other men the art of improving on yourself.'[14]

Since art, to Richardson, was secondary to teaching, he would have been startled to know how often his novels are praised as either documentary or aesthetic experience. He wrote realistically, to be sure, but the realism was to him always the vehicle, not the reason for his writing. Moral instructions and warnings, he said, were 'the very motive with me' for *Clarissa*'s being written at all (Carroll, p. 224). Critics often say that he wrote better than he knew, but his careful preservation of the commentaries he wrote on his own books show how thoroughly he considered the purpose as well as the art of fiction. As he writes, his books become more sure in their technique, more largely important, more expansively accepting of his predecessors, and so linked by allusion and resonance to a wider world of literature which in turn enriches his own. From the illustrative allusions of *Pamela* to the richly charged, invigorating analogies of *Clarissa* and *Grandison*, Richardson places his work boldly among English writing rather than the classical past. He may not have changed the world, but he established a path for fiction that was new and extraordinarily influential.

1

Pamela

Pamela was a novel, something new, and it took the world by storm. Simple villagers rang church bells to celebrate Pamela's wedding, but her solid little world exists primarily for the sake of its subject, the rape that does not happen.

Plunging straight into the middle of things, Pamela tells her mother and father that the old mistress of the house has died. Her son Mr B. vows to take care of her, giving her 'with his own Hand Four golden Guineas' which she promptly sends to her parents 'by *John* our Footman, who goes your way; but he does not know what he carries; because I seal it up in one of the little Pill-boxes which my Lady had, wrapt close in Paper, that it mayn't chink; and be sure don't open it before him'. A death, the ambivalence of being placed in the care of a young man, gold that chinks and must be hidden in a pill-box, all these are lures to raise the curiosity of the reader. Richardson wastes no time in developing the relationship between that interesting young man and Pamela. She has been scared out of her senses, she says, for in has come her young master. 'Good Sirs! how was I frightned! I went to hide the Letter in my Bosom, and he seeing me frighted, said, smiling, Who have you been writing to, *Pamela*?' Here is an invasion not only of her refuge, the lady's dressing-room, but of her private life and thoughts, and as her reaction shows, she realises that however kind, this is her master's first attack.

Conspicuous for beauty and literacy, vulnerable in a house bereft of its old order, and alert to the danger of the gold going astray or herself doing likewise, Pamela responds with instant alarm to the proximity of this young man. Her instinctive concealment of the letter in her bosom shows how she equates her inmost self with the letters which Mr B. will pursue as earnestly as he pursues her body. No wonder she can do nothing but 'curchee and cry, and was all in Confusion', but at his goodness, merely, as she thinks? She does not know, and neither yet do we.

After this promising start the story proceeds briskly. Gifts of his mother's clothes allow Mr B. to show his awareness of the body he desires, and the space within which he encroaches grows dangerously more confined. Pamela, unable to recognise an attraction to a man so greatly her superior in class, tries to stave off disaster by acting as though the worst will not happen, stays doggedly on in the house to finish a waistcoat, and defies him with her own sense of right. This wary and unstable situation is dramatically heightened by Mr B.'s unexpected abduction of Pamela just when she thinks she is on her way home. At his country house she is guarded by two monstrous warders, Mrs Jewkes and Mr Colbrand, so that even her energy and ingenuity must falter before the array of obstacles to her freedom. When she is reduced to considering suicide, her state at last convinces Mr B. of her determination not to be raped. Once allowed to go, Pamela wants to stay. She and Mr B. marry, the remainder of the book showing how their new relationship works out.

Such a tale of sexual pursuit and resistance is scarcely new, but, as has always been known, what gives it life is the particularity of its physical and psychological realism. The carefully itemised clothing that Mr B. gives to Pamela, the forty sheets of paper, the bundle of pens and the sealing wax by which she is enabled to carry on her correspondence, the letters that she sews into her petticoats or hides under the sunflower, the blister on her hand from scouring a pewter plate, the round-eared cap of her country clothes, those four golden guineas, all are present and important through the naming of their names and what they mean to Pamela. The bold Hogarthian caricature of Mrs Jewkes' 'Picture', for instance, tells us just as much about Pamela as it does about her keeper:

She is a broad, squat, pursy, fat Thing, quite ugly, if any thing God made can be ugly; about forty Years old. She has a huge Hand, and an Arm as thick as my Waist, I believe. Her Nose is flat and crooked, and her Brows grow over her Eyes; a dead, spiteful, grey, goggling Eye, to be sure, she has. And her Face is flat and broad; and as to Colour, looks like as if it had been pickled a Month in Salt-petre: I dare say she drinks!

(107)

Again, when she dresses for home, Pamela's delight in the details of her own appearance gives Mr B. a chance:

I dropt a low Curchee, but said never a Word. I dare say, he knew me as soon as he saw my Face; but was as cunning as *Lucifer*. He came up to me, and took me by the Hand, and said, Whose pretty Maiden are you? – I dare say you are *Pamela*'s Sister, you are so like her. So neat, so clean, so pretty! Why, Child, you far surpass your Sister *Pamela*!

I was all Confusion, and would have spoken; but he took me about the Neck; Why, said he, you are very pretty, Child; I would not

PAMELA

be so free with your *Sister*, you may believe, but I must kiss *you*.
O Sir, said I, I am *Pamela*, indeed I am: Indeed I am *Pamela, her own self!*
(61)

Preening herself on her show of pretty poverty, she has been tricked by her master's jest of a sister prettier than herself. To his covetous question, she declares that she belongs to no-one, for she is Pamela, her own self.

In such sparring exchanges Richardson catches the essence of unshaped human dialogue with all its repetitions, indirections, hesitations and uncertainty. Richardson was not an unconscious author as some say, but the creator, rather, of characters who are unconscious. To a large extent this results from the novel's being written (like all his novels) in the form of letters. It exists in an eternal present where the past is pored over for clues leading up to this moment, where the future is as dark to the character as it is to the reader. The sense of knowing no more than she does what will happen to her, the following of her mind as it wavers from fear to trust and love, made Richardson understandably proud of his 'new species of writing', which he called 'Writing – to the Moment' (Carroll, pp. 41, 329).

Much of Richardson's carefully constructed impression of reality derives from the theatre's characteristic conviction through the eye as well as through the ear, by means of stage-direction, costume, gesture, setting and action. For instance, Mr B. considers a rich silk and silver morning gown suitable for seduction (66). Dialogue is frequent in *Pamela*, though not necessarily witty when the dramatic situation is all. Swift and economical in its obliteration of narrative links, dialogue contrasts effectively with those meditative sections which are in essence Pamela's soliloquies. Most striking of all, the characters often accuse one another of acting as if in plays, that is, insincerely. Pamela mimics fits, says Mr B. in anger (42); his sister Lady Davers thinks that in claiming to be married she is playing a theatrical part (322). Speech and act in this book are constantly assumed to be deceptive performances, an attitude consistent with Richardson's attack on the stage in his pamphlet, *A Seasonable Examination of the Pleas and Pretensions of the Proprietors of, and Subscribers to, Play-Houses* (1735). Accuracy of disclosure is believed to belong solely to letters, which tell truth as in soliloquies. People may lie, but the letters that tell of their lies do not. In an attempt to strip off the mask, characters therefore watch one another as closely as if they are actors and audience on a shared stage, although only Pamela watches herself as well as others, explores

11

behind her own mask, and finds out the love she did not know. Plays within plays are set to catch Pamela, as in the episodes where Mr B. dresses as Nan the drunken servant and Mrs Jewkes pretends she has no mohey, and Pamela too plays her own pretty sister or stage-manages a scenario for suicide. Fielding decided that she always feigned because she sometimes feigned, but Pamela's greatest struggle is to make herself heard, believed and respected in a world where appearances are cynically assumed to be treacherous.

Like his dramatic technique, Richardson's celebrated realistic technique builds solid-seeming appearances in a world where surfaces betray. The very details that establish its actuality often contain a resonance that is not realistic, but symbolic. What differentiates his work from journalism, say, or romance, is the freedom offered to readers not simply to absorb information or submit to a dream world, but to commit themselves to their own subjective response. Richardson draws us in to be 'if not Authors, Carvers', that is, readers who choose and interpret and work. It is this above all that makes the experience seem real, when we haul his characters into our world, which we know to exist.

What, to return to that first letter, is the meaning of the golden guineas? Her fearful parents read them as the wages of sin in advance, tainted money to be hidden in the thatch and not spent. Did Pamela glimpse something of this for herself? She dissociated herself from the money by sending it to her parents, but was still proud to deserve it for her service to the old lady, and possessive of it, guarding against loss or theft and wrapping the golden guineas that they might not chink. And yet she is aroused by them not just from cupidity, for they represent a transaction between herself and her master that is not only financial. She is confused by an act that she dares only to think of as 'goodness', for to imagine it otherwise would be to make it otherwise. No reading of these events can be definitive, neither the parents', nor Pamela's, nor ours. Richardson has set up a situation full of queries about Mr B.'s motives, Pamela's response, her present, her future, and the meaning of the golden guineas. The debate over Pamela and her virtue has already begun.

'Mighty Piece of Undone', sneers Mrs Jewkes when Pamela protests against being raped (169). Derision as well as enthusiasm greeted *Pamela* when it burst upon the world in 1740, the worst attack, or rather the best, being Henry Fielding's parody in which Shamela deploys her 'vartue' to shackle Mr B. Some said that

Pamela's was not worth all the pother, while others argued that Richardson's inflammatory scenes made nonsense of his stated moral design. None of this, however, should obscure the fact that Richardson works from acute observations about women's lives to present a very enlightened point of view.

Pamela's 'virtue' and the way it is 'rewarded', as the sub-title suggests, by marriage, are problems. What, many people ask, is one sexual experience more or less? But then as now, sex had very different consequences for women than for men. Men were not expected to be chaste, but women had to stay pure for the bloodlines to run true. As Pamela remarks, 'those Things don't disgrace Men, that ruin poor Women, as the World goes' (49). In fact, beauty and virginity form Pamela's sole defence. If she loses the one, disease might ravage the other, as Hogarth's *Harlot's Progress* shows, so that, melodramatic as it sounds, it was probably true for Richardson to conclude that 'the abandon'd Prostitute, pursuing the wicked Courses, into which, perhaps, she was at first *inadvertently* drawn, hurries herself into filthy Diseases, and an untimely Death' (410). The seduction, once accomplished, could readily cause a seducer to discard her, as the story of Sally Godfrey, Mr B.'s first mistress, proves. She lives, says Mr B. complacently, in Jamaica,

and very happily too. For you must know, that she suffer'd so much in Child-bed, that nobody expected her Life . . . [R]ecommending to me, by a very moving Letter, her little Baby, and that I would not suffer it to be called by her Name, but *Goodwin*, that her Shame might be the less known, for hers and her Family's sake; she got her Friends to assign her Five hundred Pounds, in full of all her Demands upon her Family, and went up to *London*, and imbarked, with her Companions, at *Gravesend*, and so sailed to *Jamaica*; where she is since well and happily marry'd; passing, to her Husband, for a young Widow, with one Daughter, which her first Husband's Friends take care of, and provide for.   (396)

Pamela is moved, and obliquely criticises her new husband when she points out Sally Godfrey's sacrifice. 'It shew'd she was much in Earnest to be good, that she could leave her native Country, leave all her Relations, leave you that she so well lov'd, leave her dear Baby, and try a new Fortune, in a new World, among quite Strangers, and hazard the Seas; and all to preserve herself from further Guiltiness!', she says (396). Mr B. knows he embittered Miss Godfrey's whole voyage by turning up at the embarkation but accepts as inevitable her recommendation to him of 'the dear Guest' her baby as she sailed away, her handkerchief at her eyes. Richardson's master-stroke is the ten year-old negro boy who dies of smallpox a month after he is landed, sent to her little daughter by a woman who has not been guilty alone (398–9).

The episode warns Pamela, and us, about what could have happened if Mr B. had made her '*Sally Godfrey* the Second' as he wished (399): a punitive pregnancy, a difficult childbirth, a self-imposed exile from lover, friends, family and country, and an appropriation of all the shameful blame. Miss Godfrey must lie, and lose the daughter she bore with such pain, while her seducer maintains his standing in society, remains wealthy where she is beggared, has free access to the child belonging to them both, and sets out freely on a fresh path of seduction. No wonder that Pamela weeps out of compassion for the mother and joy in her own escape (393), nor that her care for the child is more passionate than married love explains.[1]

If Pamela agreed to become a kept mistress, her safety would endure only as long as her youth. Since wicked men love variety, she writes, 'poor *Pamela* must be turn'd off, and look'd upon as a vile abandon'd Creature' (49). Offered the chance of marriage if after a year Mr B. still loves her, she retorts, 'What, Sir, would the World say, were you to marry your Harlot? – That a Gentleman of your Rank in Life, should stoop, not only to the base-born *Pamela*, but to a base-born Prostitute? – Little, Sir, as I know of the World, I am not to be caught by a Bait so poorly cover'd as this!' (167). Discarded, she might return to being a servant girl again, but her education has effectively spoilt her for such a descent. When she tries to scour a pewter plate, her hand blisters in two places (78), an obliging demonstration that it wants no further part of menial work. Since she has advanced socially in the good lady's house, it would be unfair to demand her return to poverty.

Finally, she must hope and work for marriage because only that will give her a place in society, only that will make her free as dependent spinsters could never be. When she thanks God after her marriage she singles out her chance to be socially and spiritually active through the 'Opportunities put into my Hand, by the Divine Favour, and the best of Men!' (304). Richardson stresses her exultation that she will not be useless in her generation (303), for only a married woman could in the eighteenth century exercise the 'Godlike Power' of doing good (264). She dispenses money which she could not otherwise earn, and with it life and health and hope to others. It is easy to laugh at Pamela for being so very pleased with her marriage, but without it she would be either ruined or invisible. Like Charlotte Lucas who marries Mr Collins in *Pride and Prejudice*, she simply preserves her female life when she curtsies and thanks Mr B. for marrying her (289). At least she wants to, for if, as she asks, 'one's Heart is so sad, and one's Apprehensions so great, where one so extremely loves, and is so extremely obliged; What must be the Case of those poor Maidens, who are forced, for sordid Views, by their tyrannical Parents, or Guardians, to marry the Man they almost hate, and, perhaps, to the Loss of the Man they most love?' (291). It is a question to trouble Richardson in *Clarissa*.

Marriage too has its dangers. Pamela is not prudish when she writes on her wedding night of 'that sweet Terror, that must confuse poor bashful Maidens, on such an Occasion, when they are surrender'd up to a more doubtful Happiness, and to half strange Men; whose good Faith, and good Usage of them, must be less experienced, and is all involv'd in the dark Bosom of Futurity, and only to be proved by the Event' (286). Jane Austen, who knew Richardson almost by heart, laughs at Mr Woodhouse for grieving that women marry strangers, but she still marries Emma to a neighbour she knows very well indeed. Pamela's marriage, by contrast, marks an irrevocable moment of risk-taking when she commits her entire future to a man she hardly knows. Courtship is her only time of power, and the mere fact of marriage holds no guarantees of his good faith and usage. It still does not. The ambivalence of marriage as a reward for virtue will be clearly shown in the continuation.

For all that, marriage is far preferable to the loss of chastity without it. But the book also defends Pamela's right to take a stand on principle simply because she chooses to. What that principle is makes no odds. Her chastity is as dear to her as his doctrine is to the bishop burnt for his religion (77), for like other literary virgins she confronts a demon with his monstrous crew by means of the sanctity of individual belief.

Richardson knew the odds against Pamela to be enormous, for an awareness of these odds, the essence of what is now called feminism, was nothing new in his time.[2] Sectarian groups during the English Civil War had called for universal suffrage, universal education, and the right of women to be preachers, while Locke argued for girls to be educated as readily as boys. Towards the close of the seventeenth century Mary Astell had gathered up many of these ideas in two important works, one appealing for the right of women to an education, and the other attacking the inequities of marriage for women. She would have founded a college for women if the Protestant bishops had not recoiled from such a nunnery-like proposal. Richardson advocated the Protestant Nunnery for women with little money or no desire to marry,[3] and in generous encouragement of women to prove they had *minds*, he urged his women friends to write to him, directed their reading, revised their novels and printed them when they were written. Above all, in his own novels he shows women writing their way to rewards on earth and in heaven by the energetic exercise of their wits and pens. When he made Pamela defend 'her own self', he thoroughly understood the odds she must face.

As Pamela's guardian and master Mr B. has absolute power over her. For doing exactly as he likes he can demand gratitude, obedience and dependence. The four guineas of the first letter are her sole wages; she can have no other money, nor any other post without his recommendation. In his house the servants obey out of self-preservation, and are so much his creatures that they will reform when he does. Pamela's master controls the post-office and so intercepts her letters (118), nor can she appeal to the law when he is a justice of the peace (63) and member of parliament for the district.[4] A sham marriage he would have been at liberty to confirm or abrogate as he pleased (230), while Mr Peters, representative of that traditional defender of chastity, the church, refuses Pamela's plea with the remark that 'it was too common and fashionable a Case to be withstood by a private Clergyman or two', adding, 'What, and imbroil myself with a Man of the 'Squire's Power and Fortune! No, not I, I'll assure you!' (123). Since Mr B. has the right to give out church livings he can with impunity set bullies on his clergyman Mr Williams to tip him into the dam (134). Above all he is rich and Pamela is poor, and where he has social standing she has none. He can do anything he likes to a woman of no consequence at all. As Sir Simon Darnford, one of the local gentry, says, what does it matter if 'the 'Squire our Neighbour has a mind to his Mother's Waiting-maid? And if he takes care she wants for nothing, I don't see any great Injury will be done her. He hurts no Family by this' (122). Well might she complain when she is about to be sent home, 'here I am again! a pure Sporting-piece for the Great! a mere Tennis-ball of Fortune!' (212), for what indeed 'can the abject Poor do against the mighty Rich, when they are determin'd to oppress?' (95). Mr B. will willingly injure her, but will not hurt himself by marrying her. After the failure of the attempt where he disguises himself as his own servant Nan, he says arrogantly, 'But, what can I do? Consider

16

the Pride of my Condition. I cannot endure the Thought of Marriage, even with a Person of equal or superior Degree to myself . . . How then, with the Distance between us, and in the World's Judgment, can I think of making you my Wife?' (184).

He assumes the right to define her, calling her hussy, saucebox, gewgaw, speaking picture, artful young baggage; he insists that she dresses as *he* thinks fit in the cast-off clothes of his mother; he spins her around in front of Mrs Jewkes as if she were merchandise. 'See, said he, and took the Glass with one Hand, and turn'd me round with the other, What a Shape! what a Neck! what a Hand! and what a Bloom in that lovely Face!' (162). Lastly, Mr B. has power over her simply by reason of being a man. Although it was said that England was a paradise for women and a hell for horses, women, who belonged first to their fathers and then to their husbands, had very little protection in law. Pamela's declaration that she belongs to herself is therefore remarkable. With such accumulations of feudal power Mr B. can do as he wants – lock her up, deprive her of religious consolation, drive her to despair and almost to suicide. He manhandles her, shouts at her, calls her names, and against all this Pamela has nothing but her quick wit and her ready tongue:

If you mean honourably, why, Sir, should you not let me know it plainly? Why is it necessary to imprison me, to convince me of it? And why must I be close watch'd and attended, hinder'd from stirring out, from speaking to any body, from going so much as to Church to pray for you? . . . Whatever you have to propose, whatever you intend by me, let my Assent be that of a free Person, mean as I am, and not of a sordid Slave, who is to to be threatened and frightened into a Compliance, that your Conduct to her seems to imply would be otherwise abhorr'd by her – My Restraint is indeed hard upon me.   (126)

'What is left me but Words?', she asks in her despair (182), not daring to believe that her words can prove powerful against his acts.

Richardson speaks often of Mr B. and Pamela as monarch and subject, terms which would seem normal at a time when the customary superiority of men over women was used to justify the hierarchy of kings over states. This case had been wittily dismantled by John Locke, the main spokesman for the libertarians, who in the first of his *Two Treatises of Government* (1689–90) attacked Sir Robert Filmer's defence of the divine right of kings, *Patriarcha* (1680).[5] If Filmer based the people's subordination to kings on the analogy of Eve's to Adam, Locke retorted that female subordination was not the law of God but his curse, like pain in childbirth (I. 47). Dominion, he argued, was once *shared* between Adam and Eve (I. 29, 44);[6] nor could subordination be justified if claimed merely for the act of engendering. If so, mothers might claim equal power over children. Husbands and fathers therefore had no natural authority over women and children, nor (by daring extension) had kings over people.

Locke's radical convictions derive from the Christian doctrine of souls and his own theory of mind, for if all are born equal and equally capable of reason, then none is innately superior (I. 67). And if each belongs to himself and each shares in common property, why should the possession of property grant power over the life of others (I. 41)? Where Filmer proclaimed the submission of the people to a government's will and force,[7] Locke replied that men consented to surrender their rights only in exchange for protection. Thus whenever a king uses force against his subjects' interests he enslaves them, and they may resist his tyranny (II. 207), as had already happened, of course, to Charles I.

Mary Astell complained that not even Milton 'would cry up Liberty to poor *Female Slaves*, or plead for the Lawfulness of Resisting a private Tyrany [sic]' (*Marriage*, pp. 34–5), but Locke's vocabulary of 'slaves', 'tyranny' and 'liberty' may be found domesticated in many a Restoration play. Locke's influence is obvious, too, upon (for instance) the gardener's daughter Mary Leapor, whose work Richardson printed and published by subscription. Where Locke had written derisively that under Filmer's patriarchal scheme 'there will be as many Kings as there are Fathers' (I. 70), she in her *Essay on WOMAN* wrote 'Unhappy Woman's but a Slave at large', because, as she explained in *Man the Monarch*, men take to themselves the prerogatives of kings.

> Sires, Brothers, Husbands, and commanding Sons,
> The Sceptre claim; and ev'ry Cottage brings
> A long Succession of Domestic Kings.[8]

These too are the issues that Richardson dramatises in *Pamela*. Each time that Mr B. abuses his authority as a domestic king, Pamela responds with Locke's 'Fundamental, Sacred and unalterable Law of *Self-Preservation*' (II. 149). He follows Filmer and the old ideas, whereas she argues that she may legitimately resist tyranny to protect her only property, her person. This concept includes mind as well as body, since, as Locke wrote in his *Letter Concerning Toleration*, no civil power can change a mind by force of 'confiscation of estate, imprisonment, torments'.[9]

When Mr B. puts on a 'stern and majestick Air' to the servants (160), he commands obedience by fear rather than by consent. He misuses his power over Pamela his servant when he invades the dressing-room, kisses her in the summer-house, obliges her to yield to a force she cannot withstand and finally abducts her. Pamela only escapes by a miraculous 'double Strength' (42), verbal resistance, and the fits that force him into stratagems and disguises unworthy of the Man–Monarch he claims to be.

Mr B. wants Pamela to be his 'kept Mistress, or kept Slave rather' (124). 'Slavery' is the first word of Locke's first treatise of government, and he defines it as the vile and miserable estate of man under tyranny, and the exercise of power beyond right when the satisfaction of any irregular passion comes before the preservation of the people (II. 199). The word 'slave' refers pointedly to the Turks, whose treatment of women was often in the eighteenth century unfavourably compared to England's. For instance, the father of Anna Seward the Swan of Avon, in his poem *The Female Right to Literature* printed in Robert Dodsley's well-known miscellany of 1748, urges defiance of 'The coward insults of that tyrant, man' who 'looks on slav'ry as the female dow'r'. In a contrast with 'happy BRITAIN' he attacks countries where women are confined in the wanton bowers of seraglios and kept from 'th'exertions of th'enlightened mind'. If that Turk Mr B. makes Pamela a 'kept Slave', she has therefore the right to resist her domestic, her undeserving king (II. 18).

Law being the only restraint upon Men–Monarchs, Mr B. takes pains to put Pamela beyond its protection by making her look like a criminal. She is guilty, he says, of prostitution, invitations to rape, robbery, rebellion, plots and treason. But Pamela is no criminal, as she says to the coachman 'with the Look of a Hangman' who abducts her (100).

Many a critic has fallen for Mr B.'s ruse of calling Pamela a whore. Like the country wench come to town in Hogarth's *Harlot's Progress*, Pamela is deceptively young, pretty, and ripe when handed over into her rakish master's power, and the country house to which she is abducted looks very like a private bordello. To Mrs Jewkes, its bawdy '*London* Prostitute' (162), Pamela reacts not as a prude, but in shocked denial of the role being forced upon her. Mr B. behaves as though she were already his harlot when he abducts her, isolates her, sets Colbrand to watch her, or has Mrs Jewkes hold her down to be deflowered. The erotic bedroom scenes with their undressing and watching and touching and fainting all allow interpretations of Pamela, by Mr B., that it will be the business of the book to dispel. Even when Pamela is married, Lady Davers makes the same mistake. '*Chastity*', she calls her sneeringly, which vexes Pamela so much that 'I bit a Piece of my Fan out' (323). Lady Davers blurts out, 'Thou art not the first in the List of his credulous Harlots' (325), and invades the conjugal bedroom to catch them out. But Pamela has never been the silly goose of Hogarth's print. Neither credulous nor simple, she sturdily resists being cast as a whore even when appearances are against her.

If Pamela can be made to look promiscuous, Mr B. can blame his attempts on her being attractive, articulate, and there. As Ian Donaldson points out,[10] it is as if she had actually been defiled when she is tempted to copy the Roman matron who stabbed herself after being raped by a tyrannical Tarquin:

Pretty Fool! said he, how will you forfeit your Innocence, if you are oblig'd to yield to a Force you cannot withstand? . . .
He by Force kissed my Neck and Lips; and said, Who ever blamed *Lucretia*, but the *Ravisher* only? and I am content to take all the Blame upon me; as I have already borne too great a Share for what I have deserv'd. May I, said I, *Lucretia* like, justify myself with my Death, if I am used barbarously? O my good Girl! said he, tauntingly, you are well read, I see; and we shall make out between us, before we have done, a pretty Story in Romance, I warrant ye! (42)

Unlike pagan Lucretia, however, Christian Pamela draws back, with 'Hitherto, *Pamela*, thought I, thou art the innocent, the suffering *Pamela*; and wilt thou be the guilty Aggressor?' (153).

Mr B. is astounded that his maid-servant should resist ravishment by her seigneur, but if, as Locke had said, 'every Man has a *Property* in his own *Person*' (II. 27), Pamela's person is her own. Mr B.'s argument that if she is his property (259) she commits robbery in defending herself, Pamela challenges him to try by law, saying, 'Why then you are a Justice of Peace, and may send me to Gaol, if you please, and bring me to a Tryal for my Life! If you can prove that I have robb'd you, I am sure I ought to die!' (63). When in Lincolnshire she complains that she is dogged and watched worse than a thief, Mrs Jewkes replies that 'to rob him of yourself, would be the worst that could happen to him'. Pamela corrects her. Mr B. is the thief, having stolen her from herself. 'How came I to be his Property?' she asks, 'What Right has he in me, but such as a Thief may plead to stolen Goods?' (115–16).

Pamela's 'downright Rebellion' (116) next permits Mr B. to legitimise his lawless attacks by naming her a traitor. Her resistance against his kingly authority of birth, wealth, and power he calls plotting, treason, and intrigue, for what he dreads most is the exposure of his secret thoughts and papers 'by such a Sawcebox as you' (41). His obsession in Lincolnshire will be to find her methods out. Understandably when he misuses his powers she makes party with the servants against him (163) – this device, forced upon her in self-defence, would have been understood by Locke, who wrote in his *Letter Concerning Toleration* that 'there is only one thing which gathers people into seditious commotions, and that is oppression' (p. 160).

Mr B.'s descent to disguise, plots and artifice forces Pamela into like contrivances. Abducted, locked up, and tricked out of shoes and money, she turns energetically to 'Inventions' (113), pleads with the local gentry in letters sent secretly through Williams, feigns an interest in gardening to hide her correspondence under the sunflower, escapes out of the window only to find the door-key will not fit, climbs the wall only to be thrown down by a loose brick, and is prevented from flight by cows which she thinks are bulls. Mr B. may complain that plots, mischief, love and contradiction are the 'natural Aliments' of a woman (161), for the man who thinks a thousand dragons sufficient to watch a woman 'will find all too little; and she will engage the Stones in the Street, or the Grass in the Field, to act for her, and help on her Correspondence' (230). But he has driven her to it.

She in her turn concludes that 'every thing, Man, Woman and Beast, is in a Plot against your poor *Pamela*' (136). After so many failures to escape, Pamela is tempted to turn the last attempt, a mock suicide, into reality, and is saved only by the providential intervention that Locke said was the ultimate recourse of the sufferer (II. 168). At this her lowest point Mr B. proposes terms of capitulation and surrender which Pamela refuses to accept. She will not be bought by gifts for her family and friends, nor will she take the 'bait' of marriage if after a year she is found to be satisfactory. Her brave defiance of his regal strength, of his 'I will not sue meanly, where I can command' (168), forces him into his last, worst plot. Man the Monarch degrades himself when he stoops ludicrously to the disguise of a female servant and invades her bed, for

little did I think, it was my wicked, wicked Master in a Gown and Petticoat of hers, and her Apron over his Face and Shoulders. What Meannesses will not *Lucifer* make his Votaries stoop to, to gain their abominable Ends!

'O wicked, base, villainous Designer! what a Plot, what an

unexpected Plot was this!', she says. Mr B. advances on Pamela; she is held down by Mrs Jewkes, who calls out, 'What you do, Sir, do; don't stand dilly-dallying. She cannot exclaim worse than she has done. And she'll be quieter when she knows the worst' (175–6). Pamela faints, and saves herself once more.

This characterisation of Pamela as a political prisoner who is guarded, beaten, frightened and silenced (199),[11] reaches its climax after the Nan episode when Mrs Jewkes, having discovered Pamela's cache of letters, takes them in triumph to Mr B. He jests when he calls the scene a 'trial', but it is indeed one to her. Punished by those who should be punished, she – like the Israelites in her awkward paraphrase – is powerless under a strange king in Babylon (268–72). She dreads the exposure of her letters, fearing that all her private thoughts of him and all her secrets, together with the reason why she affected to be so much alone, and always writing, will be known (198). Verbal subversion has been her only recourse.

Pamela's king charges her with treasonable writing. In a nightmarish way he is to her both prosecutor and judge, in spite of Locke's advice to separate the power of making laws from the power of executing them (II. 143). Trials are favourite resolution devices in Richardson's fiction, being protected places where the powerless speak and justice prevails. Here in defiance of the arbitrariness of language the whole truth and nothing but the truth is told. In trials, too, words have evidential force: if uninterrupted, they convince, and offer true conduits to meaning.

In this mock court-room Mr B. jests about seizing the 'treasonable Papers' of a 'great Plotter', but Pamela very sullenly and gravely defends the privacy of her thoughts. 'What one writes to one's Father and Mother is not for every body', she protests, only to be answered by the arrogance of divine right: 'Nor, said he, am I every body.' Pamela has asked him to remember 'that I always declared I thought myself right to endeavour to make my Escape from this forced and illegal Restraint' (199–200). Well might she have seen herself as a sheep tried before the vulture on the accusation of the wolf (162), for when at her 'trial' she hopes pointedly for a '*just* Judge' to hear her cause, he replies as though his character has been split, 'you may hope for a *merciful* one too, or else I know not what will become of you'.

Her own lawyer to this aggressive judge and prosecutor, Pamela replies as smartly as any modern critic to the charge of encouraging Mr Williams, 'that is your Comment; but it does not appear so in the Text'. He persists in calling their contrivances against each other mere entertainment, saying, 'there is such a pretty Air of Romance, as you relate them, in your Plots, and my Plots, that I shall be better directed in what manner to wind up the Catastrophe of the pretty Novel'.[12] But when he, the dangerous plotter, tries to transform himself into an innocuously plotting novelist, Pamela rebukes him for painful light-mindedness. If she were his equal, she says, 'I should say this is a very provoking way of jeering at the Misfortunes you have brought upon me' (200–1).

Pamela's denial of her letters, and her refusal to offer an absolute veracity that he will not promise from himself, make Mr B. burst out in exasperation, 'I know you won't tell a downright *Fib* for the World; but for *Equivocation!* no Jesuit ever went beyond you.' He recalls his sexual and physical power to assault her. Are the letters in her pocket? In her stays? 'No more Questions,' she begs. 'Is this fair, just or honest? I am no Criminal; and I won't confess'. He threatens to press her to death, a sexual pun she must take seriously when he is determined to be obeyed in this 'unreasonable Matter; tho' it is sad Tyranny to be sure!' To 'expostulate with such an arbitrary Gentleman' she knows will 'signify nothing. And most hardly do you use the Power you so wickedly have got over me.' In the hope that they will not be used against her in this place of trust, she finally agrees to hand over even the most recent of her letters (203–4).

Now it is Mr B. who gives in. Moved by what she has written, he offers marriage without conditions. Pamela, accustomed to seeing plots everywhere, believes the gipsy's warning, and Mr B., angered by being thought dishonest when for once he is not, orders her to go. His surrender and her free-willed return establish a contract between monarch and subject,[13] in a trust to make plots cease.

In prison imagery translated to love talk, Mr B. says that 'the sweet Girl has taken me Prisoner; and, in a few Days, I shall put on the pleasantest Fetters that ever Man wore' (248). Pamela's prison is become her palace (293), she says, for love 'creep, creep it has, like a Thief upon me'. She has 'made an Escape, to be more a Prisoner!' Her heart, a 'perfidious Traitor', has given itself up to the proud invader 'before a Summons came, and to one too, who had us'd me so hardly!' (214–15). Having 'sufficiently tortur'd one another', as Mr B. says, they call a truce (229). The proof that things have changed comes when Pamela, again held prisoner by force by Mr B.'s haughty sister Lady Davers, vaults out of the window and flies to the protection of her husband. Miss Darnford may jeer, 'O these Tyrants! these Men!' (332), but misrepresentations fall away when as Mr B.'s wife Pamela may no longer be called actress, liar, criminal, whore, rebel, thief or treasonable subject.

Graphic though the scenes of physical knowing have been in *Pamela*, the real battle has been to decide who she is. When Mr B. gives Pamela his mother's clothes, saying 'Don't blush, *Pamela*: Dost think I don't know pretty Maids wear Shoes and Stockens?', his classing of her among other pretty maids he has dressed confounds Pamela to such an extent that 'you might have beat me down with a Feather' (31). Her own choice of the famous country clothes is the reply. When she buys from a pedlar two round-eared caps, a little straw hat, mittens, and blue hose with white clocks (53), she contemplates fondly not just the clothes, but her choice of her own self. She is 'as proud as any thing', and 'to say Truth, I never lik'd myself so well in my Life' (60). In a scene beloved of illustrators, she divides her clothes in bundles, the first her lady's, the second her master's gift ('Hay, you know, *Closet* for that, Mrs. *Jervis!*'), the third all her own, and speaks to the last as to her chosen self, 'come to my Arms, my dear third Parcel, the Companion of my Poverty, and the Witness of my Honesty' (79–80).

What she represents he wilfully misrepresents, and he makes her guard her thoughts. Mr B. seeks out secret recesses of mind as well as those of body, and although at first he has easy access to the letters that reveal them, in Lincolnshire she keeps them to herself. Mr B. fights to possess Pamela's inner life as much as her outward shape when he intercepts letters, eavesdrops on private conversations, or tries to subvert her independence by removing the means to write. Letters and clothes are equivalent from the first moment that she hides that letter in her bosom. She sews letters into her under-coat so that plots and letters swell together in mental pregnancy. 'How nobly my [Sunflower] Plot succeeds! But I begin to be afraid my Writings may be discover'd; for they grow large!', she writes (120). Mr B. relishes the undressing of Pamela's thoughts as much as the revelation of her body, and when in the trial scene he threatens to strip her, unpins the handkerchief around her neck and stoops to inspect her garters, it is letters he thinks of, not legs. But foolish Mr B. is slow to realise why Pamela objects to untacking her correspondence, and vexes himself all night that he did not strip her, garment by garment, until he had found them (207).

Pamela hands over her precious writings, asking only, 'if you please to return them, without breaking the Seal, it will be very generous'. His immediate tearing open of the letters seems fatally to anticipate the invasion of her maidenhead, but reading them changes all. Words written in substantiation of the sincerity of her professions that her honesty is dearer to her than her life, convert him. 'Walk gently before', he says, and he 'seem'd so mov'd, that he turn'd away his Face from me' (207–8). Mr B., who has lusted after Pamela's thoughts as well as her body, must learn to value both: 'her Person made me her Lover; but her Mind made her my Wife', he says at last (390). Pamela's surrender demonstrates the wonderful ways of providence, for 'the very things that I most dreaded his seeing or knowing, the Contents of my Papers, have, as I hope, satisfy'd all his Scruples, and been a Means to promote my Happiness' (261). Once she has given herself freely she may dress in rich clothes without loss of self, for his reading of her letters endorses the identity she had chosen for herself. As she says to Longman, 'you don't know how much of my present Happiness I owe to the Sheets of Paper, and Pens and Ink you furnish'd me with' (379).

The restoration of the English birthright, liberty, within love and marriage, is the real subject of this tale, an attempt like Mary Astell's to 'retrieve, if possible, the Native Liberty, the Rights and Privileges of the Subject' (*Marriage*, pp. 95–6). Not sedition, but rather the abolition of tyranny and an end to oppression will do it. 'We are *born Free*, as we are born Rational', writes Locke (II. 61); 'if *all Men are born Free*, how is it that all Women are born Slaves?' retorts Astell.[14] The free-born Englishwoman Pamela uses words like 'freedom' and 'liberty' in their full political sense, where Mr B. restricts them merely to personal and sexual connotations, as he did with 'plots'. 'Freedom' to Pamela means freedom of speech and movement, freedom from fear, constriction and censorship, but whenever she utters her true thoughts her words are called freedoms in quite another sense, that is, inadmissible defiance which Mr B. characterises as impudent and pert. Conversely his verbal 'Freedoms to his poor Servant' (34) or the physical 'Freedoms he actually took', his hand in her bosom (67), invade her personal freedom. It is a poignant moment when Pamela, fishing for carp with the rods and baits of love pictured in the emblem books, throws back her catch out of sympathy for its wretched state. 'O the Pleasure it seem'd to have, to flounce in, when at Liberty!' she says, comparing the fish with herself (120). Whenever he takes what she calls liberties with her, she resists. She wants liberty, he takes liberties; she is free with words, he makes free with her body. Mr B.'s concept of 'intrigue' as sexual relationship clashes too with Pamela's idea of plotting against her, as each tries to cancel the other's meanings out. Pamela is 'quick' in defensive repartee, Mr B. would rather have her quick, pregnant, another way (72). By limiting his meanings to sex, he debases and trivialises words whose political seriousness she struggles to sustain.

Pamela's finest moment is her response to the 'naughty articles' that will make her a kept mistress. Here Mr B. makes the same impossible demand as the God from whom his authority ultimately descends. He wants consent 'freely' given under duress, and says,

Now, *Pamela*, will you see by this, what a Value I set upon the Free-will of a Person already in my Power; and who, if these Proposals are not accepted, shall find that I have not taken all these Pains, and risqued my Reputation, as I have done, without resolving to gratify my Passion for you, at all Adventures, and if you refuse, without making any Terms at all.

[She replies] I know, Sir, by woful Experience, that I am in your Power: I know all the Resistance I can make will be poor and weak, and perhaps stand me in little stead: I dread your Will to ruin me is as great as your Power: Yet, Sir, will I dare to tell you, that I will make no Free-will Offering of my Virtue.   (166)

When she does return freely to Mr B., she will be driven by an irresistible impulse, passion coinciding with conscious choice in a 'voluntier Love' that Mr B. learns to appreciate in the person he wishes for a wife (231).

Pamela insists upon freedom of speech even when she can write to no-one. As a rebel, she preserves the privacy of her own thoughts by any means she may, committing them to paper to make a party first of her parents, then of the world in general when they are not being delivered, and always of course of us. Mr B. is right to see her literacy as the real threat, from the first account of his attacks to the prayer for her welfare that she tries to smuggle out to the congregation (171). 'That Girl is always scribbling; methinks she might find something else to do', he says angrily (37), and, 'you mind your Pen more than your Needle; I don't want such idle Sluts to stay in my House' (55). Stitching occupies a hand that would otherwise be scribbling, for of the two traditional implements for women, the needle provides him with a waistcoat, but the pen will blow him up. Writing subverts his 'state', for being private, revisionist, secret, it need neither tally with what is said nor please the 'king' whom the writer overtly obeys. Pamela is a true conspirator when she hides one pen here, and another there, and 'a little of my Ink in a broken China Cup, and a little in another Cup; and a Sheet of Paper here-and-there among my Linen, with a little Wax and a few Wafers in several Places, lest I should be search'd' (105). The sunflower scene shows her quick conspiratorial wit:

When I came near the Place, as I had been devising, I said, Pray, step to the Gardener, and ask him to gather a Sallad for me to Dinner . . . When she had stept about a Bow-shot from me, I popt down, and whipt my Fingers under the upper Tile, and pulled out a little Letter, without Direction, and thrust it in my Bosom, trembling for Joy. She was with me before I could well secure it; and I was in such a taking, that I feared I should discover myself. You seem frighted, Madam, said she: Why, said I, with a lucky Thought, (alas! your poor Daughter will make an Intriguer by-and-by; but I hope an innocent one!) I stoopt to smell at the Sun-flower, and a great nasty Worm run into the Ground, that startled me; for I don't love Worms. Said she, Sun-flowers don't smell. So I find, said I.(117–18)

But Pamela finds her perfect reader in Mr B., and they agree on meanings at last. As soon as the privacy of her letters guarantees their truth and establishes mutual trust, Mr B.'s jest that he would like to see her lose her shape Pamela can call, but not in anger, the 'freest thing you have ever yet said' (312). As soon as Mr B. by his remark that 'there can be no Friendship lasting without Freedom' accepts her meanings (311), Pamela can cease flourishing the political significances of 'freedom', 'liberty' and 'intrigue', and freely confess her love.

Pamela's trial provides the climax of her rebellion, the climax of her relationship with a tyrannical, monarchical man. Trials from without derive from Mr B., his minions and his powers, and even though they increase in seriousness as Pamela's friends and material helps are removed one by one, they prove comparatively easy to withstand. Trials from within are not. As in the traditional accounts of a saint's life[15] she is tempted by despair and passion. Pamela saves herself from drowning only by perceiving the 'Devil's Instigation' in it, and asks herself,

because wicked Men persecute thee, wilt thou fly in the Face of the Almighty, and bid Defiance to his Grace and Goodness, who can still turn all these Sufferings to thy Benefits? . . . But yet, I will add, that tho' I should have prais'd God for my Deliverance, had I been freed from my wicked Keepers, and my designing Master; yet I have more abundant Reason to praise God, that I have been deliver'd from a worse Enemy, *myself*!

Her rebellious mind has rebelled even against the divine will to whom she owes duty and resignation, for 'art *thou* to put a Bound to God's Will, and to say, Thus much will I bear, and no more?'

Providence, she learns, imposes trials and removes them. She should rely on God to order things, not vainly depend on her own 'foolish Contrivances' (153–4). She has learnt the lesson of a Christian saint, of Robinson Crusoe, of Rasselas, that humanity is fallible and contrivance presumptuous. Like Herbert in *Jordan II*, she realises that this busy bustling is pride.

Her passion, which tries her from within, she must hide even from herself. From that first letter in which she is scared out of her senses, her erotic awareness of Mr B. makes her imagery feverish and her body's responses instantaneous. She spots puns in 'quick' or 'planting' (122), and fastens on any hint of danger with a confusion that makes her conspicuous. Pamela's body seems even more alert than her watchful mind, but should she trust a body which is falling in love with a libertine? Gradually, however – and Richardson does this finely – Pamela's feelings for Mr B. become something she can dare to recognise. She cannot admit a love at first illicit, but Mr B.'s increasing kindness reveals to her a very real love for him. When Pamela hears in her prison at Lincolnshire that Mr B. has nearly drowned, she wonders to herself.

What is the Matter, with all his ill Usage of me, that I cannot hate him? To be sure, I am not like other People! I am sure he has done enough to make me hate him; but yet when I heard his Danger, which was very great, I could not in my Heart forbear rejoicing for his Safety; tho' his Death would have ended my Afflictions.

For her good lady's sake, she adds hastily, she must wish him well, but the reader is not deceived (157). Her cry, 'Why can't I hate him?' (171), is at last answered by herself. It is easy enough to resist his physical attacks, but his kindness is hard to withstand. She begins to know 'too well the Reason, why all his hard Trials of me, and my black Apprehensions, would not let me hate him' (185). Being only the poor abject Pamela and not the first lady in the land, however, she cannot as yet reply. She harps upon the sham marriage until he is angry enough to let her go to her father's house, then finds to her astonishment that she is loath to leave. She muses to herself in a language strikingly religious,

What could be the Matter with me, I wonder! – I felt something so strange, and my Heart was so lumpish! – I wonder what ail'd me! – But this was so *unexpected*! I believe that was all! – Yet I am very strange still. . . . I'll take thee, O lumpish, contradictory, ungovernable Heart, to severe Task for this thy strange Impulse, when I get to my dear Father's and Mother's; and if I find any thing in thee that should not be, depend upon

it, thou shalt be humbled, if strict Abstinence, Prayer and Mortification
will do it! (211–12)

The kindness of Mr B.'s last letter frees her at last to own that she
will never be able to think of anybody in the world but him. She
admits her body's claims, and 'before I knew what was the Matter, it look'd like Love'. This of all her trials has been the hardest,
for the weakness of her own sex is too mighty to be withstood
(214–15). Her heart, that 'credulous, fluttering, throbbing
Mischief!' may be wrong, but even as she foolishly dialogues with
herself, 'all the time this Heart is *Pamela*' (217).

And so Mr B.'s love, the cause of trials from without, is freed
of danger, and Pamela's, the cause of trials from within, is allowed
into the light of day. Both kinds of trial vanish as though they had
never been, except in nightmare. The glass slipper fits, the Beast
turns into a Prince;[16] how everything wears another face, thinks
Pamela in the giddiness of her new prospects (293).

Richardson's task now is to make plausible Pamela's acceptance
of her persecutor. As one critic wrote,

> Tho' odd the question may be thought,
> For one so very modest;
> Yet that she would forgive the fault
> To me seemed much the oddest.[17]

Fielding was right to accuse Mr B. of fumbling his chances, but
his mercy does make Pamela's acceptance of him easier. Mr B. has
not, as he argues himself, been a 'very abandon'd Profligate', and
has hitherto been guilty of 'no very enormous or vile Actions'. (That
repetition of 'very' is wonderful.) It is indeed true, as he says, that
'had I been utterly given up to my Passions I should before now
have gratify'd them, and not have shewn that Remorse and Compassion for you, which have repriev'd you more than once, when
absolutely in my Power' (184).

Richardson makes Pamela's acceptance possible by the intervention of providence in her suicide attempt and by Mr B.'s conversion. Mr B. also acknowledges the power of law. If Pamela learns
to trust God, Mr B. learns that other laws supersede those of Man
the Monarch. Contemplating the playing cards, he sees 'something
sacred' in the character of a king, but 'by the Ace, I have always
thought the Laws of the Land denoted; and, as the Ace is above
the King or Queen, and wins them; I think the Law should be
thought so too; tho' may-be, I shall be deem'd a *Whig* for my Opinion' (335–6). The section after the marriage shows not just

Pamela's acceptance by society, as is often said, but Mr B.'s change
from a domestic tyrant to a benevolent constitutional monarch
whom she may safely marry.

Pamela teaches Mr B. that there is an ordering of duties. According to the domestic conduct books which Richardson knew well,
a Christian's first duty should be to God's laws, his second to himself, and his third to social relations such as that between master
and servant. On the authority of her conscience, which she believes
to be God's will, she defends her chastity as a first duty, whereas
the duty she owes to society can only be secondary. She obeys temporal power only up to the point at which the law and God take
precedence in her conscience, saying, 'I will bear any thing you
can inflict upon me with Patience, even to the laying down of my
Life, to show my Obedience to you in other Cases; but I cannot
be patient, I cannot be passive, when my Virtue is at Stake! –
It would be criminal in me, if I was' (182). She tells Robin the
coachman that she should not be punished for her resistance, for
she is 'no Criminal, as you all know: And if I could have thought
it my Duty to obey a wicked Master, in his unlawful Commands,
I had sav'd you all the Merit of this vile Service' (103). Even the
powers of a husband Pamela resists in anticipation: when Mrs
Jewkes argues that Mr B. will procure her obedience as soon as
he rapes her, 'No Husband in the World, said I, shall make me
do an unjust or base thing' (169). She will render unto Caesar only
what she can, and no more.

The other servants, unlike her, see their duty to their master as
peremptory. When Robin pleads that he has only been obeying his
master's command in abducting her, Pamela replies tartly, 'Mighty
well, Mr. *Robert*! . . . I never saw an Execution but once, and then
the Hangman ask'd the poor Creature's Pardon, and wip'd his
Mouth, as you do, and pleaded his Duty, and then calmly tuck'd
up the Criminal'. Mrs Jewkes, too, thinks her master's commands
more important than God speaking in her conscience:

Why look ye, look ye, Madam, said she, I have a great Notion of doing
my Duty to my Master; and therefore you may depend upon it, if I can
do that, and serve you, I will; But you must think, if your Desire and his
Will come to clash once, I shall do as he bids me, let it be what it will . . .

Well, said I, you will not, I hope, do an unlawful or wicked Thing, for
any Master in the World! Look-ye, said she, he is my Master, and if he
bids me do a Thing that I can do, I think I ought to do it, and let him,
who has Power, to command me, look to the Lawfulness of it. Why, said
I, suppose he should bid you cut my Throat, would you do it? There's no

Danger of that, said she; but to be sure I would not; for then I should be hang'd; for that would be Murder. Well, said I, and suppose he should resolve to insnare a poor young Creature, and ruin her, would you assist him in that? For to rob a Person of her Virtue, is worse than cutting her Throat.

Why now, says she, how strangely you talk! Are not the two Sexes made for one another? And is it not natural for a Gentleman to love a pretty Woman? And suppose he can obtain his Desires, is that so bad as cutting her Throat? (103–4)

Mrs Jewkes' curiously modern defence that she only obeys orders is definitively answered. There is, says Pamela firmly, 'a Duty superior to that she talked of, which would oblige her to help distressed Innocence, and not permit her to go the Lengths injoin'd by lawless Tyranny' (147). Innocence, she argues, is sacred and above the laws of man. What gives her the courage to speak is her thesis (or Locke's, or Christ's) that to God everyone is equal. In words that would be echoed by her courageous literary descendants Elizabeth Bennet and Jane Eyre, she writes, 'You do well, Sir, said I, to even your Wit to such a poor Maiden as me! But, Sir, let me say, that if you was not rich and great, and I poor and little, you would not insult me so in my Misery!' (72).

Pamela is Mr B.'s spiritual equal, and in transforming him from devil to angel she restores him to his ideal shape. When he had sought to corrupt his own servant by naughty articles, or actually corrupted Robin and Mrs Jewkes, he no longer deserved a responsibility he had betrayed. Pamela in her righteousness has the courage to say so:

I said, I won't stay! You won't, Hussy, said he! Do you know who you speak to! I lost all Fear, and all Respect, and said, Yes, I do, Sir, too well! – Well may I forget that I am your Servant, when you forget what belongs to a Master.

I sobb'd and cry'd most sadly. What a foolish Hussy you are, said he, have I done you any Harm? – Yes, Sir, said I, the greatest Harm in the World: you have taught me to forget myself, and what belongs to me, and have lessen'd the Distance that Fortune has made between us, by demeaning yourself, to be so free to a poor Servant. Yet, Sir, said I, I will be so bold to say, I am honest, tho' poor; And if you was a Prince, I would not be otherwise. (35)

With the disappearance of identity and order, chaos comes again. 'You cannot then be my Master,' cries Pamela, 'for no Master demeans himself so to his poor Servant' (181).

In deserting his duties Mr B. forgoes his right to power. Since to

31

Pamela he is as guardian to ward, master to servant, man to woman, wealth and gentility to poverty and low estate, and since each relation carries with it not only rights but duties of protection for his servant, charity to the deserving poor, chivalry and delicacy to women, Mr B. sins not just in lusting after Pamela, but also by inverting his duties to her. Their social relations link into the checks and balances of earth and even heaven to make her his important angel, his reforming mentor, a pretty preacher like her contemporaries, the women of Methodism.

Mr B.'s handsome exterior promises well, for the demons of his passion make him merely look like Lucifer when 'his Vices all *ugly him over*, as I may say' (171). Because Mr B.'s wickedness is involuntary, caused by indulgent parents (366), he can excuse himself and hope that 'my present Temper will hold' until 'your Prayers will get the better of my Temptations' (188). Vice and virtue do tug until 'your white Angel got the better of my black one' (231), a very special dispensation as Sir Simon Darnford says: 'On my Soul there has been but one Angel come down for these thousand Years, and you have got her' (339).

Mr B.'s descent is plain, his corruption marked like Satan's by shape-changing and disguise. If Satan's lowest and last disguise was that of a creeping serpent, Mr B. abandons his male sphere when he dresses in the clothes of a serving maid. Pamela restores him to his true shape, a gentleman and an earthly substitute for divinity. Once dressed in proper clothes, he becomes a man she can accept. Instantly, as if by sympathetic magic, the servants too resume their own spheres, Mrs Jewkes, for instance, becoming entirely different, 'quite circumspect and decent' (315). In restoring her master, Pamela rights a world her master turned upside down.

If Mr B.'s actions have been aberration, not essence, Pamela is neither foolish nor self-interested to love her stubborn vision of him as perfect guardian, master, gentleman and man. And in time Lady Davers testifies that he is daring, courageous, generous, noble, wise, prudent, sober and magnanimous, and will not tell a lie. He gives his wife money to distribute, sings to her, and provides for her in case he dies. When the happy couple return to a prelapsarian state where sexuality is freed from lust and guilt and unfallen majesty revives (373), the Golden Age, the millennial state foreseen by Locke and Astell,[18] has come again. Pamela will bring forth children under no threat of sorrow, neither will she labour. Benefits flow from God to man, from god-like man to deeply grateful woman. The sunflower that aided her revolt now representing her obedience, she too will turn her face to her king when she accepts the 'kind Rules' he lays down for her behaviour (369), subsidiary moon to the fervent glow of his sun (334).

The second part of the book makes painful reading, for as soon as Pamela gives up her sole weapon, her chastity, she surrenders rights to her only property, her person. Reminded that she now runs the risk of committing '*Læsæ Majestatis*', a sort of 'Treason against my Liege Lord and Husband' (334) she realises the confirmation of his power over her. Bound by her vow of obedience, Pamela may no longer resist. Whatever she thinks, she may no longer say it.

Once subsumed into the role of wife, Pamela has little freedom to be 'her own self', and the habits she once resented she must now permit. Tied to her husband by law, financial dependence, and gratitude, she must suffer for instance the testing of her obedience when he is angry with Lady Davers. For 'my Wife', he says, she has too meanly stooped to this furious sister of his: '*Pamela*, said he, and made me tremble, How dare you approach me, without Leave, when you see me thus disturb'd! – Never, for the future, come near me, while I am in these Tumults, unless I send for you' (359). Pamela replies out of self-preservation, as she must, 'I will endeavour to conform myself, in all things, to your Will' (365). Mr B. lays down injunctions which she promptly codifies like the 'naughty articles' she once resisted, but her defiance is purely private:

1. That I must not, when he is in great Wrath with any body, break in upon him, without his Leave. – *Well, I'll remember it, I warrant. But yet I fansy this Rule is almost peculiar to himself. . .*

6. That I must bear with him, even when I find him in the wrong. *This is a little hard, as the Case may be!*

I wonder whether poor Miss Sally Godfrey be living or dead!

7. That I must be as flexible as the Reed in the Fable, lest, by resisting the Tempest, like the Oak, I be torn up by the Roots. *Well! I'll do the best I can! . . . yet, sure, the Tempest will not lay me quite level with the Ground neither.*
. . .

30. That if the Husband be *set* upon a wrong Thing, she must not dispute with him, but do it, and expostulate afterwards. – *Good-sirs! I don't know what to say to this! – It looks a little hard, methinks! – This would bear a smart Debate, I fansy, in a Parliament of Women.*

The list runs on for forty-eight points, leaving Pamela with only a flicker of resistance. To the rule that his imperfections be not a source of complaint for her, she replies with a flash of the old sharpness, '*To be sure, 'tis no matter how good the Women are; but 'tis to be hopd, Men will allow a little*'. She concludes, 'you'll see I have not the easiest Task in the World' (369–72). One assertion in particular, that 'there are fewer Instances of Mens than Womens loving better after Marriage' (no. 22), will certainly try her patience in the continuation of her story.

Pamela obeys. She dresses for dinner the way he likes, gets up early as he wishes, charms the rakes when they come to inspect her, gladly forgives him his temper tantrum over Lady Davers, and most important, forgives and extenuates his fault with Sally Godfrey, commenting only in response to his admission that he meant to do the same by her, 'you dear naughty Gentleman!' (399). The injustice of the scene seems particularly striking when we remember that this was the man who demanded not once but several times of Pamela to swear that she preferred him to all other men. He too is the man who at the wedding ceremony made a point of asking Pamela whether there was any impediment on *her* side, who managed not to blush when she blushed and said softly, 'None, Sir, but my great Unworthiness' (289).

She is shown off to the gentry who so conspicuously failed to help her, cruel though it is to make an emotional spectacle of her with her father. It is small revenge to kick the card table into Lady Jones' shins (251). She endures general comments upon her sex, and in order to be worthy of him dresses in a fine quilted coat, delicate green mantua silk gown and coat, and French necklace – very different from her country clothes (256). As he reminds her for the rest of the book, Mr B. values Pamela mainly for being his wife. Only briefly in the confrontation with Lady Davers do Pamela's wit and energy reappear, but when she bolts to Mr B. and gabbles out all that has passed, she is not a teller of tales but a tattletale from whom the reader recoils.

Because Pamela is now legally part of her husband, her rebellion is undeclared. Most distressing of all, she abandons her strongest principle – the important hierarchy of duties – when she remarks, as if in sympathy, to Mrs Jewkes, 'what you have done, was in Obedience to a Will which it will become me also to submit to' (234). The uncomfortable sense that all is not quite well in Pamela's world Richardson will courageously confirm in the continuation of her story.

And so we leave Pamela, that steadfast individualist, in her daily round. She will run the household, take over the family accounts, visit the sick and the poor, assist the housekeeper in making jellies, comfits, sweetmeats, marmalades and cordials, pot, candy and preserve, and make all the fine linen for Mr B. and herself. For recreation her highest hopes are an airing in Mr B.'s chariot,

And when you shall return home from your Diversions on the Green, or from the Chace, or where-ever you shall please to go, I shall have the Pleasure of receiving you with Duty, and a chearful Delight; and, in your Absence, count the Moments till you return; and you will, may-be, fill up the sweetest Part of my Time, with your agreeable Conversation, for an Hour or two now-and-then; and be indulgent to the impertinent Over-flowings of my grateful Heart, for all your Goodness to me.   (226)

If we still think of Pamela as a real person, the outlook for her is bleak. But I suspect that by this stage of the book we have given up thinking of either character as real: when they are all too often mouthpieces for conventional opinions, Richardson seems simply to have given up. He will not make the same mistake in *Clarissa*.

How revolutionary, then, is *Pamela*? If Christianity teaches Pamela rebellion, it also confirms her in obedience. Where Richardson is revolutionary, however, is in throwing the issues of sexual and class privilege open to debate among his characters, and, by extension, among us. When he explores the implications of her rise, through merit, to wealth and status, Lady Davers suggests sarcastically – in a way that many a critic would be glad to copy – that she would have her brother 'publish your fine Reasons to the World, and they will be sweet Encouragements to all the young Gentlemen that read them, to cast themselves away on the Servant-wenches in their Families' (349). Her brother can reply boldly that anyone who married a Pamela would stand acquitted since Pamela is a paragon, and unique.

Richardson presents the view – found everywhere from the Wife of Bath's Tale to *Tess of the D'Urbervilles* – that gentil is as gentil does. But if he is sharp upon Lady Davers' husband, that 'titled Ape' who acts like a fool and writes like a lord (278), he does not say how merit may more generally triumph. Faced with Lady Davers' pride of condition, Pamela rehearses only the traditional consolations of the poor, that 'we were all on a foot originally', that 'many of these Gentlefolks, that brag of their ancient Blood, would be glad to have it as wholsome, and as really untainted, as ours!', that life is short, that one cannot distinguish between the skulls of a king and a poor man, that at the last judgment their neglect of opportunities may be held against them, that the genealogy of the poor goes back at least as far as that of the rich, and that the wheel of fortune turns round:

And how can they be assured, that one hundred Years hence or two, some of these now despised upstart Families, may not revel in their Estates, while their Descendants may be reduced to the other's Dunghils?

But none of this alters the status quo, as Pamela's complacent reference to the great Chain of Being shows (222). Privilege and property remain intact, as they do in Locke.[19]

Pamela's rise does not, then, overturn the structure by which she rose. To Lady Davers' query about the difference between a beggar's son married to a lady, a beggar's daughter made a gentleman's wife, and she herself marrying her father's groom, Mr B. replies with utter assurance that the difference is that 'a Man ennobles the Woman he takes, be she *who* she will; and adopts her into his own Rank, be it *what* it will: But a Woman, tho' ever so nobly born, debases herself by a mean Marriage, and descends from her own Rank, to his she stoops to'.[20] It is one thing for Mr B. to raise up a lowly Pamela, another for a lady to set above herself 'a sordid Groom, whose constant Train of Education, Conversation, and Opportunities, could possibly give him no other Merit, than that which must proceed from the vilest lowest Taste, in his sordid Dignifier'. Lady Davers is not satisfied, and asks again, 'You are actually and really marry'd, honestly, or rather foolishly, marry'd to this Slut?', to which Mr B. can simply say that 'why, when I have a Sufficiency in my own single Hands, should I scruple to make a Woman equally happy, who has all I want?' (348–50). Mr B. overpowers his sister, but not I think the reader. He will conform to Pamela's 'almost sacred' virtue, to be sure (338), but his compliance in his own restoration merely confirms his birthright of privilege. Hurrying, perhaps, to a conclusion, Richardson does not examine property and privilege as strenuously as he will in his masterpiece, *Clarissa*.

Steadfast before a battery of arbitrary powers, Pamela is rewarded by the restoration of her little world. Her defence of individual vision could be seen, though, to anticipate the overthrow of arbitrary authority in a century of revolutions to come. Her weapon in the battle to be seen not just as a woman but as an individual is not so much her chastity as her pen. Literacy defeats the handicap of sex. 'By God,' says Chaucer's Wife of Bath, faced with Jankyn's tales of treachery in women, 'if women had written stories the way scholars do shut up in their cells, they would show more wickedness in men than all the sons of Adam might ever make up for'. As if seizing upon this hint for all women, indeed for all the dispossessed, Pamela speaks and writes. Critics may laugh at her constant scribbling,[21] but her urgent and insistent young voice, her fluency, her mastery of the word both spoken and written dominate her book, and endow with god-like power the scrattle, scrattle, scrattle of her pen.

2

From *Pamela* to *Clarissa*

Pamela was an immediate best-seller, provoking praise, blame, parodies, continuations, and associated products such as fans and flat straw hats. Richardson laboured extensively to control his audience's response. He tested the manuscript on his wife and a friend (Carroll, pp. 41–2), anticipated criticism within the book, challenged correspondents in private, and added prefatory material by friends with which to head off readers before they could even start. Fielding, to whom the puffing was intolerable, spoofed these admiring and susceptible gentlemen in his *Shamela*. Richardson resorted next to revision. Without a full comparison of editions, a compliment uncommon for novels until now, revision may go undetected, but Richardson, who apparently reasoned that if *Pamela* was vulnerable to wayward readers at least he could convince posterity, worked on it sporadically for the rest of his life, giving *Pamela* his 'last Hand' (Carroll, p. 234). His pains were to be largely ignored.[1]

Since large-scale alteration is revisionist tampering with the facts, Richardson limited himself by necessity mainly to tendency and tone. Many changes are for the worse, such as the gentrification of Pamela's cheerfully idiomatic speech,[2] and his invisible mending could anyway have little general effect. By May 1741 continuations and criticisms, of which *Shamela* was only the sharpest, had convinced Richardson that he himself must interpret to an uncomprehending world a *Pamela* 'basely Ravished' out of his hands (Carroll, p. 43). Even as he revised it he embarked upon two further volumes which, as Mrs Barbauld shrewdly remarked, were 'less a continuation than the author's defence of himself'.[3]

Pamela in her Exalted Condition (1741) is at first a ramshackle collection of fragments to answer the critics' mocks[4] which backtracks, clogs up, and stutters to a stop. No-one could possibly call it a free-standing success. Commentary is not fiction, nor can characters survive who look backwards to such a fatal degree. In fact the whole first volume makes little sense without the original *Pamela*. Richardson acts as though creative fatherhood gave him rights to change his 'children', whereas publication had liberated the characters into a space where he could neither possess nor protect them. Animated by the act of reading, they had lived out their lives in real minds, entered into real memories, and been shared and discussed as though they were truly known. By these tests they were as 'alive' as any person born of the flesh, they belonged to history as much as to fiction, and even their author could not alter what they had done.

Indeed Richardson himself endorses the reality of Pamela's world every time he draws on it for 'evidence'. Frequent cross-referencing to the first *Pamela* makes it an exhibit, the new book's subject and object, so that characters speak with bizarre effect to ghostly voices from outside. In *Pamela* the reading of letters changed lives, but now it is something to do when there is nothing to do, as her mother and father tell:

when our spirits flag, thro' the infirmity of years, we have recourse to some of your papers. Come, my dear, cry I, what say you to a banquet now? . . . and after a little while, we are as brisk, as if we had had no flagging at all, and return to the duties of the day with double delight.

(III.127)

The scribbling that once filled the tense time of entrapment becomes now the occupation of idleness. Pamela has been long silent, she writes, 'having had nothing new to entertain you with: and yet this last is but a poor excuse neither to you, who think every trifling subject agreeable from your daughter' (III. 120). Once, Mr B.'s dread of exposure justified all his plots, but now he cheerfully allows his sister to flourish Pamela's letters about the 'dark affair' (III. 154). Worse than the continuation's failure as a fiction, though, is Richardson's betrayal of his book. Contradiction and absurdity are the price of his close control, and if he is not loyal to Pamela, who will be?

All the most wounding complaints, that Pamela was too knowing, too scheming and too inflammatory, that Mr B. should not have married down, that it was wrong to forgive Mrs Jewkes, and that Mr Peters' refusal to help was a slur upon the profession, Richardson answers with marked complacency, as his page of contents shows:

[Lady Davers] Gives her reasons, why those scenes [Pamela] is so scrupulous about, were necessary to be written by her, and ought to be read by those who saw the rest of her narrations. – That they all blame her for bearing the wicked Jewkes in her sight, &c. . .
 [Mrs. B.] defends her forgiving conduct to Mrs. Jewkes. . .
 Mr. Peters desires her to mention his hearty sorrow for having formerly

deny'd her the protection of his house; and hopes, that neither religion
nor his cloth may suffer in her opinion on that account . . .
  [Pamela] Endeavours to extenuate Mr. B.'s former faults, and has no
fear for his morals . . . Her generous allowance in Mr. Peters's favour;
and her regard to the cloth . . .
  The substance of a conversation begun by Sir Jacob, of the bad precedent Mr. B. has set to young gentlemen to marry their mothers waiting
maids. Lady Davers seconds Sir Jacob. Mr. B. clears up the point to their
satisfaction.   (III. vi–ix)

But these points are not cleared up to *our* satisfaction, because as
soon as Richardson invents new stories, dialogue, and characters
to fabricate causation for their predecessors, he unfairly justifies
the whole from the happy end, by hindsight.

For those critics who thought Pamela's resistance ridiculous,
Richardson presents scenes of her saving a maid from seduction
and caring for that little memento of sin, Miss Goodwin. Other
criticisms he assigns to characters whom he then undermines. For
instance Pamela recalls an antiquated rake who accused Mr B. of
encouraging others to marry beneath them, as 'splitting his arch
face, with a broad laugh, and shewing a mouth, with hardly a tooth
in it, while he is making indecent remarks upon what he has read'.
To this unkind portrait Mr B. adds 'his dismounted spectacles, his
arch mouth, and gums of shining jet, succeeding those of polish'd
ivory, of which he often boasts, as one ornament of his youthful
days'. Typically, though, Richardson lets Sir Simon complain of
'war declar'd against my poor gums' when 'your what-shall-I-call-
her of a wife, with all the insolence of youth and beauty on her side,
follows me with a glass, and would make me look in it, whether
I will or not' (III. 115–17).

Characters witness to Pamela's saintliness and gentility, and
attest to readers who called Mr B. a booby that he is god-like in
his benevolence, or at least like Adam when he and Pamela are
compared to the 'first pair before the fall' (III. 284). Lady Davers
tackles the accusations of knowingness and 'warmth' by arguing
triumphantly that if Pamela had not 'recited all you could recite'
no bound would have been set to one's 'apprehensive imaginations,
which otherwise must have been injurious to your chastity, tho'
you could not help it' (III. 39). If, as some had said, Richardson's
ignorance of high life was revealed in Lady Davers' rudeness, she
explains that it was due to preference for a friend (III. 201), while
Mr Peters, whose betrayal Pamela actually palliates by analogy with
St Peter's in a much greater instance, is helped out by a similarly

retrospective invention of motive. He 'might think', says Pamela, that he was helping another to a wife (III. 133). And in response to the general dismay at Pamela's marriage, Richardson has her plead that Mr B. 'overcame his criminal passion, and, braving the opinion of the world, married his poor servant girl, as a reward for her virtue' (III. 131). But if Mr B. was good all along, Pamela's resistance and suffering have been pointless. Worst of all, forgiveness of Mrs Jewkes is the abandoning of her first duty to God, the principle to which she was steadfast when even the church, through Mr Peters, had betrayed it.

In such ways Richardson fought to seal off debate, but *Pamela*'s central topic, the hierarchy of duties, still troubled him. Had Pamela truly been right to forgive Mrs Jewkes? If she did so out of obedience to a violent and impetuous master (III. 56), what does her submission in marriage really mean? The old important words like 'liberties', 'criminal' and 'thief' recur apparently without their former menace, as when Lady Davers argues that her brother 'takes no glory in the blind submission of a slave; but, like a true British monarch, delights to reign in a free, rather than in an abject mind'. But she warns that he is 'jealous as a tyrant of his prerogative' (III. 86). Pamela, though grateful to her husband, does not want to 'be guilty of a meanness of spirit, and shew myself a servile creature, and such a one as would lick the dust'. She will give in on small points, but not on large ones such as nursing her child, and dreads that the 'sleeping dragon' will awake (III. 347–8). Richardson's honest doubts thus provided him with his next volume, when – in a way that became habitual to him – he reconsidered and rewrote.

So long as his mind was entangled with what was already done, Richardson could not start afresh. The first volume of *Pamela in her Exalted Condition* contains working papers, the author's queries to himself, and brief moments when his imagination is on the glow only remind us of what it could have been. Polly Darnford's sardonic view of her sister's courtship, for instance, which often anticipates Elizabeth Bennet's distress at that of Charlotte Lucas, sparks up a liveliness soon stifled by the elegant blank of her marriage with Lord Greresby. It is as dismissive a solution as Lucy Selby's with Lord Reresby in *Grandison*.

Richardson simply loses his head in the first volume of *Pamela Exalted*. Whenever he disavows his own innovation of counterpointing public against private expression the character looks self-deceived, and the author who interferes with memories seems tyrannical. Flustered by criticism, Richardson, whose real business was to defend his own technical, moral and narrative freedom of choice, denied Pamela the chance to be aware and articulate under trial. Where the layering of consciousness in the first *Pamela* held surprises for characters as well as readers, here that life-like sense of doubt, indecision, and the chanciness of the world disappear among characters so openly his puppets. Mrs Jewkes will even die for him, and Pamela delivers an essay on the Italian opera actually written by a correspondent of the author (Eaves and Kimpel, p. 145). By writing over it, Richardson obliterates his first work in what is perilously close to a cheat. Officiously author, character, critic and compliant audience all in one, he bustles in between characters and readers. As he must have realised himself, the volume raises troubling questions about the powers of the author, the extent to which he may show his hand, and his freedom to modify past events or characters already shaped. The vehement anarchy of the response to *Pamela* jolted him into breaking the rule that even authors, bound as they are by the pastness of their own work, the need for consistency, and the curious necessity of letting the reader in, have limits on their freedom. But suddenly, as he writes his way into the last volume of Pamela's story, Richardson's skill and confidence are restored.

The fourth volume of *Pamela* wastes little space. In episodes dense with significance for his future concerns, Richardson shows that domestic heavens can turn out marital hells. Pamela bitterly discovers, as Mary Astell said, that 'she who elects a Monarch for Life . . . gives him an Authority, she cannot recall' (*Marriage*, p. 37). For all her vaunts of happiness Pamela admits that subordination is indeed a penance and a curse, frankly telling Miss Goodwin that in marriage,

> which is a kind of state of humiliation for a woman, you must think yourself subordinate to your husband; for so it has pleased GOD to make the wife. You must have no will of your own, in *petty* things: and if you marry a man of sense and honour, he will look upon you as his equal; and will exalt you the more, for your abasing yourself.　　　　(IV. 392–93)

As he brooded over *Clarissa* he would spell this remarkable observation out again. 'What is called a happy Issue' in *Pamela*, he wrote in his 'Hints of Prefaces',

> was, however, owing to her implicit Submission to a lordly and imperious Husband, who hardly deserved her, that she was happy; a Submission

which every Woman could not have shewn. And yet she had a too well grounded Jealousy to contend with afterwards; which, for the time, tore her Heart in pieces.[5]

For the rest of his life Richardson would be trying to make up for the mistaken conclusion he seemed to have reached in *Pamela*, 'that sad, that inconsiderate notion, *that a reform'd rake makes the best husband*' (IV. 377), by warning that subordination is only tolerable with a man of sense and honour. Equally dreadful, argues Pamela, is marriage with a tenacious and obstinate fool, taught to 'talk of prerogative, and to call himself a *man*, without knowing how to behave as one, and I to despise him of course' (IV. 224).[6] So at least Clarissa will dismally think as she surveys her two suitors, Robert Lovelace and Roger Solmes.

Man the Monarch returns in the second volume of the continuation. The B.'s are in London, Pamela is pregnant, and Mr B. insists that she must not nurse her child. Now Pamela's obedience constrains her to a new conflict of duties. Retreating of necessity to private thoughts, she calls him arbitrary to insist that 'if the husband is determined, it is a wife's duty to obey', bravely arguing that even a husband's will is not sufficient to excuse one from a natural or divine obligation. Mr B., his precedents, like Filmer's, taken from the Old Testament, imposes limitations on her nursing. He threatens separate beds, warns that he might not love Pamela if her appearance suffers, and bribes her with promises of education. When he threatens polygamy Pamela must revolt, with '*Polygamy* and *prerogative*! Two very bad words! I do not love them', to which Mr B. quotes Moses to prove how little force the vows of the female sex have, and 'how much you are under the controul of ours'. Pamela is bewildered, and asks her parents whether a husband does have such vast prerogatives when the New Testament teaches men not to set themselves in God's place. Nor is it a compliment to him if she has no will of her own. Since she cannot trust the judgment of Mr B., who was never thought 'so nice a casuist in these serious points, as that one might absolutely rely upon his decisions', she appeals for the toleration allowed to a tender conscience by law, 'but my beloved husband, my lawgiver, and my prince' will allow her none (IV. letter 3). Mr Andrews is frightened, and advises her to give in. When she does, Mr B. meanly blames her for making him assume 'a hated, because ungenerous, necessity of pleading the privilege of a husband' and again threatens her with polygamy. He accuses her of being an encroaching subject: 'he smiled when he spoke this; but was in earnest for all that', writes poor Pamela. But, she protests in one last rebellious flash, he should have distinguished 'between a point where my *conscience* was concerned, and a *common* one', for without meaning to invade his province nor step out of hers, 'I thought I had a right to a *little* free-will, a *very* little'. Her retort to his patronising forgiveness, that she is not fully satisfied 'whether it must be I that forgive you, or you me', provokes a demand for her whole will that makes her privately protest, 'the words *command* and *obey* are not quite blotted out of his vocabulary, as he said they should be'. She cannot believe that many women would sit down so satisfied with it as she is forced to do. Finally, his rebuke for her angry tears makes her write, 'Very heroic, truly! One stands a poor chance in a contest with such a husband. It must be all pure unmixed obedience and submission' (IV. letter 5). Here Richardson's gift for the volleys and returns of verbal conflict, deepened by political significance, has obviously revived.

Richardson sends Pamela to a play, the Italian opera, and a masquerade, his imagination kindling again when she sees her husband, dressed as a Spaniard, flirting with a bold nun. If he carries out his threat of polygamy, her surrender will have been in vain. 'I liked my English Mr. B. better than my Spaniard', says Pamela pitifully (IV. 83). If submission is God's first curse upon women, the birth of her son Billy fulfils the curse of bringing forth children in sorrow, for Pamela has 'a very sharp time' that makes Miss Darnford vow that no man 'is worth running these risques for' (IV. 100). Trapped by fears of losing the hard-bought child to another woman, Pamela endures Mr B.'s accusation that he sees his 'nun' only because his wife is vapourish, jealous and inquisitive. Her old enlivening knack of writing to the moment is restored in the scene where she painfully observes that Lady S. 'would have stifled [the baby] with her warm kisses', grudges that her 'naughty lips should so closely follow mine', and feels it keenly when the treacherous child does not complain. 'I would have had *him* just then, cry, instead of me', she writes (IV. 137–41).

The offender is the accuser still, and although Mr B.'s perverse vehemence suggests that he knows it, his head is no sooner laid upon the pillow than he falls asleep, or feigns to, which is 'as prohibitory of my talking, as if he had bid me be silent'. Pamela has 'all my own entertaining reflections to myself: which gave me not one wink of sleep' (IV. 147). An anonymous letter having confirmed her fears, Pamela, who perhaps recalls that Mr B. had said the law was above him, constructs in a mock courtroom a mutual 'trial'

(IV. 154) in which she impresses Mr B. by her bold statement that she is no criminal, in a renewed resistance to his attempts to put her beyond the law's protection (IV. 158). In an anticipation of the divided love theme of *Grandison*, she offers to release him so long as she can keep her child (IV. 165). Mr B.'s statement in his own defence gives Richardson the advantage of trying out multiple points of view, of examining the subjectivity of vision, the unreliability of signs, the incompleteness of knowledge, and the difficulty of 'reading' events. By laying together Mr B.'s story, Lady S.'s, and an informant's, he moves from *Pamela*'s self-confirming journal towards the sophisticated competition for truth that marks *Clarissa*.

Miss Goodwin's adoption into the family circle introduces an important new theme: education for the young. Pamela quotes extensively from Locke's treatise, *Some Thoughts Concerning Education*, her quibbles and additions only showing how carefully Richardson has read it. Like Locke she recommends education at home, and pleads for the educational freedom of girls. Her remarks on swaddling develop for instance from his promotion of physical health:

How has my heart ached, many and many a time, when I have seen poor babies roll'd and swath'd, ten or a dozen times round; then blanket upon blanket, mantle upon that; its little neck pinn'd down to one posture; its head, more than it frequently needs, triple-crown'd, with covering upon covering; its legs and arms, (as if to prevent that kindly stretching, which we rather ought to promote, when it is in health, and which is only aiming at growth and enlargement) the former bundled up, the latter pinn'd down; and how the poor thing lies on the nurse's lap, a miserable little pinion'd captive, goggling and staring with its eyes, the only organs it has at liberty, as if it were supplicating for freedom to its fetter'd limbs!

(IV. 261–2)

The fettered child symbolises to Pamela the condition of all women, 'forced to struggle for knowlege, like the poor feeble infant' who is 'pinioned, legs, arms, and head, on the nurse's lap'. If by great chance its little arms happen to 'gain freedom, and offer but to expand themselves, [they] are immediately taken into custody, and pinn'd down to passive behaviour, by the tyrannical nurse' as, she explains, 'when a poor girl, in spite of her narrow education, breaks into notice, her genius is immediately tamed by trifling employments, and she is kept back, lest she should become the envy of her own sex, and be shunned by the other' (IV. 277).

By his denial of innate ideas, Locke attributed the cause of all morality to education, upon which as Pamela in echo says, the superstructure of the future man is erected (IV. 297). And if, as

45

Locke had said, virtue and a well-tempered soul are preferable to
Latin and languages, Pamela will learn Latin by reading the
Evangelists aloud. See what a mother can do with the privilege of
the first education (IV. 311–13), but who, she asks acutely, 'as our
sex is generally educated, shall teach the *mothers*?'. Why, therefore,
should not girls be allowed the same first education as boys, so that
they are raised above 'the imputations of some unkind men, who
allot to their parts common tea-table prattle, while they do all they
can to make them fit for nothing else, and then upbraid them for
it?' (IV. 316–17). Pamela believes that women's learning is mainly
to the benefit of others, but goes on to develop a theme understandably
dear to Richardson, that natural talent can outshine minds privileged by education. Women, she says, 'notwithstanding their cramp'd
and confin'd education', often make '*more* than an equal figure with
the men . . . in spite of the contempts pour'd upon our sex by some
whose writings I have in my eye' (IV. 319). She draws back from
the obvious conclusion that women's innate gifts make them
superior to educated men, and dares not to conjecture the cause
of this 'more than parity in the genius of the sexes'. This she says
'might lead one into too proud a thought in favour of a sex too contemptuously treated'.

Education creates hierarchy and prerogative, she argues. An-
ticipating *Clarissa*, she reasons that the 'contemptuous treatment
of one half, if not the better half, of the human species' exposes
women to profligate attacks by rendering the sex 'vile in the eyes
of the most vile', so that a woman's very excellences become 'in-
centives for base wretches to attempt her virtue, and bring about
her ruin' (IV. 321–2). Since men have no strength except in
women's weakness, the innocent heart cannot guard too watchful-
ly against their hard hearts and their breaking of promises. Richardson is already thinking of *Clarissa* when he imagines a wretch who
makes 'sport of destroying a virtuous character, and delights in being the wicked means of throwing, perhaps, upon the town, a poor
creature, whose love for him, and confidence in him, was all her
crime' (IV. 367–9). He need only combine this idea with Miss Darnford's unhappy discovery that too many women 'from fond lovers,
prostrate at their feet, find surly husbands, trampling on their
necks!' (IV. 352) to discover his new heroine, Clarissa Harlowe.

The book concludes experimentally with a series of debates on
love, Miss Stapylton's tale of first-sight love (IV. 354) and a lively
outline of a fop (IV. 362–3) which must have been useful, for instance, for *Grandison*. *Clarissa* is foreshadowed in the story of

the rich and lovely Miss Cope, who has allowed the familiarities of an imperious libertine to proceed to 'romping' before visits were prohibited. She is detected in her design to elope, 'which, had she effected, in all probability the dishonourable lover would have triumphed over her honour; having given out since, that he intended to revenge himself on the daughter, for the disgrace he had receiv'd from the parents' (IV. 355). Trustingly, lovingly, she has forgiven his rough manners just as Clarissa after the rape will hallucinate that she has made a pet of a bear. By now, Richardson has clearly found his new plot.

The story of Miss Lucas, a name surely noted by Jane Austen, looks forward rather to Lovelace. Her 'wild young man' waited with patience 'till he thought himself secure of his prey; and then would pull off the mask at once, and, if he succeeded, glory in his villainy' (IV. 357). Like Lovelace he corresponds even after his visits are forbidden. Miss Cope maintains that the cruelty of friends forces lovers upon private and clandestine meetings, as Clarissa's tyrannical father's cruelty will force her to meet with Lovelace. Given the 'continual state of war between the two sexes; one offensive, the other defensive', it is better to fear an enemy than hope a friend, comments Miss Towers (IV. 361). Men's capacity for deception Richardson will definitively demonstrate in *Clarissa*.

Miss Shafton resembles Anna Howe, Clarissa's friend. Rather too airy, with 'a great deal of that flippant wit, which makes more enemies than friends', she has 'made herself cheap and accessible to fops and rakes, and had not the worse opinion of men for being such'. She listens eagerly to stories told to the disadvantage of women, and 'held inexcusable the woman who suffer'd herself to be seduced; and declared the seducers to be much less faulty' (IV. 356). All the things that make Anna Howe a dangerous friend, her lack of seriousness, her inability to resist a handsome exterior, her persistent reading of Clarissa's relationship as love, and her love for the seducer, are here to be found in their essence.

By the end of *Pamela in her Exalted Condition* Richardson has returned to the things he does best: political conflict in the nursing debate, tense confrontation in the 'court-room' scene, sharp dialogue over the Countess, and psychological truth in Pamela's jealousy over her son. If in the young women's tales he sketched ideas for *Clarissa*, the discussion of women's education made him consider what might happen to a truly gifted woman in the society of his day. Clarissa, who is older and better educated than Pamela, cannot be patronised as she was. She is both an exception among womankind, and its vulnerable representative in a world that belongs to men. The fact that she is extraordinary and a woman will be cause enough for her family to crush her and a libertine to challenge her in a conflict to breed disaster.

In these uneven volumes, Richardson regains his nerve. The criticism that drove him to self-defence forced him also into renewed creativity, when, obsessively reading and re-reading *Pamela* for the sake of his revisions and his continuation, he steadied his mind for *Clarissa*. His last, best reply to the critics was to do it all over again.[7]

The essential elements of woman, libertine, abduction and resistance recur in *Clarissa*, the shift from comedy to tragedy solving at a stroke the problem of rewarding virtue. The story is simply told. Clarissa Harlowe, a young woman who is intelligent, lovely and beloved, antagonises her family when she refuses to marry Roger Solmes. Her sole comfort is writing to her friend Anna Howe, a lively woman who finds her own suitor Mr Hickman dull. Robert Lovelace, a dashing rake who reveals his intention to trick and seduce Clarissa to his friend Belford, helps her escape, and lures her, unwitting, to a London brothel. Here she is initially fooled by the gentility of the whores and their madam, Mrs Sinclair, but his true intent having become clear, she resists him, and attempts escape. Exasperated, Lovelace drugs her and rapes her, and Clarissa decides inexorably upon death. Cutting off all connection with Lovelace, she takes shelter with an elderly couple, and prepares to die. She is arrested for debt, and spends her last days writing on the coffin by which her body returns to her father's house. Lovelace, challenged by her cousin Colonel Morden, receives a mortal wound.

In *Clarissa*, then, Richardson boldly pursues the logical consequences of *Pamela*, richly complicating and fulfilling its hints. If Pamela was a paragon, here is what happens to a truly exceptional woman. If Pamela was treated as if she were a prostitute, Clarissa inhabits a real brothel where real whores assist in her actual rape. Pamela resists identification as a whore, resists rape, and considers suicide as the only way out, as her father knows. 'What! then,' he asks when told she is in a way to be happy, 'is she dying?' (248). Miss Harlowe, once raped, thinks herself the harlot her name implies, and she completes that drive to self-destruction. Mr B.'s sexual threat is enlarged in the ugly encroaching weight of Roger Solmes, his sexual attraction in the irresistible Lovelace. Pamela marries

Mr B. because he could not rape her, Clarissa cannot marry Lovelace because he did; Mr B.'s affection for Sally Godfrey proved him not utterly abandoned, but Lovelace's restraint over Rosebud is part of his plot to catch Clarissa; Mr B.'s scruples restrained him where Lovelace proceeds to the final outrage by any means possible. Mrs Jewkes, who held Pamela down in an attempt at rape, becomes Mrs Sinclair, an actual madam, and where Pamela prevented rape by taking fits, Lovelace induces the stupefaction that permits it. *Clarissa* is Richardson's definitive answer to critics of *Pamela*, for its logical development from first premises to final tragedy meant that they had to take seriously the 'Mighty Piece of Undone' they once had mocked.

Clarissa improves startlingly upon *Pamela*. Where in his first novel actions had often seemed random, in *Clarissa* they derive from the nature of the characters. For instance, Pamela's arbitrary abduction becomes a complex scene in which Clarissa is being half-forced, half-tricked into an act she does not altogether resist. Pamela's isolation is imposed upon her by Mr B., whereas Clarissa's results from family disputes about her marriage fate. Where Pamela's humble parents had no real power over her, the Harlowes actively reject their daughter. Their house is no pastoral Eden, but a mansion filled with envy and greed. Clarissa's impulse to love and to revere clashes with awareness of her parents' tyranny, and she flees to the villain–hero because he seems less of a threat than her family or marriage with Solmes. And, having convinced himself in the continuation that heroines are subdued in marriage, Richardson in *Clarissa* wisely reverts to courtship, the scene of women's power. The result is a plot subject not to authorial whim, but to necessity.

In *Clarissa* Richardson returns to his proper place, the umbrage of the editor. After forcing perfection on Mr B. he now creates a villain–hero, and instead of reforming a Mrs Jewkes, does not flinch from a Jezebel who dies roaring, unrepentant and gangrenous. Working on his sequel had taught Richardson to prefer different versions of a story to direct editorial intervention, and he had only to make them compete for our sympathy as they so markedly do in *Clarissa* to create a narrative wonderfully absorbed in itself. *Clarissa* is long, but it does not digress. He learnt too to let characters speak for themselves. Even when shouting his head off Mr B. was muted by Pamela's narration, but Lovelace writes himself into immediate life. After experimenting in only one letter with Mr B.'s delighted telling of his plots, his rakish wit with its quick exchanges, smart exclamatory turns and comradely frankness, his swearing and slang and cant of hunting (III. 320–4), Richardson evolves a style for Lovelace that would enchant his dazzled readers. With a new shapeliness of plot, the novel begins in January and ends in December. Clarissa leaves home in spring, is raped at Midsummer (a dreadful irony when this is the time for lovers to find out their true loves), and dies in September just before the autumnal equinox. Lovelace is killed a few days before the winter solstice, in December.[8] Characters and episodes are complementary in new ways: for instance, Anna Howe's resistance to a good man whom she does not like reflects Clarissa's to a bad one whom she might like. Voices balance when, speaking frankly to their friends and dissembling to each other, Lovelace tells his plots to Belford and Clarissa her fears to Anna. The inability of the confidants to intervene allows dramatic irony to operate to a far greater extent than in *Pamela*. Above all, *Clarissa* faces the nagging objection to *Pamela*'s sub-title, *Virtue Rewarded*: what if the outcome does not justify the event? Lady Betty Darnford's blurted question, 'what would the world have said, had it not?' (III. 27), provides the imaginative germ for *Clarissa*. Without that punctilious attentiveness to his critics, Richardson might never have pushed himself into writing a masterpiece.

3

The extraordinary woman

If Pamela is moon to her husband's sun, Clarissa is nobody's satellite, but a comet which blazes briefly, disastrously, once in a lifetime, to the astonishment of all. Her name, which means both 'famous' and 'full of light', promises that like Halley's Comet she will be 'eccentric', and soar outside her proper sphere.[1] 'Pushed into blaze' in the very first letter, she is a radiant beauty who with shining hair, dazzling fire in her starry eyes, diamond snaps, and a sky-blue riband surmounting all, flashes upon Lovelace 'all at once in a flood of brightness'. Even the embroidered violets on her gown are filled with gold and silver light, so that the exultant Lovelace might well take off his hat to see if the lace is scorched, 'supposing it had brushed down a star' (399–402).[2] Bolder and braver than Sidney's Astrophel, he has forced his Stella down to earth (521).

Clarissa's father, mother, sister, brother, suitor, friend, and lover all endeavour to bring down to their level this sun among faint twinklers (129) for one reason only, that she is special. Trapped in the body of an earthly woman, fettered by the dangerous condition of being female, she is to her family a mere daughter, a commodity, a love-object born to marry, obey and breed. This heavenly comet they will lower into earthly Harlowe–harlot, as they say: 'the celebrated, the blazing Clarissa – Clarissa, *what?* – *Harlowe*, no doubt – and Harlowe it will be to the disgrace of us all!' (509). Clarissa's resistance to the awesome battery of powers by which these earth-dwellers deny her mind, her reason, her identity, and her right to be responsible for herself provides the story of Richardson's masterpiece.

The beauty that attracts Lovelace and the merit that won her grandfather provoke the Harlowes to push this child, to whom all her blessings are a curse, into marriage with Solmes. In exchange for Clarissa, Solmes promises to leave his estate not to his own hated family but to the Harlowes, and with the two estates lying contiguous, they hope thus to advance themselves into the nobility.[3] Inflamed by Lovelace's rejection of Clarissa's sister Arabella, as well as by his courtship of herself and his animosity to her brother

James, they drive Clarissa into a forbidden correspondence and eventually to flight.

At the start of the novel Clarissa enjoys queenly privileges. In Harlowe Place, which Lovelace compares with aristocratic scorn to Versailles, 'sprung up from a dunghill within every elderly person's remembrance' (161), she dresses (like Marie Antoinette) as an elegant dairy-maid in her dairy (1468). As if from a throne she grants haughty audience to her clumsy courtier Solmes, who awkwardly strides backward as he retires 'till the edge of the opened door, which he run against, remembered him to turn his welcome back upon me' (319). Her brother and her sister continually cabal against Queen Clarissa, their master-plan being to force her to marry Solmes in Uncle Antony's deserted, moated house.

Actual queens like Mary or Elizabeth need obey no man, as Locke points out (I. 47), but the princely soul of this 'Gloriana' (418) being confined in an eighteenth-century woman's body, every man – whether father, brother, husband, or lover – can become her Domestic King. A Lockeian woman in a household of Filmerian men,[4] Clarissa is therefore subject to a father, a brother, and two uncles. Just as to Filmer the right of parents over the children they begat was '*Supreme Power*, and like that of Absolute Monarchs over their Slaves, Absolute Power of Life and Death', as Locke witheringly describes it (I. 51), to Mr Harlowe filial obedience is an absolute and peremptory requirement, its test and its punishment the unlovely suitor Solmes.

Like God in the Old Testament, Clarissa's father is omnipotent, invisible, absolute, and unjust. Anna calls him tyrannical and despotic (86) and even Clarissa admits that he is arbitrary (95). Existing only as a strong voice demanding to be obeyed, he is heard but not seen when from the next room 'this sentence I heard thundered from the mouth of one who had a right to all my reverence: Son James, let the rebel be this moment carried away to my brother's – this very moment – she shall not stay one hour more under my roof!' The door she presses on flies open, to throw her humiliated into an empty space (312). Mrs Harlowe has resigned the power over her offspring that Locke said belonged equally to mothers (I. 55), and has anyway no influence in the family of a tyrant. She feebly apes her husband's power when, ignoring Clarissa, she continues 'looking into a drawer among laces and linen, in a way neither busy nor unbusy' (102), and, though conscious of what she every day forgoes and undergoes, is willing for the sake of peace to sacrifice her daughter. Clarissa marvels at the prerogative of manhood that allows her father to dominate a woman who brought him so much wealth, regretting too that her mother has not always by her sacrifices found peace (105).

Like God in the Garden of Eden, Clarissa's father challenges the independence and obedience of a creature he has made. Since her independence derives from the inheritance, the Harlowes resent her for having it, fear what she will do with it, and want it for themselves. To get it they will marry her to Solmes. Clarissa's crime is that as 'his *youngest* grandchild! a *daughter* too!' (194) she was not the first-born son. Her brother believes daughters to be 'chickens brought up for the tables of other men'. This means that the idea of Clarissa wielding more power as a single woman than she would as a wife enrages her father, who 'could not bear that I should be made sole, as I may call it, and independent, for such the will as to that estate and the powers it gave (unaccountably, as they all said), made me' (77–8). Aware that their claim depends upon force, not right, they rush to conclude the marriage before Morden's arrival makes her independent of them all.

Her grandfather's will bestows on Clarissa a free will in the marriage choice that Bella insanely resents:

I do not doubt but it is Miss Clary's aim . . . to get her estate into her own hands, and go to live at *The Grove*, in that independence upon which she builds all her perverseness. And, dear heart! my little love, how will you then blaze away! Your mamma Norton, your oracle, with your poor at your gates, mingling so *proudly* and so *meanly* with the ragged herd! Reflecting, by your ostentation, upon all the ladies in the county, who do not as you do. This is known to be your scheme! And the poor *without-doors*, and Lovelace *within*, with one hand building up a name, pulling it down with the other! (199)

The Harlowes also covet the money for its own sake. Traditional emblems of avarice, they 'fret on, grumble and grudge, and accumulate; and wondering what ails them that they have not happiness when they have riches, think the cause is want of more; and so go on heaping up till Death, as greedy an accumulator as themselves, gathers them into his garner!' (68). They hate Clarissa's moderation and generosity. Her most earnest charge against Solmes, and she has many, is a 'diabolical parsimony' that would circumscribe her in his 'narrow, selfish circle!' (153).

Believing that wealth will bring her round as it would them, the family orders patterns of the richest silks from London. What rich suits, jewels, pin money she will have, exults her mother like Mrs Bennet to Elizabeth; great encouragement indeed, adds Clarissa sarcastically, to adorn oneself to be the wife of Mr Solmes (190). Bella knows how it torments her to spread the silks upon her sleeve and run on with apparent tranquillity, '*This*, Clary, is a pretty pattern enough: But *this* is quite *charming!* I would advise you to make your appearance in it. And *this*, were I you, should be my wedding night-gown – and *this* my second dressed suit!' (203).

The Harlowes select Solmes because he will return to them property otherwise lost in marriage: for the sake of a peerage they will give Clarissa to a man she cannot endure. When she logically proposes to surrender her estate to Bella so that she can marry Solmes, they will not hear of it. 'Are *you*, who refuse everybody's advice, to prescribe a husband to your *sister?*', asks Uncle John Harlowe rudely (260). Intolerably for the Harlowes, their happiness depends upon her. Fearing to appear a fool with no authority over his own daughter, Mr Harlowe plans, as Bella gloats, that his '*living* will shall control your grandfather's *dead* one' (199) as soon as the 'I will' of marital obedience to Solmes over-rides both Clarissa's free will and her grandfather's will and testament.[5]

To the awesome list of 'hatred to Lovelace, family aggrandizement, and this great motive *paternal authority!* – What a force *united!* – when, *singly*, each consideration is sufficient to carry all before it!' (82), Father Harlowe makes a last addition, violence. Whether she trembles behind the yew-hedge as he goes by (327), fears she will be dragged away by violence to her Uncle Antony's house (229), or has her writing supplies torn from her in an act of violence (321), Clarissa has to combat strength multiplied among his minions. Father Harlowe also delegates his power to James, his first-born son, for not having '(any more than my brother) a kind opinion of our sex' (64). He confirms the rights that James already holds over Clarissa by virtue of being her brother, older, and a '*man*' (157).

Much of James' power derives from education, the foundation of all hierarchy, for what are colleges, asks Clarissa, 'but classes of tyrants, from the upper students over the lower, and from them to the tutor?' (139). She argues, like Locke, that the main aim of a university education is not knowledge but morality; the brandishing of a Latin tag proves, she says to James, that if humanity were a branch of his studies at the university, 'it has not found a genius in you for mastering it' (219). James, who is not possessed of sufficient parts to make his learning valuable to himself or to anybody else (367), feels threatened by intelligent women, and says, 'I know not what wit in a woman is good for, but to make her

over-value herself, and despise everybody else.' Like those dismayed
by Mrs Wesley and her sister sectarians, he cannot stand the 'saucy
lecturing' of 'such a conceited and pert preacher and questioner'
as Clarissa.

In the face of men's educational privilege Clarissa suggests that
she has taught herself more than James ever learnt at university
(137–8). She proclaims the superiority of the Bible and the dictates
of her own heart, and exchanges the folk wisdom of proverbs with
Mrs Betty the servant, whose gift for repartee is smarter, she says,
than things heard at table from some of her brother's fellow col-
legians. Thus Clarissa, her education compounded by natural
advantages, outshines the men and the women too (264).

To this imperious man, her brother (61), she is neither servant
(137) nor slave (111), but sister. But once privileges such as making the tea, having a personal servant, running the household and
writing letters are stripped away, Clarissa's only power is vested
in her only property, her person. This she must fight to preserve.
When her brother says to Solmes, 'take the rebel daughter's hand;
I give it you now; she shall confirm the gift in a week's time', she
snatches it away. 'What right have YOU to dispose of my hand?
– If you govern everybody else, you shall not govern *me*; especially in a point so immediately relative to myself, and in which you
neither have, nor ever shall have, anything to do' (306). She protests against the 'tyrant word AUTHORITY, as they use it' (239);
'AUTHORITY!', as Anna says, 'what a full word is that in the
mouth of a narrow-minded person, who happened to be born
thirty years before one!' (85). Even Mrs Harlowe admits her husband to be needlessly jealous of male and especially paternal
prerogatives (96). How then may Clarissa reconcile her loving filial
obedience with her free will?

A slave under tyranny, she legitimately resists. In what she herself
calls a liberty of speech she takes verbal freedoms with James (126),
and though prohibited to correspond with Anna, like Pamela before
her she uses the artifice and contrivance forced upon her to do so
clandestinely (66–7). Soon Clarissa is seen as being in a state of
'actual rebellion' (168), her justified resistance and principled
steadiness labelled stubbornness, obstinacy, and prepossession 'by
those who have a right to put what interpretation they please upon
my conduct', as she says. Her family punishes the criminal by
means of an unjust merging of executive and judicial powers. 'The
authors of my disgrace within doors, the talkers of my prepossess-
sion [for Lovelace] without, and the reporters of it from abroad,

were originally the same persons', objects Clarissa (106–8), when she is confined, banished and insulted to enforce her consent to be what she never will be. 'Can you think I am such a slave, such a *poor* slave, as to be brought to change my mind by the violent usage I have met with?' (307). She is above fear in points where her honour and the true dignity of her sex are concerned (216), and will not be brought to marry what she calls the implement of her cruel brother's undeserved persecution, Roger Solmes (318).

To Clarissa, happiness in marriage seems to be rare. Indeed, an equal relationship must have been difficult at a time when women were considered politically and intellectually second-rate. Love was a natural enough passion, but it could scarcely be expected to flourish in eighteenth-century marriages. Anna Howe for one knows how women are tricked, 'cajoled, wire-drawn, and ensnared, like silly birds, into a state of bondage or vile subordination: to be courted as princesses for a few weeks, in order to be treated as slaves for rest of our lives' (133). Clarissa's own indictment of marriage is stark and comprehensive:

To be given up to a strange man; to be engrafted into a strange family; to give up her very name, as a mark of her becoming his absolute and dependent property: to be obliged to prefer this strange man to father, mother – to everybody: and his humours to all her own – Or to contend, perhaps, in breach of a vowed duty for every innocent instance of freewill: to go no-whither: to make acquaintance: to give up acquaintance – to renounce even the strictest friendships perhaps; all at his pleasure, whether she think it reasonable to do so or not. Surely, sir, a young creature ought not to be obliged to make all these sacrifices but for such a man as she can approve.   (148–9)[6]

Left to herself, Clarissa would gladly renounce her female constraints to live chaste and single in a life of mind, but that is forbidden her. 'Were ours a Roman Catholic family, how much happier for me, that they thought a nunnery would answer all their views!', she writes longingly (83), and Anna too dreams of escaping from female destiny to live charmingly together, 'and despite them all!' (133). Mary Astell's idea of a Protestant Nunnery Richardson praised in *Grandison* (III. 9), for in such a place, unconstrained by vows, a woman like the classicist Miss Elizabeth Carter could freely have used her mind. In her *Ode to Wisdom*, which he included in *Clarissa*, Carter's wish to give up fortune, ambitions, beauty, for 'empire o'er my mind' (232) runs parallel to that of a heroine who knows like her namesake, 'grave Clarissa' in Pope's *Rape of the Lock*, that only the cultivation of the mind can defeat time and death (186). The Protestant Nunnery that many women longed for was, however, defeated by a bishop who smelt Popery in it, and Clarissa's intellectual haven would not exist for two hundred and fifty years more.

Clarissa's choice of chastity makes her family suspect the sincerity of her offer to live single, or never to marry at all, or never but with their full approbation (95). Bella calls her preference 'one of your fetches to avoid complying with your duty' (139), and a cover for her secret love of Lovelace. Elizabeth's freedom is denied her: she looks in vain to the example of the virgin Tudor queen, because, being an ordinary woman, she must be an ordinary wife.

Anna cynically surveys the field. 'All men are monkeys more or less, or else that you and I should have such baboons as these to choose out of is a mortifying thing, my dear' (210). But Clarissa, who knows she must yield to marriage as her destiny, asks only the right to say no, if she does not love. 'What law, what ceremony, can give a man a right to a heart which abhors him more than it does any of God Almighty's creatures?', she demands (87). Solmes' proposals have been accepted, she says, as if her choice, happiness and free will were not of the least signification (159), and she warns the 'embattled phalanx' of her family who unite to break her spirit and make her a fit wife for this man that if they take meekness and gentleness for servility, they mistake her (150–1).

Solmes is chosen to humiliate her. Like Satan 'squat like a Toad' at the ear of Eve in *Paradise Lost* (IV. 800), he is a 'bent and broad-shouldered creature' who moves on splay feet to a chair and draws it 'so near mine, squatting in it with his ugly weight, that he pressed upon my hoop' (87). He gnaws the head of his hazel stick, a carved head almost as ugly as his own; he presumes, he encroaches unbearably:

The man stalked in. His usual walk is by pauses, as if (from the same vacuity of thought which made Dryden's clown whistle) he was telling his steps: and first paid his clumsy respects to my mamma, then to my sister; next to me, as if I were already his wife and therefore to be last in his notice; and sitting down by me, told us in general what weather it was. Very cold he made it; but I was warm enough.   (114)

She is to be wedded to a '*monster*', cries Clarissa in despair. His animality revolts her, and yet she is careful to explain that she has not 'only maidenly objections against a man I never can abide' (95–6). Can a man whose person reveals his mind, a man who offers terms to rob his own relations, be truly honest and virtuous? (92). Roger Solmes is her moral and intellectual inferior. He

SAMUEL RICHARDSON

enjoys 'but a very ordinary share of understanding, is very illiterate, knows nothing but the value of estates and how to improve them, and what belongs to land-jobbing, and husbandry' (62). His letters are 'as indifferently worded as poorly spelled' (158). All she asks, pitifully, is that if she must be compelled, let it be for a man that can read and write, 'that can *teach* me something: for what a husband must that man make, who can do nothing but command' (151).[7] Persuaded by the example of her parents that married life is disadvantageous, she pleads only for 'something of an alleviation, if one must bear *undue* control, to bear it from a man of sense' (112).

But it is Solmes, one of 'the noble lords of the creation' (129), who is to be lord of the horrified Clarissa. She recoils from his

disagreeable person, his still more disagreeable manners; his low understanding – understanding! the glory of a man! so little to be dispensed with in the head and director of a family, in order to preserve to him that respect which a good wife (and that for the justification of her own choice) should pay him herself, and wish everybody to pay him.   (111)

'What a degree of patience, what a greatness of soul, is required in the wife, not to despise a husband who is more ignorant, more illiterate, more low-minded, than herself?', she writes (241). Clarissa will not be sold to a man who diminishes what she is. Nor will she marry for gain, for it concerns her not a little that 'my friends could be brought to encourage such offers on *such* motives as I think a person of conscience should not presume to begin the world with' (81).

If, as Locke argued, women might avoid pain in childbirth, then logically they should also be freed from God's other curse, submission to their Adams. He almost dared to say so before recollecting the constraints of custom, temporal law, and nature (I. 47). Solmes, however, has no such liberal qualms. Like her father and her brother he claims a '*mannish* superiority' (62), and has 'all the insolence of his sex, without any one quality to make that insolence tolerable' (241). James delegates the additional right of violence to king Solmes, who duly shows 'a countenance whitened over, as if with malice, his hollow eyes flashing fire, and biting his underlip to show he could be *manly*' (319). He delights in 'curbing and sinking the spirits of a woman he had acquired a right to tyrannize over', and threatens that she might have cause to repent her usage of him to the last day of her life (241–3).

In Solmes' capacity to break sexually this 'termagant' and

58

'tyranness', James takes an ugly pleasure. As Clarissa protests, she is 'considered as an animal to be baited to make sport for my brother and sister, and Mr Solmes. They are all, all of them, wanton in their cruelty – *I*, madam, see the man!' (322–3). Now is the time to resist, before she is irrevocably bound by her vow of obedience, as Anna points out. 'I know of old, my dear, your meek regard to that little piddling part of the marriage vow, which some prerogative-monger foisted into the office to make that a *duty* which he knew was not a *right*.' Even if she married Lovelace, Clarissa would be brought 'so *prettily*, and so *audibly*, to pronounce the little reptile word OBEY, that it will do one's heart good to hear you. The *Muscovite* wife takes place of the *managed* mistress' (277–8).[8] But no man deserves obedience from Clarissa, let alone a cloddish, sadistic Solmes. 'What a dreadful thing must even the love of such a husband be!', writes Anna, and yet 'this is the man they have found out, for the sake of considerations as sordid as those he is governed by, for a husband (that is to say, for a lord and master) for Miss Clarissa Harlowe!' (129–30).

In an appalling foreshadowing of Lovelace's last trick the family plan to marry her at the moated house even if she is unconscious. Clarissa asks desperately, who would presume to look upon such an act of violence as a marriage (365), but clearly the Harlowes can. She turns as a last resort to reason, to the idea that words need only to be heard to be understood, and like Pamela welcomes formal confrontation. But the Harlowes pervert all that she says and wants. Secret witnesses behind the wainscot ('I saw just the gown of my sister, the last who slid away') are inflamed instead into irrational violence (303), and her brother prevents her reasonable words from working on Solmes when he erupts into the room shouting, 'This prating girl has struck you all dumb' (317). Clarissa's trust in a benevolent and reasonable world is thus reluctantly overturned. 'One half of mankind tormenting the other, and being tormented themselves in tormenting!', she writes in despair (224). By the end of the second volume her speech is attenuated, lapsing into frequent exhaustion, silence and sighs. When Betty challenges her claim that her writing supplies are gone, Clarissa is too worn to fight:

What's that [napkin] for, said I?
Only, miss, one of the fingers of your right hand, if you please to look at it. It was inky.
I gave her a look: but said nothing.   (345)

The Harlowes assume that Clarissa is irrational, because female, and must therefore be in love. Resistance to Solmes indicates love for Lovelace, and when Anna presumes the same, she throws her friend first into their hands, then into Lovelace's. Though smart, shrewd and vehement, Anna – like Mary Crawford in *Mansfield Park* – cannot think seriously on serious subjects. With a fatal levity that helps push Clarissa to destruction, she sees in Solmes a Hickman and in Lovelace a lover she never had. Persuading herself that she is of one mind with her friend, she presumes identity in return. She loves her as never woman loved another, she writes (40), as if they were two halves of one whole, with Clarissa 'a little too grave, methinks; I, no doubt, a little too flippant in your opinion'. No third love can come between them, she says (131), while inviting a third love to do just that.

Freely offering advice, Anna insists that Clarissa should make herself independent without seeing how that provokes her tormentors. Clarissa has no friends to support her claim, nor can she seek Hickman's protection before Anna is married to him. Anna, who cannot conceive of the pressure put on her friend to marry, clings to romantic notions of living single in a foolish scheme of going off privately to live and die together (331), but for all her assertions that 'a woman going off with a woman is not so discreditable a thing, surely! and with no view but to avoid the fellows!', Clarissa knows it would ruin both their reputations (354). Anna underestimates the difficulties of getting to London, nor is it so light a thing to flee there. Clarissa is understandably fearful about what her youth, her sex, and her 'unacquaintedness with the ways of that great, wicked town' might expose her to (335) – she knows what a young woman of her time cannot easily do. Anna articulates more vigorously what Clarissa can only hint, but not being Clarissa, she can afford to. She may love to 'engage in knight-errantry, now and then' (331), but what is sport to her is death to Clarissa.

Because Anna tyrannises over Hickman, she urges Clarissa to lord it similarly over Solmes. She loves to 'mortify proud and insolent spirits', she boasts, and bears Hickman only because 'the man is humble and knows his distance' (68). He would suit Clarissa, she says unkindly, being 'mighty sober! mighty grave! and all that' (207). Since the power of courtship is short-lived, she argues, she must torment him while she can:

At our alighting . . . My mamma's hand was kindly put into his, with a simpering altogether bridal; and with another, How do you do now, sir? – All his plump muscles were in motion, and a double charge of care and obsequiousness fidgeted up his whole form, when he offered to me his officious palm . . . With an averted supercilious eye, and a rejecting hand, half-flourishing – I have no need of help, sir! – You are in my way. (274)

Luckily for Anna, Hickman is driven not to violence but to withdrawal of his suit. Nor need Anna loathe Hickman as Clarissa must loathe Solmes, for his avarice, animality, family feuding, illiteracy, cruelty, and sadistic tyranny.

Anna can write cheerfully that in marriage 'I shall watch how the imperative husband *comes upon him*; how the obsequious lover *goes off*; in short, how he *ascends*, and how I *descend*, in the matrimonial wheel, never to take my turn again, but by fits and starts, like the feeble struggles of a sinking state for its dying liberty'. She understands the parallel between marriage and the state, and echoes Locke closely on the need to separate legislative from executive powers (II. Ch. xii):

The suiting of the tempers of two persons who are to come together is a great matter: and yet there should be boundaries fixed between them, by consent as it were, beyond which neither should go: and each should hold the other to it; or there would probably be encroachments in both. If the boundaries of the three estates that constitute our political union were not known, and occasionally asserted, what would become of each? The two branches of the legislature would encroach upon each other; and the executive power would swallow up both. (277)

Lightly translating political prerogative into domestic terms by saying, 'I desire my hoop may have its full circumference. All they're good for, that I know, is to clean dirty shoes and to keep ill-mannered fellows at a distance' (292), she forgets how horribly Solmes had squatted on Clarissa's hoop. For Anna encroachment is mere theory, while her friend endures the practice.

Because she is attracted to Lovelace, Anna thinks Clarissa is too. Out of disdain for Hickman's comparative lack of sprightliness she admires Lovelace by proxy, her sympathy being confidently transferred to Clarissa. 'I *know* you love him!', she writes (248). Earnestly she pleads for this wet, woebegone lover, this '*poor* man (Shall I pity him for *you*, my dear?)', who has run great risks for her, and perhaps all for nothing (275). But Anna's belief that Clarissa, once loved, will love in return, reduces her friend to the heroine of romantic tragedy. Some cause for this exists in the early hints of *Romeo and Juliet*, like the duel that sets two families at odds, the idea that Lovelace will wade into her favour through the blood of her brother (40), and Clarissa's promise that she will 'even consent to enter into the awful vault of my ancestors, and to have that bricked up upon me, than consent to be miserable for life' (305).[9] Lovelace too seems like Romeo with his 'is it not a confounded thing to be in love with one who is the daughter, the sister, the niece, of a family I must eternally despise?' (142). But literary allusions deceive: Clarissa is not the love-struck heroine of Anna's heated imagination. Dangerously, Anna leads her friend's response, asking her, 'don't you find at your heart somewhat unusual make it go throb, throb, throb, as you read just here?' (71). To Anna love is simply romantic *eros*, whereas to Clarissa it is *agape*, that is, divine love in all its relative, social and superior duties.[10]

And so Clarissa, betrayed by her powerlessness, her body and her friend, submits to go away with Lovelace. Is she in love? Her jealousy over Lovelace's pretty Rosebud certainly shows how much his suffering affected her when, after lurking in the coppice, his wig and his linen 'dripping with the hoar frost dissolving on them!', he got a great cold and almost lost his voice (270). Now she remarks angrily that his hoarseness was perhaps acquired 'by a midnight revel, singing to his wild-note singer – and only increased in the coppice!' (286). But she readily believes him innocent, and in conciliatory mood agrees to meet him at the gate.

Like Anna ennobling herself by romanticising Clarissa, Lovelace aggrandises the difficulty of his task, which, he says, would be 'a rape worthy of a Jupiter!' (165). Since the higher he raises her the greater the triumph in lowering her, he plans to recreate her as a heavenly love-object. To a goddess-maker like him, his imagination fired by poets, Clarissa Harlowe is a woman worth working on (143). She responds shrewdly to his flatteries, saying, 'you never knew so bold a supposer. As commentators find beauties in an author which the author perhaps was a stranger to, so he sometimes compliments me in high strains of gratitude for favours, and for a consideration, which I never designed him' (128), but she cannot know that as the result of being jilted Lovelace has vowed revenge on all womankind (143). Since all that is excellent in her sex is in her, Clarissa will do, one for all.

Lovelace's plan is to make her mortal by making her sexual. There are people who remember that she was born, he exults, 'that she came not from above, all at once an angel!' In prophetic echo of Pope's dark poem *Eloisa to Abelard* about sexuality denied, separation and despair, he reasons that '*matrimonial* or *equal* intimacies' will make her less than angel (145–7). Clarissa already endures constant irritation and danger because Lovelace, an expert in teaching many a one to dress, and helping them to undress, extravagantly relishes her body, her charming flesh and blood, her wavy ringlets 'wantoning in and about a neck that is beautiful beyond description', or the white handkerchief above her stays, concealing still more inimitable beauties, as he observes, when 'all the way we rode, the bounding heart; by its throbbing motions I saw it! dancing beneath the charming umbrage' (399–400).

In reality a tyrannical Filmer, Lovelace poses as a liberal Locke. Clarissa mistakenly deduces from his indignant sympathy with her being 'actually confined and otherwise maltreated by a father the most gloomy and positive; at the instigation of a brother the most arrogant and selfish' (142) that at worst he would surely not confine her prisoner in her chamber, forbid her correspondence with her friend, take her mistressly management from her, or force on her an insulting servant and tyrannising women (183). His scorn of 'the compulsory methods' (170) used on Solmes' behalf allow her to hope that because he attacks her father's prerogative and authority (168) he himself may be trusted. His vow that he wishes only to free her from imprisonment and restore her free will (349) must touch a woman starved of kindness, especially when he suffers in health for her sake, or promises to effect her dearest wish, reconciliation with her family (259). Most grateful of all, his claim to be 'still more captivated with the graces of my *mind*' than those of her body restores her power of conviction through reasonable words. For her sake, he says, he could overcome his prejudice against matrimony (169).

Her shorthand term 'the man' for all that is tyrannous in the sex proves, however, to be right. She cannot know that Lovelace has in fact named himself king and emperor (148) in a territorial campaign where Clarissa, he says, will be won without a long siege. He will force the family to creep to him, and the 'sordidly-imperious' James to kneel at the footstool of his throne (145). He usurps all their kingly powers by his vow to be 'father, uncle, brother, and as I humbly hoped, in your own good time, a *husband* to you, all in one' (377), and at St Albans he pretends, ominously, to be her brother (388). As she rapidly suspects, she has only escaped from one confinement to another. Like her other tyrants Lovelace employs guile and force, and although she always recognised in him an '*art*; fierceness, and a temper like what I have been too much used to at home' (270), she cannot know that through a servant he dances Mr Harlowe upon his own wires (145). Like the Harlowes he intrigues, and he writes a great correspondence of which he is 'as secret and careful as if it were of a treasonable nature' (74), treason against Queen Clarissa. A lordly proprietor to women, he calls Clarissa '*his*, and [she] *shall* be *his*, and he will be the death of any man who robs him of his PROPERTY' (223). His prophetic vow, 'may I perish eternally if your will shall not be a law to me in everything!', she is right to suspect. 'Must I never be at liberty to follow my own judgement!', she cries at the garden gate (376–9).

Though startled by the prompt disappearance of her letter, when 'in all probability there was but a brick wall of a few inches thick between Mr Lovelace and me at the very time I put the letter under the brick' (263), out of sheer weariness Clarissa considers flight. Persecution at home, the threat of forced marriage, a proposed trial in an 'awful court' with the 'poor prisoner' made to sign by her parents (346), force her to it. At the gate mind and body fail again. Panic seizes her, and although she struggles vehemently, crying out, 'I will sooner die than go with you!', she is drawn protesting away by Lovelace's gentle force. A voice calls that they are discovered, Lovelace draws his naked sword, takes her hands, and urges her to fly before murders are done. Terrified and looking back, like Eve abandoning Eden, Clarissa flees (letter 94).

In the shock that the letter form allows, disjunctive and out of sequence, comes the pitiful announcement to Anna, 'you will soon hear (if already you have not heard from the mouth of common fame) that your Clarissa Harlowe is gone off with a man!' (370). Her dream about Lovelace can now symbolically come true, that

seizing upon me [he] carried me into a churchyard; and there, notwith-standing all my prayers and tears, and protestations of innocence, stabbed me to the heart, and then tumbled me into a deep grave ready dug, among two or three half-dissolved carcases; throwing in the dirt and earth upon me with his hands, and trampling it down with his feet. (342–3)

Lovelace now stands forth the exuberant conqueror, his once muted and disguised voice bursting out in triumph to Belford. Revelling in the odds against him, he relishes a difficult success. Pride has been the real stake in what is to him 'far, very far, from an amorous warfare' (401). Carelessly, viciously, to Leman his servant helper (the name ironically means 'lover'), he reveals his expertise in the cure of a termagant wife. 'I can teach thee how to break her heart in a twelvemonth', he writes (385). Reliving the heady instant of success, he recalls that hearing the door unbolt he was sure of her, his heart bounded to his throat, he trod air, 'and hardly thought myself a mortal'. Thus, he writes, he became her emperor and she subject to his imperial will and pleasure. She is his conquest, a queen, a conquered fortress whose garrison, 'with General *Prudence* at the head, and Governor *Watchfulness* bringing up the rear, shall be allowed to march out with all the honours due to so brave a resistance'. The volume ends with a paean of jubilant exhilaration. 'My whole soul is joy. When I go to bed I laugh myself asleep: and I awake either laughing or singing.'

How it swells my pride to have been able to outwit such a vigilant charmer! – I am taller by half a yard, in my imagination, than I was! – I look *down* upon everybody now! – Last night I was still more extravagant. I took off my hat, as I walked, to see if the lace were not scorched, sup- posing it had brushed down a star; and, before I put it on again, in mere wantonness and heart's ease, I was for buffeting the moon. (letter 99)

4

King Lovelace

After his anatomising of domestic tyranny among the Harlowes, Richardson examines King Lovelace's siege of Clarissa within a brothel proclaimed to be a respectable house. A broken-down Irishman poses as Captain Tomlinson, intermediary to the family, and Lovelace himself swallows ipecacuanha to feign illness and test her affection. The fire scene in which he flushes her, dishevelled, from her room, alarms her to such an extent that she flees to Hampstead. Here Lovelace easily tracks her down.

Exiled by her father's curse, Clarissa fights to defend her identity in the brothel to which she has been lured. Frequent allusions to *Paradise Lost*,[1] the work which explains how hierarchical power was first assigned to men, will universalise her defence of mind and body, as she comes to represent all women – from Eve to Queen Elizabeth – who long for freedom from restraint. In the interval between abduction and escape, Lovelace plays various parts such as the Devil, Don Juan, King, General, and Man, to lull her wariness almost to the point of deception.

Father Harlowe's curse, like God's, punishes his daughter's independence and disobedience. As Clarissa realises even at St Albans, his thundered wish that she may meet her punishment 'both *here* and *hereafter*, by means of the very wretch in whom you have chosen to place your wicked confidence' (509) will be fulfilled in the same loveless/Lovelace lust imposed upon the fallen Adam and Eve. 'Here,' she says, 'like the first pair, I at least driven out of my paradise, are we recriminating' (393). As unquestioningly as Eve she accepts that she has deserved her sorrow for setting her own judgment against that of her parents. In a symbolic funeral they nail up in the closet her portrait in the taste of Vandyke, painter to Stuart princes, hoping thus to lower her dignity to the dust, and make her a common creature, a beggar along London streets (509–10). Would that the cruel curse had turned, as Lovelace protests, 'to a mortal quinsy, and sticking in his gullet had choked the old execrator, as a warning to all such unnatural fathers' (518). But 'miserably fallen and . . . unhappy', her woes blamed on an Eve-like 'correspondence against prohibition' with her Satan,

Clarissa speaks of her error as the evil root from which such bad branches spring (479). Hers is the guilt, she believes, and its consequence will be a knowledge of sin and death figured forth in the gross 'mother' Mrs *Sin*-clair with her monstrous brood, and in Death the King, Death the Lover, King Lovelace who stabbed and trampled Clarissa in her dream.

Clarissa, like Eve in Paradise, was 'immensely happy, above the happiness of a mortal creature' before she knew Lovelace. Everybody almost worshipped her, and 'envy itself, which has of late reared up its venomous head' against her was awed by her superior worthiness into silence and admiration (578). Like Eve, Clarissa is forced into curvings from the plain simple truth upon which she was wont to value herself (484). Lovelace's '*rattle*' may well warn her of the snake (439), for he in his bravado, leadership, envy, lying and remorse is connected in numerous references to Satan. Beelzebub to 'a set of infernals' (549), he prowls about the Harlowe estate, and no disguise can hide the gracefulness of his figure (352). Just as the Devil spied on Adam and Eve, his spying on Rosebud and her lover provokes an all too brief self-censure that he acts the part of the 'grand tempter' (534). He lies, he rejoices in setting one against another, every step he takes is a wry one, says Clarissa (527). Like Satan journeying to Eden to confirm his leadership, he has to corrupt Clarissa to prove himself worthy of being 'the prince and leader of such a confraternity as ours!' (416). As a Satan, Lovelace tempts Clarissa to disobedience and deceit, and as an Adam, he destroys her by his lust. As both, he trails delusively sympathetic traces of his former glory, for his tragedy, like Medea's, is to know the better but follow the worse (*Grandison*, II. 138).

Lovelace reduces Clarissa from natural queen to woman in the way that Eve was reduced, boasting – in an image from that other poem of Fall, Pope's *Rape of the Lock* – that 'the lady must fall, if every hair of her head were a guardian angel, unless [the Harlowes] were to make a visible appearance for her, or, snatching her from me at unawares, would draw her after them into the starry regions' (440). Like the lock become a star, like a comet 'soaring upward to her native skies' and only to be kept 'with us sublunaries' by another offer of marriage (518), Clarissa's very heavenliness precipitates this envious Satan's plots, as he admits:

But it is so discouraging a thing, to have my monitress so very good! – I protest I know not how to look up at her! Now, as I am thinking, if I could pull her down a little nearer to my own level; that is to say, could prevail upon her to do something that would argue imperfection, something to repent of; we should jog on much more equally, and be better able to comprehend one another: and so the comfort would be mutual, and the remorse not all on one side. (450)

The whores, resentful that he spares her when he had not spared them, urge just as vehemently that she should be brought to their level (729).

Robert Lovelace is as much a baroque poet, hero and courtier as his Cavalier namesake Richard Lovelace, who called his own love-object Lucasta, meaning 'chaste or pure light', and who was buried in St Bride's, as Richardson himself would be.[2] But Richardson could have derived his test of Clarissa's chastity from the trial that another Lord Lovelace made of the actress Mrs Bracegirdle, who acted tragic roles similar to Clarissa's. She died in 1748, the year the novel was published. Richardson's friend Colley Cibber wrote of Mrs Bracegirdle's resistance and its monetary reward, her charity to the poor, the vengeful plan to abduct, rape and marry her that ended in a fatal duel, and the paradoxical reputation of this 'Romantic Virgin' that she was said to be at once sensual and cold.[3] Certainly Robert Lovelace claims, like Lord Lovelace to Mrs Bracegirdle, that he acts only for Clarissa's good. Is virtue 'to be established by common bruit only? – Has her virtue ever been *proved*?', he asks (427). For the public interest he will prove to the whole sex that there was once a woman whose virtue no trials, no stratagems, no temptations, even from the man she did not hate, could overpower. Lastly, Lovelace tests her virtue because he plans to marry her. Since by a sexual lapse a wife may obtrude another man's children into her husband's possessions, women's chastity matters more than men's, he says. Since Lovelace's wife should be no more suspect than Caesar's, if she nobly stands her trial, he will have an angel for a wife (429–31).

In fact, Lovelace pursues Clarissa because he must, for like Don Juan he is insatiable, obsessed and doomed. Here Richardson drew closely, I think, upon Thomas Shadwell's play *The Libertine*. This particularly vicious version of the theme was first played in 1676 by a famous colleague and contemporary of Mrs Bracegirdle, Betterton – the name given to Lovelace's mistress – and was a general favourite in the decades before *Clarissa* was written.[4] Shadwell's Don Juan defies his own conscience and the laws of God and society to live by nature and reason. His two murders, first of his father, then of Maria's brother at the garden gate, Richardson realistically mutes to Lovelace's dream of killing Lord M. (611), the duel with James Harlowe, and the scuffle at the gate when he frightens Clarissa by crying murder, although the Christian reference in the scene offers the chance of redemption. Lovelace is as violent with his servants as Shadwell's Don Juan, whose servant Jacomo, like Tomlinson, turns against his master. Don Juan boasts of spectacular rapes to retain the leadership of his gang, and remarks like Lovelace, 'What an excellent thing is a Woman before enjoyment, and how insipid after it!' He imagines himself as the Grand Signor when an 'inundation of Strumpets' hang about him and claim to be his wives, as the whores hang about Lovelace. One of them stabs herself like Lucretia, as Clarissa will offer to do. His proposal, that in the name of liberty men should change brides as regularly as other natural creatures, resembles Lovelace's St Valentine's Day scheme (p. 873), while Shadwell's central episode of Don Juan fleeing from the law in storm and shipwreck seems to have inspired Richardson's third edition 'restoration' in which Lovelace plans to throw Hickman overboard and rape Anna Howe, her mother, and her servant on the way to the Isle of Wight (see p. 83). Don Juan and his friends land, after planning to throw Jacomo into the sea (like Hickman, he cannot swim), and meet a hermit with whom they discuss free will and the idea that constitutions formed by nature are unalterable. They force an old woman, and take 'these Toys, they call *Maidenheads*' of Don Francisco's two daughters. Later they use fire to force them from their refuge in a nunnery, as Lovelace tricks Clarissa in the fire scene, or dreams of setting fire to the brothel (1430). Don Juan vows to thaw one daughter even 'if she were Ice', and kills Leonora, who seeks to save him, by poison. In a hint that Richardson would pick up for *Grandison*, Jacomo is almost gelded by angry shepherds, but the hermit's belief is like Clarissa's (1444), that only magistrates should punish rapes and murders. The daughters like Lovelace speak of 'expiation', but it is the supernatural in the shape of the ghosts of the people Don Juan has murdered that rise up against him, as they will for Lovelace at the point of death, when the clock strikes twelve. The play ends with the triumph of providence as devils welcome Don Juan to a hell where Lovelace himself expects to go.

Lovelace is indeed as dark, anarchic and anti-authoritarian as Shadwell's exuberant villain, the Don Juan whose prototypes are the shape-changers Satan and Jupiter to whom Lovelace proudly compares himself. A marriage-hater, he longs to prevail upon Clarissa to live with him without real change of name (431), and grieves that '*one* man cannot have every woman worth having –

pity though – when the man is such a VERY clever fellow!' (416).
He takes maidenheads only, and though he has created all the
harlots in Mother Sinclair's house, never frequents whores (674).
Many of his women have died without testifying against him, not
even Miss Betterton, because of his care once he has ruined them:

These were the rules I laid down to myself on my entrance into active life:
To set the mother above want, if her friends were cruel, and if I could
not get her an husband worthy of her; to shun common women – a piece
of justice I owed to innocent ladies, as well as to myself; to marry off a
former mistress, if possible, before I took to a new one; to maintain a lady
handsomely in her lying-in; to provide for the little one, if it lived, according to the degree of its mother; to go into mourning for the mother if she
died. And the promise of this was a great comfort to the pretty dears as
they grew near their times.   (II. 148)

Clarissa and her friend offer a double challenge. 'So lively the one,
so vigilant, so prudent both, who would not wish to outwit such
girls, and to be able to twirl them round his finger?' (416). A month
would suffice to break the virago Anna, he thinks. Imperial,
polygamous Turk as he is, he imagines 'how sweetly pretty to see
the two lovely friends, when humbled and tame, both sitting in the
darkest corner of a room, arm in arm, weeping and sobbing for
each other! And I their emperor, their then *acknowledged* emperor,
reclined at my ease in the same room, uncertain to which I should
first, Grand Signor-like, throw out my handkerchief!' (II. 369).[5]

But if Clarissa's body is a trap to her, Lovelace is oddly helpless
in his. Even at church he falls prey to Satan's snares (419), for 'are
we not devils to each other? They tempt us; we tempt them' (II.
185). So abandoned is he, says Belford, 'that to give thee the best
reasons in the world against what thou has once resolved upon, will
be but acting the madman, whom once we saw trying to buffet down
a hurricane with his hat' (559). The beats of that 'triangular varlet'
his heart choke him (520). 'How does this damned love unman me!',
he exclaims in desperation after the failure of his fire plot (742).
His body's reactions and the energy consumed by his teeming, fertile plots combine to make him almost impotent.

Lovelace delights in seduction more than the crowning act, 'for
that's a vapour, a bubble!' (616). Preferring a difficult chase to an
easy one, he teaches Belford to 'fly at nobler game than daws, crows,
and wigeons':

Thou knowest nothing, Jack, of the delicacies of intrigue; nothing of the
glory of outwitting the witty and the watchful; of the joys that fill the mind
of the inventive or contriving genius, ruminating which to use of the

different webs that offer to him for the entanglement of a haughty charmer, who in her day has given him unnumbered torments. Thou, Jack, who, like a dog at his ease, contentest thyself to growl over a bone thrown out to thee, dost not know the joys of the chase, and in pursuing a winding game. (II. 30)

As his Hobbesian animal imagery shows, Lovelace's Satanic, Don Juanish body dominates his reason. To Richardson, as to many of his contemporaries, love of bodies drives out mind, as Belford explains. 'See what fools this passion makes the wisest men! What snivellers, what dotards, when they suffer themselves to be run away with by it!' (713). But Clarissa must be his, says Lovelace in defiance, though his damnation were to be the purchase (593).

Clarissa's body also betrays her, by attracting and reacting against her will. Even her 'sweet disorder in the dress', as Robert Herrick would have called it, draws amorous attention. 'Oh what additional charms,' writes Lovelace after the fire scene, 'did her struggles give to every feature, every limb, of a person so sweetly elegant and lovely!' When she falls at his feet, and 'in the anguish of her soul, her streaming eyes lifted up to my face with supplicating softness, hands folded, dishevelled hair; for her night head-dress having fallen off in her struggling, her charming tresses fell down in naturally shining ringlets, as if officious to conceal the dazzling beauties of her neck and shoulders; her lovely bosom too heaving with sighs, and broken sobs, as if to aid her quivering lips in pleading for her' (725–6), she is the very image of an erotic Mary Magdalen, a Bathsheba to arouse a David. 'These women, Jack', he says, 'have been the occasion of all manner of mischief from the beginning!' (540).

Lovelace's two desires, to deflower her and to make her love him, are mutually contradictory. Believing that she can be caught by praise, his proof that he once, in the streets of London, saw 'a well-dressed handsome girl laugh, bridle, and visibly enjoy the praises of a sooty dog, a chimney-sweeper' (II. 21), he is astonished to find Clarissa immune. But he can tell nothing new to a woman impatient with praise. Clarissa's anger when he draws aside 'the handkerchief that concealed the beauty of beauties, and pressed with my burning lips the charmingest breast that ever my ravished eyes beheld', makes him argue that she should descend from goddess-hood into humanity, the signs of her female sex altering to maternal emblems. 'Let me perish, Belford, if I would not forgo the brightest diadem in the world for the pleasure of seeing a twin Lovelace at each charming breast, drawing from it his first sustenance' (705–6). He denies her spiritual life, for his own sake:

> We have held that women have no souls: I am a very Jew in this point, and willing to believe they have not. And if so, to whom shall I be accountable for what I do to them? Nay, if souls they have, as there is no sex in ethereals, nor need of any, what plea can a lady hold of injuries done her in her lady-*state*, when there is an end of her lady-*ship*?[6]　　　　(704)

Belford's plea to his friend not to rob her of those purities which to her constitute the difference between angelic and brutal qualities (713) proves that he at least comprehends her dualism:

> She is, in my eye, all mind: and were she to meet with a man all mind likewise, why should the charming qualities she is mistress of, be endangered? Why should such an angel be plunged so low as into the vulgar offices of domestic life? Were she mine, I should hardly wish to see her a mother unless there were a kind of moral certainty that minds like hers could be propagated. For why, in short, should not the work of bodies be left to *mere* bodies? . . . it would be a million of pities to ruin a lady in whose fall none but devils can rejoice.[7]　　　　(555)

Even Lovelace, who wonders if she ever romped, sees that if for her (as for a vestal virgin) it is sacrilege but to touch the hem of her garment, how can this 'consecrated beauty' think to be a wife? (646). Even as 'her sweet bosom, as I clasped her to mine, heaved and panted!' (723), her eloquence proves that her mind is superior still.

Can Clarissa love? Anna and Belford think so, as they watch her waver. She admits that she 'never saw a man, whose *person* I could like, before this man', knowing all the while that he is a 'trifler with his own happiness; the destroyer of mine!' (II. 167). The single life attracts her, and yet her anxiety when Lovelace pretends to be ill proves that she could indeed have liked him. Once again her family drives her to him, accusing her as of old that she prefers her will to theirs for 'a transitory preference to *person* only; the morals of the men not to be compared with each other's' (504). To the Harlowes, who are incapable of seeing why Lovelace with his quick, well-read mind, loving devotion, and wide knowledge of the world makes him as exhilarating to Clarissa as Rochester to Jane Eyre or Darcy to Elizabeth Bennet, morality is merely sexual, whereas Clarissa's larger criticism includes Solmes' avarice, disloyalty to his family, illiteracy, and the reflection of his brutish mind in his brutish body.

Anna too pushes her friend towards Lovelace. Although passionately loyal to Clarissa, she matches him in levity, disdain for the other sex, tyrannising, and contrivances, even in her emphatic and exclamatory style. Clarissa often protests against Anna's inappropriate sense of fun in a case that will not bear it (481), for Richardson, who could write very funny scenes himself, genuinely feared Lord Shaftesbury's test by laughter (443), and argued that the most immaculate virtue is not safe when a man 'makes a jest of the most solemn vows and protestations' (605). 'I despise his whole sex', says Anna in a generalisation which leads her to undervalue Hickman's real benevolence and his loyalty to the outcast Clarissa. Drawn to Lovelace by her 'wicked eye' (474–5), she argues that if Clarissa cannot have everything in one man, she should settle for appearance. Her view of Lovelace coloured always by her dissatisfaction with Hickman, she writes that Lovelace 'will always keep up attention; you will always be alive with him, though perhaps more from fears than from hopes: while Mr Hickman will neither say anything to keep one awake, nor yet by shocking adventures make one's slumbers uneasy' (514–15). Vixen to Lovelace's fox (653, II. 248), she likes Clarissa's lively lover better than her own.

Anna longs, like Lovelace, for variety, and says that if politeness is necessary 'to induce us to bow our necks to a yoke so unequal', a little intermingled insolence is required

to keep up that interest, when once it has got footing. Men must not let us see that we can make fools of them. And I think that *smooth* love, that is to say, a passion without rubs; in other words, a passion without passion, is like a sleepy stream that is hardly seen to give motion to a straw. So that, sometimes to make us fear, and even, for a short space, to *hate* the wretch, is productive of the *contrary* extreme.

Where Hickman's 'whining, creeping, submissive courtship' sends her to the harpsichord, 'Lovelace keeps up the ball with a witness, and all his address and conversation is one continual game at racquet' (466). Her vision of life as a game makes her look so much like Lovelace that Clarissa must remind her of what he really says. 'Do you think it is to the credit of Mr. Lovelace's character that he can be offensive and violent?', she asks (II. 180–1). Anna, who spiritedly defies her mother's prohibition on correspondence, refuses to give up a suffering friend (477), but Clarissa, who has painfully discovered that girls need protection from 'the vultures, the hawks, the kites and the other villainous birds of prey that hover over us with a view to seize and destroy us, the first time we are caught wandering out of the eye or care of our watchful and natural guardians and protectors' (480), fears the results of this zealous love. Anna's behaviour confirms Lovelace's assertion that this girl is 'a devilish rake in her heart. Had she been a man, and one of us, she'd have outdone us all in enterprise and spirit' (634).

Anna is most treacherous as a woman and a friend when, actually looking as if with the eyes of a man, she says,

I do not think a *man-woman* a pretty character at all: and as I said, were I a *man*, I would sooner choose for a dove, though it were fit for nothing but, as the play says, to go tame about house and breed, than a wife that is setting at work [the servants], those of the stud not excepted; and who, with a besom in her hand, as I may say, would be continually filling me with apprehensions that she wanted to sweep me out of my own house as useless lumber.

Identifying with Lovelace's resentment of powerful women, she promotes Clarissa as one who will 'move in her proper sphere' of needle, pen, dairy, and benevolence (476). Her advice is for all these reasons deeply compromising. Clarissa's merit must always be undervalued, she writes flippantly, therefore 'marry whom you will' (II. 105). If thrown upon a fool, she should marry him as a punishment 'since you cannot as a reward. In short, as one given to convince you that there is nothing but imperfection in this life' (604). She rushes officiously to 'save the wretch then, if we can, though we soil our fingers in lifting him up from his dirt' (588), and urges Clarissa to encourage Lovelace simply because, as Jane Austen's Mary Crawford would also argue, the world expects it (467). She speaks far too lightly of the probability that once married, Lovelace 'husband-like, will let nobody insult you but himself' (432), and worse still, that the affair may end in murder or rape (474). Even when convinced that he is more consistently mean, revengeful, and proud than either of them imagined, she still advises marriage (498–9), nor does the knowledge of Miss Betterton's destruction deflect her. 'Wicked as the man is, I am afraid he must be your lord and master', she writes (586).

Clarissa must be swayed. Lovelace's kind behaviour and her own low-spiritedness bring her to some verbal concessions (513), because of 'your opinion' (591). But when Anna finds that their letters have been intercepted and altered, her outburst of scorn steels him, and the chance is lost again.

To Clarissa, genuine relationship includes respect for mind. Hickman she praises as a 'man *before* whom and *to* whom she may open her lips secure of his good opinion of all she says, and of his just and polite regard for her judgement' (482), unusual at a time when parents make light of 'that preferable part in girls, which would improve their minds and give a grace to all the rest' (529).

But women fatally lack experience, as Lovelace knows. 'Cunning women and witches, we read of without number. But I fancy wisdom never entered into the character of a woman. It is not a requisite of the sex' (573). Clarissa is prodigiously learned in theories, but a mere novice in *'practices'* and *'experimentals'* (538). Lovelace can confidently make an assumption – common from stories of Amazonian communities[8] to Tennyson's *The Princess* – that clever women simply fall harder. 'How I love these reasoning ladies!' says Lovelace, for it is all over with them 'once love has crept into their hearts: for then will they employ all their reasoning powers to *excuse* rather than to *blame* the conduct of the *doubted* lover' (II. 214).

Marriage, Clarissa knows, guarantees at least some good usage, but Lovelace's proposals come with unacceptable conditions or in awkward circumstances. For instance, in exchange for her promise never to marry another man while he is living and single, he carefully, modestly, salutes her, and delighted by this more than by the ultimatum with any other woman (413), offers a speedy solemnisation. She recalls that she has asked for a period of probation, and fearing that acceptance might look like encouragement of free treatment, hesitates. To Anna's comment that she has modestied away her chance to marry, Clarissa must repeat that her motives arise, as with Solmes, 'not *altogether* from maidenly niceness', but from her need to control who she is (596). Lovelace's uncomprehending complaint that she is ice (600) has been followed by many another man's since.

Lovelace too dreads that 'like the fly buzzing about the bright taper, I had like to have singed the silken wings of my liberty'. Never, he says, 'was man in greater danger of being caught in his own snares – all his views anticipated: all his schemes untried; and not having brought the admirable creature to town nor made an effort to know if she be really angel or woman'. Overcome by her sweet tearful face 'as my arms still encircled the finest waist in the world, sinking upon my shoulder' (as Eve's did upon Adam's), when he no more intended 'all this ecstatic nonsense than I thought the same moment of flying in the air!', he sees her power, and that he, not she, must fail in the arduous trial (492–3). He dreads that they will turn into a 'happy pair . . . dozing and nodding at each other in two opposite chimney-corners in a winter-evening, and over a wintry love', instead of being always new to each other, and having always something to say (521).[9]

Lovelace recoils also from that necessary preliminary to marriage, his own reformation. The denunciations of the Bible, which come 'so slap-dash upon one, so unceremoniously, as I may say, without even the by-your-leave of a rude London chairman, that they over-turn one, horse and man', make him uneasy. Clarissa concludes him to be worse than a wild Indian, for 'a man who errs with his eyes open, and against conviction, is a thousand times worse for what he knows, and ten thousand times harder to be reclaimed, than if he had never known anything at all' (II. 88–9). Almost succumbing to a major crisis of conscience, he overcomes it only after a protracted struggle (658).

Clarissa longs above all else to be able to define herself, but this her woman's destiny will not permit. Just as the conditions she set upon the idea of daughter and wife were unacceptable to her family, her definition of love is intolerable to Lovelace. Exemplary like all those other women from Greek times to the present whose lives had been collected to inspire her sex, Clarissa is formed upon the high and complex models of queen and Eve, but when like a queen she refuses to marry down, or when like Eve she falls, her fatally attractive, fatally feeble body gives her new identities as an outcast, a runaway, and a whore.

Knowing that by her flight she has forfeited all her power as an example, Clarissa resigns herself to being a warning to women instead (453). Anna lightly agrees. Clarissa, she says, will help those giddy creatures who would otherwise 'leap walls, drop from windows, and steal away from their parents' house to the seducer's bed, in the same day' (577). Lovelace too gloats that her humility will bring her to anything (427), but Clarissa has here identified a new and important role for herself. When Anna implies that her trial is Christ-like, the inevitable, desirable result of her descent to human form, when she says that 'ADVERSITY is your SHINING-TIME' (579), she offers Clarissa a challenge that her friend will gladly, whole-heartedly embrace.

If Lovelace's peremptory body and maggoty brain create him Don Juan, his Filmerian convictions render him tyrannical. 'King' Lovelace wields arbitrary power over his subjects:

Preferments I bestow, both military and civil. I give estates, and take them away at my pleasure. Quality too I create. And by a still more valuable prerogative, I *degrade* by virtue of my own imperial will . . . What a poor thing is a monarch to me! (569)

Three imperial passions remind him he is king: 'love, revenge, ambition, or a desire of conquest' (719) – that is, he loves Clarissa;

he vows vengeance on her, all womankind, and the Harlowes; and he has gained sovereignty over Clarissa by right of conquest (657). Having 'read in some place *that the woman was made for the man*, not *the man for the woman*' (429), he believes man to be the woman's sun, and woman the man's earth (660). General as well as king, he fills up his speech with martial imagery of gunpowder, mines and marches to glorify his private crime into public triumph:[10]

Had Hannibal been a private man, and turned his plotting head against the *other sex*; or had I been a general, and turned mine against such of my fellow-creatures of *my own*, as I thought myself entitled to consider as my enemies because they were born and lived in a different climate – Hannibal would have done less mischief – Lovelace more – That would have been the difference.   (718)

Criminals and kings differ only in extent from himself, he says, and if Caesar slew nearly 1,200,000 men, 'are not you and I, Jack, innocent men, and babes in swaddling-clothes, compared to Caesar, and to his predecessor in heroism, Alexander, dubbed for murders and depredation *Magnus*?' (II. 424).[11] Since sexual conquest is, he assumes, the inevitable consequence of military triumph, he believes therefore that

with this active soul, I should have made a very great figure in whatever station I had filled. But had I been a prince! – To be sure I should have made a most *noble* prince! I should have led up a military dance equal to that of the great Macedonian. I should have added kingdom to kingdom, and robbed all my neighbour sovereigns in order to have obtained the name of *Robert the Great*. And I would have gone to war with the Great Turk, and the Persian, and the Mogul, for their seraglios; for not one of those Eastern monarchs should have had a pretty woman to bless himself with, till I had done with her.   (762)

Lovelace believes that the law was not made for such a one as he, an arch-criminal who (like Captain Macheath in *The Beggar's Opera*) would be miraculously pardoned on his way to be hanged:

let us look down, look up, look round, which way we will, we shall see all the doors, the shops, the windows, the sign-irons and balconies (garrets, gutters, and chimney-tops included) all white-capped, black-hooded, and periwigged, or crop-eared up by the *immobile vulgus*: while the floating *street-swarmers*, who have seen us pass by at one place, run with stretched-out necks, and strained eyeballs, a round-about way, and elbow and shoulder themselves into places by which we have not passed, in order to obtain another sight of us.

Such a parade would create him king for a day, as it does a lord mayor, a general, an ambassador, or a monarch at his coronation (II. 423).[12]

Lovelace cannot understand why Clarissa behaves like a scornful beauty at the height of her power and pride, and defies him, who is lord of her destiny (423), but Richardson takes care to show how even honest people seek power. Clarissa's mother, who is weak, laments 'what a torment is it to have a will without a power!' (586), while Lovelace, who is strong, asks, 'what signifies power, if we do not exert it?' (610). Anna, whom Lovelace calls a tyrant 'conqueress' (635), may deny that her abuse of power will endure in marriage, but her belief in the necessity for fear, her anger, and her Hobbesian 'natural' images are remarkably like Lovelace's. Men no more than women, she says, are moderate in power, and

if I do not make [Hickman] quake now and then, he will endeavour to make me fear. All the animals in the creation are more or less in a state of hostility with each other. The wolf, that runs away from a lion, will devour a lamb the next moment. I remember that I was once so enraged at a game-chicken that was continually pecking at another (a poor humble one, as I thought him), that I had the offender caught, and without more ado, in a pet of humanity, wrung his neck off. What followed this execution? – Why that other grew insolent, as soon as *his* insulter was gone, and was continually pecking at one or two under *him*. Peck and be hanged, said I – I might as well have preserved the first; for I see it is the *nature of the beast*. (487)

In a comic variation on the theme Antony Harlowe proposes marriage to Mrs Howe, avariciously foreseeing them reckoning up their 'comings-in together; and what this day and this week has produced – Oh how this will increase love!', but his demand that he 'must have all in my own power, while I live: because, you know, madam, it is as creditable to the wife as the husband, that it should be so' (624–5) makes her rear back. 'I have now been a widow these ten years; nobody to control me – And I am said not to bear control: so, sir, you and I are best as we are', she says (631). Lovelace's servant Joseph Leman likewise seeks power over Betty, the only power he has. 'We common fokes have our joys, and plese your Honner, lick as our betters have; and if we be sometimes snubbed, we can find our underlings to snub them agen; and if not, we can git a wife mayhap, and snub her; so are masters somehow or other oursells' (II. 146). Lovelace laughs at what his man has learnt. 'Crow, Joseph, crow! A dunghill of your own in view: servants to snub at your pleasure: a wife to quarrel with, or to love, as your humour leads you' (497).

If all husbands are kings, this woman Clarissa's claim to superiority over him is intolerable. 'To be *despised by a* WIFE! – What a thought is that! – To be *excelled by a* WIFE too, in every part of praiseworthy knowledge! – To *take lessons*, to *take instructions*, from a WIFE!' (658). Lovelace's dread after his defeat in the fire scene is that he would be only the second person in his own family, her property rather than his own. How can he bear it that a Harlowe daughter should excel the last and not the meanest of the Lovelaces (734)? His conquest ought to have been followed by possession: Clarissa is to him both a land to be subdued, as in Donne's *Elegie: Going to Bed*, and a symbol of plenty in a conquered land, when he imagines her with twins at her breast.[13] Being an unattached woman whom anyone may attempt, she must be his 'lawful prize', for 'whose property, I pray thee, shall I invade, if I pursue my schemes of love and vengeance? – Have not those who have a right in her, renounced that right?', he asks (717). Like Mr B. he can then claim that it will be the greatest of felonies if she steals herself from her 'injured lover, and acknowledged husband' (757), as Clarissa wretchedly confirms: 'the man who has had the assurance to think me, and to endeavour to make me, his *property*, will hunt me from place to place, and search after me as an estray: and he knows he may do so with impunity; for whom have I to protect me from him?' (754).[14]

Only money, as the angry Harlowes found, can stand against power and possession. Lovelace predictably calls it foolish to make a wife financially independent 'of her emperor, and a rebel of course', for like the contending wives of 'the honest patriarchs' (polygamists all) a powerful wife could refuse to think only of his pleasure. And so, he argues, if men are born monarchs, women are born to be controlled, as the poet Waller said. A tyrant husband thus makes for a dutiful wife (669–70). Nothing, he says, 'sooner brings down a proud spirit, than a sense of lying under pecuniary obligations', just as a hen, brought to accept the 'dirty pearl' of barley-corn from the cock, will accept more from this 'Grand Signor of a bird' (449). Clarissa therefore acts simply to protect herself when she refuses money from Lovelace, let alone the rich silks that must remind her so keenly of home (414). Even when close to marrying him, she makes it a condition that she will yield her will where her husband's real honour is concerned, but must have her own money to dispense in charity. His prompt encroachment reminding her of what she gives up, she tears the papers of settlement almost in two. 'Will not she, who allows herself such

SAMUEL RICHARDSON

liberties as a maiden lady, take greater when a married one?', asks
Lovelace anxiously (653–65).

Faced with the reluctance of his 'property' to hand herself over,
Lovelace turns to violence, the last resort of tyrants. Enraged by
her escape, he vows that *'art and more art, and compulsion too, if
she make it necessary (and 'tis plain that nothing else will do)*, shall
she experience' (742). Cruelty he justifies as 'natural' to man, evolv-
ing as in Hogarth's *Four Stages of Cruelty*, to appear in 1751, from
the torture of animals to human murder. If an epicure's daughter
is taught without the least remorse 'to roast lobsters alive; to cause
a poor pig to be whipped to death; to scrape carp the contrary way
of the scales, making them leap in the stew-pan, and dressing them
in their own blood for sauce' (II. 248),[15] he, who beat out his
servant's teeth, can complacently remark, 'We begin with birds
as boys, and as men go on to ladies; and both perhaps, in turns,
experience our sportive cruelty'. A woman is a bird, an 'ensnared
volatile'[16] which beats about the cage, lays itself down panting and
'seeming to bemoan its cruel fate and forfeited liberty', but finding
it cannot escape, 'hops about from perch to perch, resumes its
wonted cheerfulness, and every day sings a song to amuse itself,
and reward its keeper' (557). He once knew a caged bird to starve
itself and die with grief, he says, but never a lady who was so silly.
If other people can put out the eyes of birds with burning knitting
needles (as in Hogarth's first print), why, he asks defensively, does
an honest fellow like himself, who prevails upon 'a mewed-up lady
to countenance her own escape, and she consents to break cage,
and be set a flying into the all-cheering air of liberty', cause an out-
cry? (II. 246–7). The 'liberty' he offers Clarissa, however, will prove
a new cage.

Because Lovelace seeks wholly to possess her, Clarissa like Pamela
must guard both mind and person. 'We are both great watchers
of each other's eyes; and indeed seem to be more than half afraid
of each other', she writes (460). Mental penetration complements
physical knowing, and here she baffles him. Each corresponds with
a friend, not with the other, and 'never was there such a pair of
scribbling lovers as we – yet perhaps whom it so much concerns
to keep from each other what each writes' (416). It vexes him that
although she writes her whole mind hourly and under the same roof,
he dares not break into a correspondence that defeats all his devices.
Their terse letters to each other after the fire scene only divide them
further.

'Penetration' means also the strong feeling preliminary to

repentance. 'What heart but must have been penetrated' by her pathetic pleas in the fire scene, asks Lovelace (726). But it endangers him to know her, because then he becomes like her. The bashful Lovelace, who 'has a good deal of the soul of a woman; and so, like Tiresias, can tell what they think and what they drive at, as well as themselves' (441),[17] becomes, like Tiresias, all-knowing, but hermaphrodite, impotent, and blind to the failure of his plots. In Hercules' gesture of abdication from manhood he says he would even dress as a woman in order to understand Clarissa, as Clodius had done with Portia and Calpurnia (420). And if, as Clarissa defines it, to be a gentleman is a distinction not necessarily deserved by a prince, Lovelace's imperial manliness is undermined again if he cannot exercise the very power, violence and tyranny that make him know he is king. Excluded from Clarissa's mind, or if included, threatened as a man, Lovelace will turn to brute force in order to 'know' and possess Clarissa.

Empress Clarissa is a clear match for this self-appointed king:

All sweetly serene and easy was the lovely brow and charming aspect of my goddess, on her descending to us; commanding reverence from every eye; a curtsy from every knee; and silence, awful silence, from every quivering lip. While she, armed with conscious worthiness and superiority, looked and behaved as an empress would among her vassals; yet with a freedom from pride and haughtiness, as if born to dignity and to a behaviour habitually gracious. (534)

Even Mrs Sinclair 'minces in her gait. She prims up her horse-mouth. Her voice, which when she pleases, is the voice of thunder, is sunk into an humble whine. Her stiff hams, that have not been bent to a civility for ten years past, are now limbered into curtsies three deep at every word. Her fat arms are crossed before her; and she can hardly be prevailed upon to sit in the presence of my goddess' (537). Indeed, Clarissa in her rich emblematic dress closely resembles the Gloriana that Lovelace several times names her.[18] Like the virgin queen Elizabeth, Clarissa has the body of a woman but the soul of a prince; though 'lion-hearted', her 'body is not equally organized. The unequal partners pull two ways; and the divinity within her tears her silken frame. But had the same soul informed a masculine body, never would there have been a truer hero' (647).

Who then is superior to whom? Lovelace in the fire scene submits 'to my beloved conqueress' (726), but more often their royalties tensely clash:

Who's modest now, thought I! Who's insolent now! – How a tyrant of a woman confounds a bashful man! – She was my Miss Howe, I thought; and I the spiritless Hickman.

At last, I *will* begin, thought I.

She a dish – I a dish.

Sip, her eyes her own, she; like a haughty and imperious sovereign, conscious of dignity; every look a favour.

Sip, like her vassal, I; lips and hands trembling, and not knowing that I sipped or tasted.

[She talks of the weather to her maid] I had no patience – Up I rose. Down went the tea-cup, saucer and all – Confound the weather, the sunshine, and the wench! . . .

I cast myself at her feet – Begone, Mr Lovelace, said she, with a rejecting motion, her fan in her hand; for your own sake leave me! – My soul is above thee, man! With both her hands pushing me from her! – Urge me not to tell thee how sincerely I think my soul above thee! – Thou hast a proud, a too proud heart, to contend with!   (644–6)

At such times Robert Lovelace sounds remarkably like Robert Devereux Earl of Essex, the military leader who offended Elizabeth by asking her to marry him. Their mutual attraction, her refusal to marry, his high treason, and her inability to save him from death all match Clarissa's story, as Lovelace himself suggests. 'Have I not known even a *virtuous woman*, as she would be thought, vow everlasting antipathy to a man who gave out that she was *too old for him to attempt*? And did not Essex's personal reflection on Queen Elizabeth, that she was *old and crooked*, contribute more to his ruin than his treason?', he writes (II. 249). In echo of Essex he bursts out, 'I hate her, hate her heartily! – She is old, ugly, and deformed – But Oh, the blasphemy!' (634), and complains of this queenly woman, 'Curse upon her perverse tyranny! How she makes me wait for an humble audience' (II. 100).

Against Queen Clarissa, her 'Essex' plots obsessively. 'I love, when I dig a pit, to have my prey tumble in with secure feet and open eyes: then a man can look down upon her, with an Oh-ho, charmer! how came you there!' (465). His plots feed his vanity. 'What a matchless plotter thy friend! Stand by and let me swell! – I am already as big as an elephant; and ten times wiser! mightier too by far! Have I not reason to snuff the moon with my proboscis?' (473). So many contrivances swarm up from his fertile brain, crowding for preference, that he does not know which to do first (672). In his itch to deceive Clarissa, he alters himself and other people, creates scenes, and makes the unreal substantial, but the disguise that exhilarates him seems to Clarissa satanic, like the fair forms that hide foul selves in the *Faerie Queene.* 'He is so light, so vain, so various, that there is no certainty that he will be next hour what he is this', she writes in despair (462).

King Lovelace appoints himself Jupiter, prototype to Don Juan, and shape-changer who in the form of various animals raped and destroyed mortal women like Semele (II. 98).[19] He is 'a perfect Proteus', a chameleon who turns his black self white (II. 82), for 'Ovid was not a greater master of metamorphoses than thy friend', he boasts (412). He passes Clarissa off as his sister, transforms whores into honest women, and makes of Deb an illiterate 'Dorcas' in order secretly to copy her letters. Mindful even of stage properties, he scatters pious books around the house (522–6) to create a respectable setting in which, he argues, they must claim to be married. His real reason is that if a court-case follows, these 'good women' can testify she was known as Mrs Lovelace. Developing his quite imaginary, cunning plans to take Mrs Fretchville's house, in order to 'show to all the world that her choice was free' (662), he pretends that marriage will reconcile her family to her. When it comes to the point, though, Clarissa will not own marriage to Captain Tomlinson the imposter, having 'resolved that I will appear to my uncle's friend, and to my uncle, as *I am*' (689). To prevent reconciliation, Lovelace devises a complicated new threat of kidnapping by her brother, and 'there's a faint sketch of my plot. – Stand by, varlets – Tanta-ra-ra-ra! – Veil your bonnets, and confess your master!' (539).

Clarissa's drift towards acceptance, drawn by hope and pushed by fear, provokes wilder schemes yet. In an episode which Richardson developed from Shadwell's play and restored from the manuscript to the third edition, Lovelace plans to take Anna, Mrs Howe, and a maid-servant by ship to the Isle of Wight and there rape them, with Lovelace 'the princely lion' taking Anna as his share. Hickman they will push overboard, 'popping up and down, his wig and hat floating by him; and paddling, pawing, and dashing, like a frightened mongrel'. After their trial and inevitable pardon, they will kidnap James and Solmes, for 'a man, Jack, would not go into exile for nothing' (II. letter 109).

Like Queen Elizabeth, however, Clarissa is always watchful. Wary of the whores and antagonistic to the four 'Hottentot' friends whom he passes off as gentlemen (574), she protests against the lie she is sure of, the pretence that they are married, knowing that he delights in obliquity and crooked ways (527). Lovelace in turn calls her papers treasonable (573), but in fact he overplots himself:

Here have I been at work, dig, dig, dig, like a cunning miner at one time, and spreading my snares like an artful fowler at another, and exulting in my contrivances to get this inimitable creature absolutely into my power. Everything made for me – Her brother and uncle were but my pioneers: her father stormed as I directed him to storm. Mrs Howe was acted by the springs I set at work: her daughter was moving for me, and yet imagined herself plumb against me: and the dear creature herself had already run her stubborn neck into my gin, and knew not that she was caught; for I had not drawn my sprindges close about her – and just as all this was completed, wouldst thou believe that I should be my own enemy, and her friend? – that I should be so totally diverted from all my favourite purposes, as to propose to marry her before I went to town, in order to put it out of my own power to resume them?   (517–18)

Galled to find that Clarissa's and Anna's 'plot, conjuration, sorcery, witchcraft' are all going forward (633), he is 'mad with love – fired by revenge – puzzled with my own devices – My inventions are my curse – my pride my punishment' (694). He may challenge Belford that without inside knowledge he could not have been able, any more than the lady, to have guessed what was to befall her until it came to pass, but admits that in the fire scene devised to frighten her into his arms he had faltered before Clarissa's pathetic pleas. She puzzled him, she beat him out of his play (715–17). He had 'retired like a fool, a woman's fool, as I was!', he writes. 'This was my mine, my plot! – And this was all I made of it!' (727).

Belford, asking what glory, what triumph there can be, given his plots and her relations, her lack of protection and the deceptions of the brothel, hastens to dissuade him from the final act (501). His prediction that however she reasserts her purity, whether she kills herself like Lucretia or wastes away from grief, she will make Lovelace's life a torment of torments to him (710), seems rapidly to be coming true when Clarissa in the fire scene snatches a pair of scissors to her breast and cries out, 'give me but the means, and I will instantly convince you that my honour is dearer to me than my life!' (724–5).

Meanwhile Anna has unravelled everything. Urgently she writes to Clarissa the truth about the whores, their house, 'Tomlinson' and 'Fretchville', establishes Lovelace's character as a ruined libertine, guesses his motivations to be revenge and pride, works out all his plots and begs her friend to flee the house, adding, 'Oh that your heart would let you fly *him!*' (751). But Clarissa, alerted by the fire plot, has already fled to Hampstead. Like Cleopatra grieving after Antony leaves her, Lovelace mourns his loss,

I have been traversing her room, meditating, or taking up everything she but touched or used: the glass she dressed at I was ready to break, for not giving me the personal image it was wont to reflect, of *her*, whose idea is for ever present with me. I call for her, now in the tenderest, now in the most reproachful terms, as if within hearing: wanting *her*, I want my own soul, at least everything dear to it. What a void in my heart! what a chillness in my blood, as if its circulation were arrested! From her room to my own; in the dining-room, and in and out of every place where I have seen the beloved of my heart, do I hurry; in none can I tarry; her lovely image in every one, in some lively attitude, rushing cruelly upon me, in differently remembered conversations.

Undone and outwitted by an 'inexperienced traitress' who impudently contrives to rob him of the dearest property he ever purchased, disgraced by being outwitted by such 'an infant, in stratagem and contrivance' (letter 228), he swears perverse revenge on the 'virago' who has armed her like the women warriors in Spenser's poem to Gloriana, *The Faerie Queene*. He resolves that at least he will have Miss Howe if he cannot have her more exalted friend, then 'if there be so much flaming love between these girls as they pretend, what will my charmer profit by her escape?'

Like another Miss Godfrey, Clarissa longs for exile abroad; like Job before her she asks,

Oh why was the great fiend of all unchained, and permitted to assume so specious a form, and yet allowed to conceal his feet and his talons, till with the one he was ready to trample upon my honour, and to strike the other into my heart! – And what had I done that he should be let loose particularly upon me!
(753–5)

It is all too simple for Lovelace to hunt her down. '*Io Triumphe!* Io Clarissa, sing!', he writes vaingloriously,[20] for to know her whereabouts is to have her in his power (757). Since, he declares, it is not fit that a woman of any age, or in any state of life, should be independent, he will turn this flight to his advantage, as all crushed rebellions can be turned to the advantage of the sovereign in possession. She will surely repent her insults, he assures himself, she will implore his forgiveness, beg to be reinstated in his favour, and plead to see buried in oblivion her heinous offence against the God of Love and Lovelace his votary. 'And now, dressed like a bridegroom,' he writes in glee, 'I am already at Hampstead!' (760–1).

5

Death and the maiden

'And now, Belford, I can go no farther. The affair is over. Clarissa
lives' (883). After all the mystifications, the play-acting and the complicated closing in, Lovelace commits an act simply physical and
brutal. Consummation proves a bubble indeed, when at the brothel
to which his false cousins have lured her, he rapes her while she
is unconscious from an opiate. Driven by his attributes as Satan,
Faust, Don Juan and Domestic King, he falls, like Hamlet, prey
to his own devices. Clarissa appeals to the law, and the pit to catch
charmers gapes as a hell-mouth for him and a grave awaiting her.[1]

At Hampstead Lovelace becomes openly satanic. As he himself
tells it,

I unbuttoned therefore my cape, I pulled off my flapped, slouched hat;
I threw open my great-coat and, like the devil in Milton (an odd comparison
though!),

> I started up in my own form divine,
> Touched by the beam of her celestial eye,
> More potent than Ithuriel's spear! –   (772)

After the rape when he can neither 'fly from himself', nor, like
Macbeth, sleep (904), the price of victory is the same as Faust's.
'Have you really and truly sold yourself to [Satan]? And for how
long? What duration is your reign to have?', asks Clarissa. 'Poor
man! The contract *will* be out; and then what will be your fate!'
(894). To his demonic darkness she is a heavenly brightness, blazing upon him 'in a flood of light, like what one might imagine would
strike a man who, born blind, had by some propitious power been
blessed with his sight, all at once, in a meridian sun' (772). When
Clarissa, like the angels in *Paradise Lost*, penetrates his disguise, this
'reptile kneeler, the despicable slave, no more the proud victor' (930)
will be shorn of his satanic contrivances, and become but a common man (907). She knows the fire scene was meant to destroy her,
guesses about Mrs Sinclair's house, and deduces that a chance to
escape to another 'mother' masquerading as a noblewoman is a
plot. But her mistrust of Lovelace's 'cousins' comes too late, and
although Tomlinson trembles to feel in his conscience 'a sudden

flash from her eye, an *eye-beam* as he called it, dart through his shivering reins' (824), the hope of family reconciliation still blinds her to his feigning.

To Clarissa's Hampstead protectors, Lovelace represents her fears as merely sexual. 'She'll get over all these freaks if once she be a mamma', they say knowingly (766). His vengeance revived by her resistance, and alive only in a whirlwind of doing, he plans to seduce Clarissa, the Hampstead women, and Anna, whose cruelty to the male–virgin Hickman proves that women 'like not novices', he says complacently (802). At other times Lovelace longs to pass his journey with Clarissa (870), weeps with pity, or finds his conscience seize his pen, but 'already have I not gone too far? Like a repentant thief, afraid of his gang and obliged to go on in fear of hanging till he comes to be hanged, I am afraid of the gang of my cursed contrivances.' In a prolonged, bloody, sadistic scene he murders conscience, a woman who looks very like Clarissa, 'Eternally resisting! – Eternally contradicting!',[2] and admits like Macbeth that she dies hard. As Belford has said, he is 'a machine at last, and no free agent' (848).

In the full knowledge that he dooms them both, Lovelace draws Clarissa, wearily hopeful of family reconciliation if she consents to marry him, back to Mrs Sinclair's, where she sinks disordered to his feet, and 'down on her bosom, like a half-broken-stalked lily, top-heavy with the overcharging dews of the morning, sunk her head with a sigh that went to my heart'. Mrs Sinclair, the 'old dragon', the compound and epitome of Lovelace's animal imagery, straddles up to her,

with her arms kemboed again – her eyebrows erect, like the bristles upon a hog's back and, scowling over her shortened nose, more than half-hid her ferret eyes. Her mouth was distorted. She pouted out her blubber-lips, as if to bellows up wind and sputter into her horse-nostrils; and her chin was curdled, and more than usually prominent with passion. (881–3)

With her help, Clarissa is drugged, then raped. The affair is over indeed.

Now, Lovelace acknowledges too late how much his deeds have been determined by his nature, his environment, and fate (870). Another world must exist, says Belford, or 'could the divine SOCRATES, and the divine CLARISSA, otherwise have suffered?' (884). He can even pity Lovelace, 'caught in thy own snares! Thy punishment is but beginning!' (964).

A king because he is a man, Lovelace has relished 'playing the tyrant over what I love' (789), and resents being 'insulted and defied by a rebel in one's power, what prince can bear that?' (818). When, after the rape, he claims the new authority of a husband, his sexuality makes him even more dangerous to her than James Harlowe. She calls him simply '*man*', which means to her all that is vile. 'Keep thy distance, *man*', she cries (794), and 'I am sick of thee, MAN!' Unexpectedly though, the rape of Clarissa, once accomplished, makes Lovelace impotent politically as well as sexually. He fears her now she is in his power, or, as Mrs Sinclair vividly puts it, 'I never knew such work in my life, between a chicken of a gentleman, and a tiger of a lady!' (935). Lovelace knows that his lust is insatiable, like Satan's, like Faust's, like Don Juan's. 'What indeed is an imperial crown itself, when a man is used to it?', he writes even before the rape (815), and after it he muses again,

Caesar never knew what it was to be *hypped*, I will call it, till he came to be what Pompey was; that is to say, till he arrived at the height of his ambition: nor did thy Lovelace know what it was to be gloomy, till he had completed his wishes upon the charmingest creature in the world.

(888)

These are three tragic heroes for whom the reader must feel as much sympathy as revulsion. So too for Hamlet, the fourth of Lovelace's prototypes. Like the prince compelled by revenge to act a villain, Lovelace, who in his self-conscious 'soliloquies' seeks excuses for delay or finds conscience makes him a coward, alludes to *Hamlet* (inaccurately) when he observes that 'there is no difference to be found between the skull of king Philip and that of another man' (885); Clarissa, abused in her sexuality, sounds like a suicidal Ophelia when she quotes from the play in her scraps which have 'method and good sense in some of them' (894). Belford, like Laertes, vows that had he been her brother 'her violation must have been followed by the blood of one of us' (884), and her death will precipitate a fight over the possession of her body. Lord M. is another Polonius with his 'bead-roll of proverbs' (784), who cannot by his prudential wisdom compass the tragic magnitude of a Lovelace, nor can Belford his Horatio comprehend all of his friend's philosophy.

Lovelace is especially like Hamlet in his use of plays to catch Queen Clarissa. Author, designer, director and leading actor all in one, he writes the scripts, assigns the parts, clothes and trains the actors, improvises, and sweeps up members of the audience into his dramatic scenes. He justifies his deceptions because already all the world's a stage. He cites as instances relatives at a man's

death-bed, pretending 'for decency's sake, to whine over his ex-
cruciating pangs – to be in the way to answer a thousand impertinent inquiries after the health of a man thou wished to die', and
consulting with 'a parcel of solemn would-seem-wise doctors, and
their officious zanies the apothecaries, joined with the butcherly tribe
of scarificators; all combined to carry on the physical farce, and
to cut out thongs both from his flesh and his estate' (849).
Turning his own world into a stage in order that he may control
it, he sets the scene and pulls back the curtain:

And here, supposing my narrative of the dramatic kind, ends Act the First.
And now begins

ACT II. SCENE, Hampstead Heath continued

Enter my Rascal (764)

In Hamlet's style he rehearses his 'cousins': 'no over-do!,' he tells
them, 'Easy and unaffected!' They practise before a pier glass, then
'a dram of Barbados each – And now we are gone' (876–7). Often,
though, he must improvise. At Hampstead he is frantic to intercept
Anna's letter, and whisks Mrs Bevis into his play to impersonate
a Clarissa bloated, dropsical, and not the woman she was (856).
He turns his Hampstead actors into audiences, and his audiences
into actors, to catch Clarissa. 'What a happy man shall I be if these
women can be brought to join to carry my marriage into consummation!', he says (788). Above all, he manipulates Clarissa both
as actor and as audience when he directs her to play love-object
and wife, or stages scenes to deceive her. Clarissa, however, resists
the roles he assigns, and will choose her own disguise for her escape.
    At times Lovelace over-reaches himself. For example, Clarissa
sees through his signalling system with Tomlinson, who rebels
briefly against his playwright:

If thou *art* dough, *be* dough; and I slapped him on the shoulder – Resume
but thy former shape – and I'll be answerable for the event.
    He bowed assent and compliance: went to the glass; and began to un-
twist and unsadden his features: pulled his wig right, as if that, as well
as his head and heart, had been discomposed by his compunction; and
once more became old Mulciber's and mine. (838)

But usually Lovelace succeeds, and by rewriting letters he makes
Anna her friend's destroyer. Her accusation of 'lurking love' tells
Clarissa that she has lost everyone (932).

89

Lovelace's theatrical illusions supplant Clarissa's truth, and he mocks the sincerity that makes her guileless:

A dear silly soul! thought I, at the time, to depend upon the goodness of her own heart, when the heart cannot be seen into but by its actions; and she, to appearance, a runaway, an eloper, from a tender, a most indulgent husband! – to neglect to cultivate the opinion of individuals, when the whole world is governed by appearance! (789)

Her 'violent tragedy speech, and the high manner in which she uttered it' out-Herod Herod and confirm his diagnosis of frenzy. As she struggles to discover the truth in this wilderness of doubt and error, he has anticipated every charge she might bring. 'These ladies will certainly think you have fallen among robbers; and that I am the chief of them,' he says cunningly. 'So you are! so you are!,' she says, stamping, 'I shall be quite distracted!' (775–7).

His mystifications are legion. In addition to the euphemism '*innocent* house' for Mrs Sinclair's brothel, which makes Clarissa complain that 'long have my ears been accustomed to such inversions of words' (951), he employs the delusions of flattery. His proud family, he claims, will cheerfully resign themselves to her sovereignty,

But thus, angrily, did she disclaim the compliment.
Yes, indeed! – (and there she stopped a moment, her sweet bosom heaving with a noble disdain) – Tricked out of myself from the very first – a fugitive from my own family! renounced by my relations! insulted by you! – laying humble claim to the protection of yours! is not this the light in which I must appear not only to the ladies of your family, but to all the world? (840)

His baroque phrase for her tears, 'charming fountains' (932), reflects his preference for elaboration and deceit over Clarissa's for plain words, while his habitual shorthand shows his liking for private codes. In tacit rejection of Locke's vision of consensus, he assigns his own meanings to words, replacing, for instance, the common definition of the '*right sort of love*' with his own (III. 156–7). He denies that friendship between Clarissa and Anna has any sense:

these vehement friendships are nothing but chaff and stubble, liable to be blown away by the very wind that raises them. Apes! mere apes of *us*! they think the word *friendship* has a pretty sound with it; and it is much talked of; a fashionable word: and so, truly, a single woman who thinks she has a soul, and knows that she wants something, would be thought to have found a fellow-soul for it in her own sex. But I repeat that the word is a *mere* word, the thing a mere name with them; a cork-bottomed shuttlecock, which they are fond of striking to and fro, to make one another glow in the frosty weather of a single state; but which, when a *man* comes in between the pretended *inseparables*, is given up . . .   (863)

He denies the very existence of 'rape', arguing that women always give way with a 'yielding reluctance, without which I will be sworn, whatever rapes have been attempted, none ever were committed, one person to one person' (719), and like Mrs Jewkes scoffs at 'the romantic notions of a girl who supposes *that* to be the greatest which is the slightest of evils' (836). Can Clarissa, raped, and a true ex- ample of penitence, 'be said to be ruined, undone, and such sort of stuff? – I have no patience with the pretty fools who use these strong words to describe the most transitory evil; and which a mere church-form makes none' (869). In Lovelace's definition she has but 'run the fate of a thousand others of her sex – only that they did not set such a romantic value upon what they call their *honour*; that's all' (885).

Lovelace thus invades Clarissa's interpretations as well as her body, even in her correspondence where 'her delicate and even mind is seen in the very cut of her letters' (811). Priding himself on being able to 'trace human nature, and more particularly female nature, through its most secret recesses' (843), he hankers after her pocketfuls of letters, 'tied round [women], as ballast-bags, I presume, lest the wind, as they move with full sail from whale-ribbed canvas, should blow away the gypsies' (569–70). Since letters mirror minds, to intercept and alter Clarissa's correspondence obliterates her innermost self, as Lovelace explains:

familiar letter-writing . . . was writing from the heart (without the fetters prescribed by method or study), as the very word *correspondence* implied. Not the heart only; the *soul* was in it. Nothing of body, when friend writes to friend; the mind impelling sovereignly the vassal-fingers. It was, in short, friendship recorded; friendship given under hand and seal; demonstrating that the parties were under no apprehension of changing from time or accident, when they so liberally gave testimonies, which would always be ready, on failure or infidelity, to be turned against them.   (II. 431)

In her longing for trustworthy communication, Clarissa hungrily 'holds out her sweet face' with 'the most earnest attention, as if she would shorten the way which [Tomlinson's] words were to have to her heart' (824). Fluency must be suspect to a woman who thinks brevity is truth, and complications alert her. 'I abhor your expe- dients, your inventions – I have had too many of them,' she says. How can she trust a man who appears in vile disguises, tells gentlewomen invented stories, and falsely asserts a husband's right over her? But, as Lovelace replies, how otherwise could he have come at his goal, her speech (829)?

The rape, which proves once and for all that Lovelace is a man who never yet told her truth (890), severs all communication just when he longs to marry her. Words, which have deceived her, she will not use. 'I will promise nothing', she says (943). His messenger returns without the 'four requested words' of church and date (955), and his letters are met by silence. In the madness which is sanity's response to the fracture of her body and her world view, Clarissa at last sees clearly. Exploring the rape in allegory, quotations, and letters that she does not send, she tries to comprehend this unspeakable act through ideas of rational causation. Lovelace's brutal deed she explains by the Hobbesian story of a bear tearing to pieces the lady who fed it; her family's wishes have been fulfilled in her humility; she 'knew not that you were vice itself!' (891–2). But the fragmentary nature of her papers shows how much the deed is beyond her reasoning.[3] Curiously though, where Lovelace's delusions once silenced her, he now stammers before her moving, Lucretia-like oratory (900). He can neither think nor write, and some characters in his letters are 'so indistinct and unformed' that they are hardly to be made out (936). Others that describe the rape are too dreadfully distinct to be obliterated. 'Scratch out, erase, never to be read, every part of my preceding letters, where I have boastingly mentioned it', he writes in vain to Belford (952).

Like Portia in *The Merchant of Venice* Clarissa turns to law, her ultimate guarantee of fixed meanings and protective contract. She implicitly subscribes to Locke's belief that the law preserves and enlarges that '*Liberty* [which] is to be free from restraint and violence from others', just as Lovelace maintains a definition that Locke calls its opposite, a '*Liberty for every Man to do what he lists*' (II. 57). In a speechless, emblematic agony, Clarissa holds up to the witness of heaven the marriage licence by which Lovelace has gulled her, a scene likened by Lovelace to 'the poor distressed Catalans' who 'held up their English treaty, on an occasion that keeps the worst of my actions in countenance' (887).[4] Mocking and fearing the power of pedantic words, he spins a wild scheme to rewrite the marriage laws. If partners changed every Valentine's Day, he says, rapes, adultery, fornication, polygamy, jealousy and barrenness would thereby all be annihilated, domestic quarrels would end, expectation would invigorate, and termagants, old maids and tyrant power disappear. 'Dost think that *old prerogative Harlowe*, for example, must not, if such a law were in being, have pulled in his horns? – So excellent a lady as he has would never else have *renewed* with such a gloomy tyrant: who, as well as all other tyrants, must have been upon good behaviour from year to year' (873).

Lovelace lives not by the world's laws but by the laws of love. Since Jupiter laughs at the perjuries of lovers (847), he can swear that his false cousins are real, in lovers' oaths, that is (910). In love, law is relative, and he forms his judgment of the nature of things and actions not so much from what they are in themselves as from the characters of the actors. 'Thus it would be as odd a thing in such as we to *keep* our words with a lady, as it would be wicked in her to *break* hers to us' (767). Clarissa is wise not to trust a man 'too *brave* to have any regard either to moral or divine sanctions' (942), and complains, like Pamela, that the 'cause must be well tried, where the offender takes his seat upon the same bench with the judge' (827).

The law that supports Clarissa's right to go free will hang Lovelace for the rape (965). Her trust in society exemplified by her bold attempts to escape, she throws up the sash window to call to the passers by, and Lovelace in a rapid improvisation has to trick the constable (905–6). Unable to stage lies, she again sets up quasi-legal occasions to discover truth, instructing Tomlinson,

You may say all that you please to say before these gentlewomen. Mr Lovelace may have secrets. I have none. You seem to think me faulty: I should be glad that all the world knew my heart. Let my enemies sit in judgement upon my actions: fairly scanned, I fear not the result. Let them even ask me my most secret thoughts, and, whether they make for me or against me, I will reveal them.

Here in the privileged surroundings as of a courtroom, Clarissa calls upon these witnesses to respond objectively; here she may safely speak, and move Tomlinson to true feeling (822–3). She even transforms Lovelace's own attempt at a court-room scene – with the whores sitting in judgment upon her – into an occasion for her 'glorious power of innocence' to shine forth, and her threat of suicide in the penknife scene terrifies her audience with her emphatic 'the LAW shall be all my resource: the LAW' (949–50). The gathering of the evidence has in fact begun. Clarissa's letters provide ample proofs of villainy, while Lovelace's own reveal everything to Belford, who is already taking 'minutes of examinations, accusations, and confessions, with the significant air of a Middlesex Justice' (963).

Richardson's novel, then, though overtly about bodies, has more to do with minds. Setting Lovelace's change against Clarissa's fixed meanings, it challenges him to possess her, soul and body. In a combat mental as much as physical, his eager eyes must seek 'for a lost heart in hers, and [endeavour] to penetrate to her very soul' (851), but she, with her wonderful 'penetration', has mastered him instead (903). In the rape Clarissa loses both mind and maidenhead: they have 'killed my head among you', she writes (895). But her mind proves independent of her body as Lovelace's fatally is not. 'Soul all over', she makes him wonder 'how came the dear soul (clothed as it is with such a silken vesture) by all its steadiness?' He acknowledges at last her superiority to him in what Clarissa calls proudly 'a disunion in minds' (850-2).

Lovelace had been forced to put her wary mind out of action with the opiate because 'all the princes of the air, or beneath it, joining with me, could never have subdued her while she had her senses' (899). His very art subverted his victory, as he always knew:

There's no triumph over the will in force! This I know I have said. But would I not have avoided it if I could? – Have I not tried every other method? And have I any other recourse left me? Can she resent the *last outrage* more than she has resented a *fainter effort?* – And if her resentments run ever so high, cannot I repair by matrimony? – She will not refuse me, I know, Jack; the haughty beauty will not refuse me, when her pride of being corporally inviolate is brought down; when she can tell no tales, but when (be her resistance what it will) even her own sex will suspect a yielding in resistance; and when that modesty, which may fill her bosom with resentment, will lock up her speech. (879)

The whores' demand for the completion of her breaking-in forces Lovelace to one last attempt. He realises too that the drug prevented him for ever from knowing what her will '*would have been* in the arduous trial' (III. 275-6), but his plan to find it out by raping her again when she is conscious falters before her keen perception. Clarissa's soul is intact where her body is not; she seems 'to tread air, and to be all soul' (949).

If, after the rape, Lovelace finds he is Hamlet caught in his own trap, Clarissa too finds her old identity gone. 'I don't know what my name is!', she writes in her stupefaction and shock, for she is 'no longer what I was in any one thing' (890). She has become 'but a cipher, to give him significance and myself pain' as she has said (567). No longer Harlowe but harlot (909), she asks to be placed in a private madhouse. When all that she has left against this Hobbesian, anarchic man is Locke's belief that 'no other Man has a Power over [one's person], but the free Disposal of it lies in

himself' (II. 190), she demands to know if she is to be 'controlled
in the future disposal of myself' or if in 'a country of liberty' she
is to be kept a prisoner (901). Claiming a right 'from which it is
an illegal violence to withhold me', insisting upon the 'freedom
which is my birthright as an English subject' (933–4) that Locke
promised (II. 55, 57), she maintains that at least her life is in her
own power. 'I dare to die, Lovelace – and the person that fears
not death is not to be intimidated into a meanness unworthy of her
heart and principles!' (940). Lovelace may argue that the opiate
mercifully absolved her from responsibility (887–8), but Clarissa
accepts no extenuation. A woman violated in body only and 'no
slave in my will!' (930), she identifies with that symbol of liberty
against tyranny, Lucretia, and is twice tempted to stab the body
that betrayed her (900).

When Clarissa appealed to the legal protection of marriage
against Lovelace's freedom without it, like him she sought her own
version of liberty. Clarissa could whole-heartedly have loved
Lovelace, being 'not capable of resolving to give my *hand*, and –
nothing but my hand' (828), and Lovelace, who loved Clarissa,
perversely justified the last trial by arguing that 'if I find in that
resentment less of hatred of *me*, than of the fact, then shall she be
mine in her own way. Then, hateful as is the *life of shackles* to me,
will I *marry her*' (838). His anxiety about the figure he will make
in the rakish annals if he takes so much trouble merely for a wife
(846) rings more true, however. Each senses in sex more than a
trap to catch charmers. If she dies, says Clarissa, he must 'dig a
hole deep enough to cram in and conceal this unhappy body: for,
depend upon it, that some of those who will not stir to protect me
living, will move heaven and earth to avenge me dead!', while marriage, says Lovelace in a fit of Lear-like revulsion from women,
is 'tumbling into the pit, which it was the end of all my plots to
shun!' (911–12).

The rape ironically reverses their ideas. Lovelace hopes for a
pregnancy, for a charming boy, to make her marry him, and just
when Clarissa is set irrevocably against him, abjures elaboration
to say simply, 'I love her beyond expression; and cannot help it'
(959). But he returns from his uncle's sick-bed to find her gone.
Clarissa had been before this the confined one, but when Lovelace
resisted Tomlinson's plea, '*No farther, I beseech you*' (830), and pro-
ceeded to the rape, his triumph could indeed 'go no farther'. The
whores may jeer and ask, 'have I gone so far, and am I afraid to
go farther?', but he has already sinned, as he knows, beyond

forgiveness (943). Clarissa's implacable declaration that *'the man who has been the villain to me you have been, shall never make me his wife'* (901) tells Lovelace that his strategies are done. 'What to do with her, or without her, I know not', is all he can now say (907).

Clarissa at last escapes. In the security of the Smiths' shop she repossesses her mind along with her body, and starts to press every responsibility home. Her refusal to prosecute and Lovelace's triumph in his 'trial' convince almost everyone that they will marry, but her arrest and imprisonment on a trumped-up charge of debt shock her so profoundly that her new friends realise that instead, she will die.

Her letters now freed from Lovelace's distortions, Clarissa can deploy her skills of writing to cross-examine witnesses, uncover inconsistencies, and so find out the truth of his contrivances. She discovers that Anna has not been seriously ill as he had said, that her family never assembled to receive her messages, and that they never planned with Singleton and Solmes to kidnap her. Lady Betty Lawrance denies that she arranged to meet her or that she knew Tomlinson, whose identity Clarissa carefully checks, Anna confirms Lovelace's theft and forgery of her vital letter exposing the vile house, and the Hampstead women explain his ruse to have Anna's other letter received by an imposter. Clarissa's recognition that all his 'dreadful perjuries, and inhuman arts, as he went along, were to pass for fine stratagems; for witty sport; and to demonstrate a superiority of inventive talents!', force from her the bitter protest that Belford, her self-proclaimed friend and advocate, has hidden Lovelace's baseness from her in the name of male friendship (1077–8).

Like Philomela who was raped by Tereus, had her tongue torn out, and was turned into a nightingale (1038), Clarissa, though raped and silenced, sings. She tells Anna everything she knows about the altered letters, the impersonations, the return to London, her faintness that allowed Mrs Sinclair to force the potion upon her, and the entry into the 'fatal inner house'. Led a 'poor sacrifice into the old wretch's too well-known parlour' and forced to drink two dishes of tea whose odd taste, the women assured her, was due to the London milk, she was tricked, like Persephone, into eating the food of hell. Dreadful scenes followed, 'female figures flitting, as I may say, before my sight; the wretched woman's particularly', and delirious days (letter 314), until London, 'the place of all others, to be private in' (1018), paradoxically allows her to speak out. Because the cruel spoiler would scarcely have had recourse to unprecedented arts, stupefying potions, and the most brutal and outrageous force had she been wanting in duty, the truth, she believes, is her best defence (988). Her uncommon openness of heart astonishes Belford, when she asks why she should conceal that disgrace from others which she cannot hide from herself (985). Lovelace is, rather, appalled by a general liberality of communication which will 'put it out of my power to redress those wrongs, with any tolerable reputation to either of us' (III. 491), and for his own honour and that of his 'wife and my illustrious progeny' demands his letters back (1041). But Belford disobeys.

Mrs Howe urges prosecution for the general good. 'What murderers, what ravishers, would be brought to justice if *modesty* were to be a general plea, and allowable, against appearing in a court to prosecute?', she wants to know. Is Clarissa afraid, ashamed, or in love? Anna too urges her friend to copy the custom in the Isle of Man where a woman is offered a rope, a sword and a ring, that is, the choice of death or marriage for her violator. Clarissa, who wants neither, astounds them by refusing to proceed (1016–19).

Instead of a public trial, Lovelace undergoes a private one, by family. Confronted by Clarissa's evidential letters, he quickly exchanges the part of accused for that of lawyer, arguing 'he must be a silly fellow who has not something to say for himself, when every cause has its black and its white side – Westminster Hall, Jack, affords every day as confident defences as mine'. He wins his judges by laughter when he says he could not help it, and again when he says that she was the only woman in the world 'who would have made such a rout about a case that is uncommon only from the circumstances that attend it' (letter 323). The family, who are impressed by Lovelace's testimony to her merits and duped by the fluency of his confession, self-condemnation and promises, undertake to mediate with the fair accuser to get her 'justice', that is, marriage (1034), which makes Lovelace dread that 'by a single hair, hangs over my head the matrimonial sword. And thus ended my trial.' Clarissa is equally trapped. If she refuses marriage it will now look as if it is her fault (1040–1), but as she wearily says, this 'was a cause before another tribunal' (1077).

Lovelace, who knew it was better for him to tell his own story than to have an adversary tell it for him, brilliantly transforms his arraignment into a 'comedy' (1038–40), and his merriment at the sympathetic 'nose-music' of his family (1029) moves Belford to complain that 'an air of levity runs through thy most serious letters'

(1077). 'I cannot be grave six minutes together, for the blood of me', replies his friend. 'I am a descendant of old Chancellor More, I believe; and should not forbear to cut a joke, were I upon the scaffold' (1098).

If the criminal Lovelace gets off by means of his own advocacy, the plaintiff Clarissa is turned into a criminal. Arrested for non-payment of the lodging she never wanted at Mrs Sinclair's, she struggles against going 'with *men*! – Must go with *men*! – I am not used to go with *strange men*!', but a gentleman in the crowd finds they have authority for what they do, and pities her as he leaves her (1051). Like the characters in Otway's *Caius Marius* and Shakespeare's *Romeo and Juliet*, who find 'The world no friend of his, nor the world's law' (1069), Clarissa here sees the law act as unjustly against her as the laws of love, in which 'male-delinquents', says Lovelace, have the advantage of the other sex, 'for while they, poor things! sit sighing in holes and corners, or run to woods and groves to bemoan themselves for their baffled hopes, we can rant and roar, hunt and hawk; and by new loves banish from our hearts all remembrance of the old ones' (1086).

By his lively image of the fairground wheel of fortune, Lovelace disclaims all responsibility.[5] Rakes naturally set down one pretty girl to pick up another, he says, 'just as the fellows do with their flying-coaches and flying-horses at a country fair – with a *Who rides next! Who rides next!*'. Clarissa skims from booth to booth in the fairground of the world, followed by a string of suitors,

One pretty little fellow called Wyerly, perhaps; another jiggeting rascal called Biron, a third simpering varlet of the name of Symmes, and a more hideous villain than any of the rest with a long bag under his arm, and parchment settlements tagged to his heels, ycleped Solmes; pursue her from raree-show to raree-show, shouldering upon one another at every turning, stopping when she stops, and set a spinning again when she moves . . .

Tempted to try the 'one-go-up, the other-go-down picture-of-the-world vehicle', she slily pops in, turns giddy, and dashes out her pretty little brains. 'Who can help it!', asks Lovelace, 'And would you hang the poor fellow whose *professed trade* it was to set the pretty little creatures a-flying?' (letter 294). And so, by his patronising, witty appeal to necessity and custom, Lovelace dismisses the gravity of the crime.

In truth he suffers as he has never done before. 'Ruined, un-done, blown-up, destroyed, and worse than annihilated' (969), he grieves, like Donne in the *Nocturnall upon S. Lucies Day*, that 'having lost her, my whole soul is a blank: the whole creation round me, the elements above, beneath, and everything I *behold* (for nothing I can *enjoy*) is a blank without her!' She is all the world to him, and 'light, air, joy, harmony, in my notion are but parts of thee' (1023). Helpless to prevent his own plots carrying on horribly without him, he selfishly claims to suffer worse than she does: where Locke had humanely allowed women to avoid child-bed pain, Lovelace the Filmerian maintains that the female sex 'is made to bear pain. It is a curse that the first of it entailed upon all her succeeding daughters, when she brought the curse upon us all.' He is sadistic to argue that women love those best who pain them most, but his own suffering confesses love:

> Every cushion or chair I shall sit upon, the bed I shall lie down upon (if I go to bed), till she return, will be stuffed with bolt-upright awls, bodkins, corking-pins, and packing-needles: already I can fancy that to pink my body like my mind, I need only be put into a hogshead stuck full of steel-pointed spikes, and rolled down a hill three times as high as the Monument.[6]   (1069)

His savage misery enlarged by the wretchedness of his friend Belton, who dies in the knowledge that his sons are not his (1099), Lovelace must attend to Belford's warning that rakes turn solitary and conquerors lose,

> Reduced, probably, by riotous waste to consequential want, behold them refuged in some obscene hole or garret; obliged to the careless care of some dirty old woman, whom nothing but her poverty prevails upon to attend to perform the last offices for men who have made such shocking ravage among the young ones.   (III. 483)

The obvious solution is marriage. Little harm will then have been done

> if it can be so easily repaired by a few magical words; as *I, Robert*, take thee, Clarissa; and I, Clarissa, take thee, Robert, with the rest of the for-better and for-worse legerdemain, which will hocus-pocus all the wrongs, the crying wrongs, that I have done to Miss Harlowe, into acts of kindness and benevolence to Mrs. Lovelace.

He knows, though, that if he marries, he will have been plundering his own treasury (III. 412).

Lovelace has in fact as good reason to satirise marriage as Hogarth has in *Marriage à la Mode*. Given the lack of education for women, clever men could hardly stay interested in one woman alone. Only the chase keeps love alive for him, love which is 'hardly ever *totally* extirpated, except by matrimony indeed, which is the grave of love, because it allows of the end of love' (1040). As Milton wrote,

> Among unequals what societie
> Can sort, what harmonie or true delight?
>
> *(Paradise Lost,* VIII. 383–4)

To Lovelace, living together outside wedlock promises a 'generous confidence', rather than, as in marriage, 'a *life of doubt and distrust,* surely, where the woman confides nothing, and ties up a man for his good behaviour for life, taking Church and State sanctions in aid of the obligation she imposes upon him' (III. 510). But the illiberal attitudes of his time, of which he himself is so lavish an example, make his proposal outrageous.

Nor will he share power in marriage. Pointing with some justice to the contemptuous behaviour that Anna has learnt from Mrs Howe, 'one of the most violent-spirited women in *England,* whose late husband could not stand in the matrimonial contention of *Who should?* but tipped off the perch in it, neither knowing how to yield, nor how to conquer' (III. 476), he remarks.

A charming encouragement for a man of intrigue, when he has reason to believe that the woman he has a view upon has no love for her husband! What good principles must that wife have, who is kept in against temptation by a sense of her duty and plighted faith, where affection has no hold of her!
(1086)

Lovelace, forgetting that Clarissa, like Cleopatra, is all variety, imagines marriage as tedious and predictable,

And what a couple of old patriarchs shall we become, going on in the mill-horse round; getting sons and daughters; providing nurses for them first, governors and governesses next; teaching them lessons their father never practised, nor which their mother, as her parents will say, was much the better for!
(III. 474)

Consoling himself by the thought that once married he will have easy access to Anna Howe (1040), he must wonder if even Clarissa, who 'according to the old patriarchal system' should 'go on contributing to get sons and daughters with no other view than to bring them up piously, and to be good and useful members of the commonwealth', can be trusted now she has let 'her fancy run a gadding after a rake'. Her idea of reforming him he mocks as spiritual pride, saying,

She had formed pretty notions how charmingly it would look to have a penitent of her own making dangling at her side to church, through an

applauding neighbourhood . . . And then, what a comely sight, all kneeling down together in one pew, according to eldership, as we have seen
in effigy, a whole family upon some old monument, where the honest
chevalier, in armour, is presented kneeling with uplift hands, and half a
dozen jolter-headed crop-eared boys behind him, ranged *gradatim*, or step-
fashion, according to age and size, all in the same posture – facing his
pious dame, with a ruff about her neck, and as many whey-faced girls,
all kneeling behind *her* . . .   (970)

It is true, Clarissa allows, that 'once I could have loved him –
ungrateful man! – had he permitted me, I *once* could have loved
him. Yet he never deserved my love' (992). Building on this hint,
Lovelace's family, Mrs Howe and Anna press her to marry. Anna
advises compromise, arguing like Jane Austen's Mary Crawford
that the gilding of a rich marriage will hide many stains. Honourable
family, noble settlements, noble presents, writes Anna glibly, and
since few know of his base brutality, Clarissa's exposure of what
has passed should be more sparing (1042–3). Even while Anna
declares that marriage is the only means left to make her future
life tolerably easy, she must add, '*happy* there is no saying' (1087).
Her advice, 'if you *can*, to get over your aversion to this vile man'
(1113), her temptations of wealth, rank, and a patched-up reputation estrange Clarissa from her worldly, corruptible friend. 'Love
me still,' she writes, 'But let it be with a weaning love. I am not
what I was when we were *inseparable* lovers, as I may say – Our
views must now be different' (1088). Talk of money inevitably
frightens Clarissa, whose evils arose originally from avarice. Even
in prison she steadfastly resists financial obligation, refusing money
from Lovelace by crying out 'No, no, no, no! several times with
great quickness'. For a three-guinea debt to Mrs Lovick she gives
a valuable diamond ring, and in her determination to pay the doctor's fee herself sells two rich dressed suits, saying that she 'would
not be obliged to anybody when she had effects by her which she
had no occasion for' (letters 339–40).

She has other reasons not to marry. Sexual assault has induced
in her antipathy to all men, and in dreadful echo of the wedding
service she cries out, 'I charge you . . . as you will answer it one
day to my friends, that you bring no gentleman into my company.'
Indeed, the whores want her to be broken in, as they themselves
were. She scruples to admit the apothecary's visit 'because he was
a MAN' (1059–63), until the kindness of the doctor keeps her in
charity with his sex (1082). To men, because of Lovelace, she has
a justifiable aversion, 'nor, having such a tyrant of a father, and

such an implacable brother, has she reason to make an exception in favour of *any* of it on *their* accounts'. She greets Belford with 'No – No – go, go; MAN, with an emphasis', and to his compliment returns quickly, 'Do you flatter me, sir? Then are you a MAN' (1064–70). Only his assistance in restoring her to her lodgings wins the trust of a lady who has reason to suspect every man she sees to be a villain (1076).

Deceiving men betray themselves through their oaths, like Lovelace at Hampstead. She cannot believe a swearer, for 'if you yourself think your WORD insufficient, what reliance can I have on your OATH!' (1071). Clarissa is not priggish when she objects to men's careless oaths. What offends her is their capacity to deceive, and it is Lovelace's deceit, above all, that makes marriage with him impossible. She herself, who was taught never to disguise the truth or be guilty of a falsehood (988), believes that without plain dealing all civil communication and all society break down. Veracity is especially indispensable in the character of a gentleman (982), for the contractual nature of the society as laid out in the domestic conduct books demanded both duties and rights together – not just models of behaviour, but safeguards of each to each. He, a gentleman, has broken the social contract when his vows and inventions were 'all for what? – Only to ruin a poor young creature whom he ought to have protected; and whom he had first deprived of all other protection' (1079). His deceptions rank with his assault, for 'in the shocking progress to this ruin', wilful falsehoods, repeated forgeries and numberless perjuries 'were not the least of his crimes', says Clarissa (985). She explains,

This last violence you speak of is nothing to what preceded it. That cannot be atoned for; nor palliated: this may: and I shall not be sorry to be convinced that he cannot be guilty of so very low a wickedness – Yet, after his vile forgeries of hands – after his personating basenesses – what are the iniquities he is not capable of? (1076)

Lovelace in return accuses Clarissa of exaggeration, saying in comradely fashion to Hickman, 'I don't doubt but a lady of her niceness has represented what would appear trifles to any other, in a very strong light.' He was merely desirous to have '*all that* without marriage', and when 'a thing is done and cannot be helped, 'tis right to make the best of it. I wish the lady would think so too.' Hickman replies stoutly, 'I think, sir, ladies should not be deceived. I think a promise to a lady should be as binding as to any other person, at the least' (1093–4). But Lovelace is bound still to the Father of Lies; he is a damned devil, says Lord M. (1037), one who in parody of Richard III calls out, '*A line! a line! a kingdom for a line!*', with his malignity as unswerving as Iago's, his black purpose as inexorable as Othello's or Macbeth's. Just as Satan's serpent children begotten upon Sin his daughter spawn ceaselessly in *Paradise Lost*, so Lovelace's contrivances work on through a 'brood' of 'dragon and serpents', Mrs Sinclair and her daughters whom he himself seduced (1047).

Clarissa summarises the reasons why she cannot marry Lovelace. Just as she could not vow duty to Solmes, a man she despised, she is once again too proud to make that man her choice whose actions are and ought to be her abhorrence:

What! – shall I, who have been treated with such premeditated and per-fidious barbarity as is painful to be thought of, and cannot with modesty be described, think of taking the violator to my heart? Can I vow duty to one so wicked, and hazard my salvation by joining myself to so great a profligate, now I *know* him to be so? Do you think your Clarissa Harlowe so lost, so *sunk* at least, as that she could for the sake of patching up in the world's eye a broken reputation, meanly appear indebted to the generosity, or *compassion* perhaps, of a man who has, by means so inhuman, robbed her of it? Indeed, my dear, I should not think my penitence for the rash step I took anything better than a specious delusion, if I had not got above the least wish to have Mr Lovelace for my husband.

Yes, I warrant, I must *creep* to the violator, and be thankful to him for doing me poor justice!

Having rejected Solmes because she could not obey a man she despised, she must now reject Lovelace when sinful compliance with a man entitled, after marriage, to her obedience, might 'taint my own morals, and make me, instead of a reformer, an imitator of him'. She despises him, she pities him, but 'I love him not, therefore! My soul disdains communion with him' (1116). She is 'no wife: and now I never will be one' (1105).

What Clarissa dreads is the power of marriage to merge her iden-tity with Lovelace's, just as when she fled the brothel, her lost self, her best self, the old Clarissa Harlowe, did not escape (974). Alienated on an earth which persecutes innocent and benevolent spirits (1020), she embraces a new identity of her own choice: her name '*was* Clarissa Harlowe – but it is now Wretchedness!', she says. In the spunging-house she insists on staying in the prisoners' room, and, like Job, whose story she reads, allows the false com-forters Sally and Polly to torment her. 'Let my ruin, said she, lifting up her eyes, be LARGE, be COMPLETE, *in this life!* –

for a *composition*, let it be COMPLETE' (letter 333).

Her new lodging does indeed enhance the 'composition' into which Belford's account moves like a camera,

A horrid hole of a house, in an alley they call a court; stairs wretchedly narrow, even to the first-floor rooms: and into a den they led me, with broken walls which had been papered, as I saw by a multitude of tacks, and some torn bits held on by the rusty heads.

The floor indeed was clean, but the ceiling was smoked with variety of figures, and initials of names, that had been the woeful employment of wretches who had no other way to amuse themselves.

Emblems of decay, death, loss of identity and madness fill the room, the furniture is worm-eaten and broken down, and the penny candle offers only a twinkle against the dark. The 'old looking-glass, cracked through the middle, breaking out into a thousand points; the crack given it, perhaps, in a rage, by some poor creature to whom it gave the representation of his heart's woes in his face', hints at the destruction of Clarissa's self-approving reflection, and the stone bottle, filled with 'baleful yew as an evergreen, withered southernwood, and sweet-briar, and sprigs of rue in flower', inevitably recalls the mad Ophelia, as Belford's gaze finally falls on Clarissa, lover and shedder of light, kneeling by the dismal window and 'illuminating that horrid corner' (letter 334).

Clarissa, without friends, believes she deserves none (1054). Her dearest friend had leapt to the assumption that love, intoxicating love, made Clarissa return to the fatal house, and though she could not know that her letter had been intercepted, betrayed her friend cruelly by her mistrust (993). Reconciliation with the Harlowes becomes even more unlikely after Anna's expressions of contempt, while her impolitic appeal to Arabella hastens Mrs Howe's plan to remove her daughter to the Isle of Wight (1112). Anna undoubtedly loves Clarissa, 'the joy, the stay, the prop of my life' (1045), but she makes Clarissa's life even more difficult by her zeal.

Only in death, when like the angels and the saints she will shake off the encumbrance of body, can Clarissa's identity be restored (974), only in death can she return to being single, chaste, exemplary, and protected from the consequences of being a woman. She is not so much a Christ-figure as a nun, a bride of Christ, who calls upon Jesus with her last breath. Lovelace is prophetic to think of country funerals, where, for a dead companion, 'especially if she were a virgin, or *passed for such*, [young women] make a flower-bed of her coffin' (1002), for this too will happen to Clarissa, a virgin who has not really fallen, a young lady remarkable for having been 'equally above temptation and art; and, I had almost said, human frailty'. Before Lovelace knew her, he 'questioned a soul in a sex, created, as I was willing to suppose, only for temporary purposes' (1036–7): that is, he denied women the chance for spiritual or eternal life. He may boast that their minds open to him as easily as their bodies, writing of her letters that 'the seal would have yielded to the touch of my warm finger (perhaps without the help of the post-office bullet), and the folds, as other plications have done, opened of themselves, to oblige my curiosity' (1085), but Clarissa defeats him by her steadfast separation of mind from body, as he says:

early I saw that there was no credulity in her to graft upon: no pretending to whine myself into her confidence. She was proof against amorous persuasion. She had *reason* in her love. Her penetration and good sense made her hate all compliments that had not truth and nature in them.
(III. 473)

By abandoning her body she can become all mind, the 'angel of a woman' for whom Belford already feels a kind of holy love (1080).

Clarissa chooses death when to dispose of herself is her only freedom.[7] Even if she may neither marry her deceiver nor resume the single life in which she was preacher and teacher (1117), she asserts that from the brothel she has taken 'nothing away that is not my own' (1053). A pilgrim passing through Vanity Fair, the Slough of Despond and Giant Despair's castle to arrive at the shining city, Clarissa is promised a heavenly reward by Mrs Norton for her suffering, patience and resignation (980). Like Christian rejoicing to feel his sins fall away in sight of the heavenly city, like Hamlet seeking the bourne from whence no traveller returns, Clarissa welcomes death as a release,

And what, after all, *is* death? 'Tis but a cessation from mortal life: 'tis but the finishing of an appointed course: the refreshing inn after a fatiguing journey: the end of a life of cares and troubles; and, if happy, the beginning of a life of immortal happiness. (1117)

Lovelace, attempting to trivialise her pain by sexualising it, asks why Belford uses such 'true women's language' when he has seen and heard of 'so many *female deaths* and *revivals*' (1084). Just like Sally the whore calling Clarissa ridiculously prudish, 'squeamish and narrow-minded' (1056), he will not accept what the rape means to her. By the time he has made one tour to France and Italy, he says confidently, she will marry him, her sufferings forgotten (1085).

Is Clarissa's drive to death suicidal? Sally thinks so when she will not eat in prison. 'Your religion, I think, should teach you that starving yourself is self-murder', she says sneeringly (1054). The doctor diagnoses a love-case, believing like his counterpart in *Macbeth* that she must be her own doctoress and 'do more for yourself than all the faculty can do for you' (1081). Lovelace, like another Hamlet, calls it cowardice to slide basely out of a world of persecutions, disappointments, and contumelies by means of a pistol, a halter, or a knife (1058), to which Clarissa replies that she does not mean 'like a poor coward [to] desert my post, when I *can* maintain it, and when it is my *duty* to maintain it' (1117).[10] It is not she but Lovelace who dreads annihilation and repeats Claudio's terrible meditation, 'Ay, but to die, and go we know not where', from a play in which another nun challenges the injustice of the world's law, *Measure for Measure* (1148–9).

At last Lovelace admits the truth of Clarissa's meaning. She vengefully encourages another lover, he tells Hickman:

Well, but the wretch she so spitefully prefers to me is a misshapen, meagre varlet; more like a skeleton than a man! Then he dresses – you never saw a devil so bedizined! Hardly a coat to his back, nor a shoe to his foot: a bald-pated villain, yet grudges to buy a peruke to hide his baldness: for he is as covetous as hell, never satisfied, yet plaguy rich.

His name, he shouts suddenly at Hickman, 'is DEATH! – DEATH! sir, stamping, and speaking loud, and full in his ear; which made him jump half a yard high' (1097). In a bony, greedy courtship, the traditional figure of avaricious Death sidles up to yet another Maiden.

6

Clarissa's will

As Clarissa waits for death to liberate her from the cruelty of her family and pressures to prosecute or marry, she rejects Parson Brand to become, radical and Protestant woman as she is, her own priest. Taking control as she never has before, she ensures her mind's preservation in her letters, and orchestrates the death that will marry her to Christ in her Father's house. Meanwhile the exposure of Lovelace's plots deprives him of his play and his leadership, and new strategies to see her fail.

Spiteful and vengeful as ever, the Harlowes renew their power along with their communications to demand Lovelace's prosecution, while Anna, Belford and Lovelace himself urge marriage. Clarissa's thoughts are however fixed elsewhere. Such is her anguish that her father's curse will make her as miserable in heaven as it has on earth that he agrees to lift it, but grudgingly and without forgiveness. Her last attempts at reconciliation meet the old avarice and power head on. As Uncle Antony explains, 'you may be suffered to have some part of your estate, after you have smarted a little more' (1196). Clarissa's mother complains of her own sorrows with the insistent selfishness of the weak, and Arabella swells the chorus of condemnation by insinuating that her sister simply grieves for a failed affair. 'It is too probable, Miss Clary,' she writes, that 'had you gone on as swimmingly as you expected, and had not your feather-headed villain abandoned you, we should have heard nothing of these moving supplications: nor of anything but defiances from *him*, and a guilt gloried in from *you*' (1180). Uncle John Harlowe shocks Clarissa by demanding to know if she is pregnant (1192), to which Uncle Antony adds mercilessly that after several weeks of free living she cannot take up the accusation and 'wipe your mouth upon it, as if nothing had happened' (1195).

Clarissa finds a new champion when her cousin Colonel Morden returns, accuses James of doing more to ruin his sister than Lovelace himself, and threatens them in the only way they understand. He will make her, he says, his only heir (1324–7). But it is all too late. Clarissa's reasons to refuse prosecution are lucid and sensible. Having met clandestinely with Lovelace and lived under the same

107

roof without cause for complaint, she knows she could easily be made to look guilty; she shies away from telling her story in a public court where her most serious pleas might be 'bandied about, and jested profligately with'; and she knows how easily his family might obtain a pardon 'for a crime thought too lightly of, though one of the greatest that can be committed against a creature valuing her honour above her life' (1253). Lovelace of course would welcome confrontation – he who, as he boasts, can 'make a bad cause a good one at any time. What an admirable lawyer should I have made! And what a poor hand would this charming creature, with all her innocence, have made of it in a court of justice against a man who had so much to *say*, and to *show* for himself' (1287). Belford's innocently incriminating visits make prosecution even more inadvisable, nor will Clarissa accept Arabella's vengeful idea that Lovelace be sent to the gallows and herself to Pennsylvania (1256–8). Lastly, Morden 'has indelicacy enough to have gone into the nature of the proof of the crime upon which they wanted to have Lovelace arraigned' (1314), and such an examination Clarissa could never bear.

Aunt Hervey's advice that she marry Lovelace, wicked as he has been, prompts Clarissa's strong resistance, for as she says,

shall we wonder that kings and princes meet with so little control in their passions, be they ever so violent, when in a private family, an aunt, nay, even a mother in that family, shall choose to give up a once favoured child against their own inclinations, rather than oppose an aspiring young man who had armed himself with the authority of a father, who, when once determined, never would be expostulated with? (1260)

Lovelace's crimes, as she reminds them, have set her above him, so that if she were to perform her duty, marriage would simply reward the violator (1301). But even her dearest friend Anna presses her to 'think, my dear, and *re*-think' (1133).

In a bravura scene, Richardson confronts Anna with her friend's rapist at a ball, even as that friend is dying. 'All glowing with indignation', Anna at first refuses his request for a quarter of an hour's explanation, saying, 'Not for a kingdom, fluttering my fan – I knew not what I did – But I could have killed him.' Flustered and stammering she tells him, 'I abhor you! – from my soul, I abhor you, vilest of men!', and not knowing what she does, snaps her fan in his face so that 'the powder flew from his wig'. Although knowing full well he is a devil, she rapidly succumbs, praising him as patient and audacious in a way that makes Hickman seem 'too meek for a man'. She may mock her fellow women as 'unthinking

CLARISSA'S WILL

eye-governed creatures!', but she herself is profoundly impressed that

nobody was regarded but him. So little of the fop, yet so elegant and rich in his dress: his person so specious: his manner so intrepid: so much meaning and penetration in his face: so much gaiety, yet so little of the monkey: though a travelled gentleman, yet no affectation; no mere toupet-man; but all manly; and his courage and wit, the one so known, the other so dreaded, you must think the *petits-maîtres* (of which there were four or five present) were most deplorably off in his company: and one grave gentleman observed to me (pleased to see me shun him as I did) that the poet's observation was too true, that the generality of ladies were *rakes in their hearts*, or they could not be so much taken with a man who had so notorious a character.

What Mrs Howe, Anna, and Hickman read sentimentally as remorse and a touched conscience (letter 367), Clarissa interprets otherwise. His gay unconcerned behaviour and intrepidity make her wonder how Miss Howe could imagine she could think of such a man for a husband: 'poor wretch! I pity him, to see him flutter-ing about; abusing talents that were given him for excellent pur-poses; taking courage for wit; and dancing, fearless of danger, on the edge of a precipice!', she writes (1141). Anna has failed to give him her friend's decisive negative as she promised, not yet understanding that Clarissa will not marry or even live.

The clamour for marriage mounts. Both Belford and Lovelace's family plead for him, and Lovelace vows that he will have her 'though I marry her in the agonies of death' (1184). But Clarissa, who reads her own story as a warning against preferring a liber-tine to a man of true honour, argues that experience proves that in hardly one out of ten tolerably happy marriages does the wife keep the hold on the husband's affection which she had on the lover's (1319). Considering Lovelace's principles with regard to women, his enterprises upon many of them, his cruelty, the sportiveness of his invention, and the high opinion he has of himself, any wife of his must be miserable, 'and more miserable if she loved him' (1161).

Not even pity, she writes, can 'purchase a sponge that will wipe out from the year the past fatal five months of my life', and she refuses to '*sanctify*, as I may say, Mr Lovelace's repeated breaches of all moral sanctions, and hazard my *future* happiness by a union with a man, through whose premeditated injuries, in a long train of the basest contrivances, I have forfeited my *temporal* hopes' (1140–1). To the argument that for honour's sake she should rather

109

die a Lovelace than a Harlowe (1169), Clarissa replies decisively that Lovelace cannot wish to raise into his family a person he abased into a companionship with the most abandoned of her sex (1172).

Anna hears clearly at last, realising that

you think more highly of a *husband's* prerogative, than most people do of the *royal* one – These notions, my dear, from a person of your sense and judgement are no-way advantageous to us; inasmuch as they justify that insolent sex in their assumptions; when hardly one out of ten of them, their opportunities considered, deserve any prerogative at all. Look through all the families we know; and we shall not find one third of them have half the sense of their wives – And yet these are to be vested with prerogatives! – And a woman of twice their sense has nothing to do but hear, tremble, and obey – and for *conscience*-sake too, I warrant! (1152)

Men creep and cringe in courtship, says Anna, and are a vile race of *'reptiles* in *our day,* and mere *bears* in *their own'.* How could she herself, who could hardly bear control from a mother, take it from a husband, 'from one too, who has neither more wit, nor more understanding, than myself? Yet he is to be my instructor! – So he will, I suppose; but more by the insolence of his will than by the merit of his counsel' (1312).[1] At last Anna comprehends how much more a Clarissa must suffer from a Lovelace husband than she from a Hickman. Anyway, Morden and Lovelace have already sparked up like two barrels of gunpowder when they met, and thus made marriage impossible. 'Damn me,' vows Lovelace, 'if I'd marry an empress upon such treatment as this' (1284).

Clarissa chooses another path. She has never been like other women: she 'had *other* views in living, than the common ones of eating, sleeping, dressing, visiting, and those other fashionable amusements which fill up the time of most of her sex' (1128). Since men take advantage of women corrupted by reading 'inflaming novels, and idle romances' (1279–80), women must instruct themselves, for their own souls' sake. The spiritual teaching transmitted by Mrs Norton derives therefore not from the university education reserved for men like Parson Brand, but from the inner light and the Bible, whose style is more 'truly easy, simple, and natural' than that of pagan authors, says Belford. Men such as Lovelace think themselves lords of the creation, when they are dependent upon other creatures for their food and raiment,

for what has he of his own, but a very mischievous, monkey-like, bad nature? Yet thinks himself at liberty to kick, and cuff, and elbow out every worthier creature: and when he has none of the animal creation to hunt down and abuse, will make use of his power, his strength, or his

wealth, to oppress the less powerful and weaker of his own species!
(1125–26)

Like Bacon in *The Advancement of Learning* he attacks these arrogant 'smatterers' in learning who 'move round and round (like so many blind mill-horses) in one narrow circle, while we imagine we have all the world to range in' (1131). Richardson is as radically Protestant as his heroine in ranking reason, conscience, and a Bible that everyone may read above authority, learning, and status. Serving as her own priest, as Milton recommends, Clarissa composes her own meditations upon the sacred books because 'GOD ALMIGHTY WOULD NOT LET ME DEPEND FOR COMFORT UPON ANY BUT HIMSELF' (1356).

Parson Brand represents by contrast the hierarchy, elitism, and traditional classical learning of the universities. Pedantically throwing about 'to a Christian and country audience scraps of Latin and Greek from the pagan classics' (1167), he in awkwardness and lack of Christian charity is a true ancestor of Mr Collins.[2] 'Persons of his cloth,' he says, 'should be very cautious of the *company they were in*, especially where *sex* was concerned, and where a lady had *slurred her reputation.*' He responds carelessly to the news that Clarissa is ill, with 'her disappointments must have touched her to the quick: but she is not bad enough, I dare say, yet, to atone for her very great lapse, and to expect to be forgiven by those whom she has so much disgraced' (1190), and he hints scandalously to John Harlowe that Clarissa receives money from Belford in private visits (1294). Vicar of Bray enough to be her chaplain if she is penitent, he even thinks of marrying her (IV. 311–12). Such a corrupt and self-serving priest isolates her all the more.

To Mrs Norton, Clarissa's evils are a fortunate fall: 'the greatest good may, for aught we know, be produced from the heaviest evils', she writes (1155). Belford too, contemplating what a fine subject for tragedy her injuries would make, maintains that her virtue is not here being punished, since we can 'look forward to the rewards of HEREAFTER, which, morally, *she* must be sure of, or who can?' Perhaps, he adds more mundanely, her reward is simply to miss such a man as Lovelace (1205). Clarissa is not the Magdalen Brand thinks her, but one who is 'upon a better preparation than for an earthly husband' (1121). Never was bride so ready as she is, she says. Even her wedding garments are bought, 'the easiest, the *happiest* suit, that ever bridal maiden wore' (1339).

Her choice, like Job's (7:15), of 'strangling, and death rather than life' (1192), is regarded as mad and suicidal, even though she engages to avoid all wilful neglects (1130). But only thus can she escape such shocking questions as Antony Harlowe's when she is 'tired and fatigued – with – I don't know what – with writing, I think – but most with myself, and with a situation I cannot help aspiring to get out of, and above!' (1194). Lovelace calls her drive to death 'downright female wilfulness' (1346), and like Shakespeare in the Sonnets calls on 'breed' to defy death. She 'fancies she is breeding death, when the event will turn out quite the contrary', he says confidently (IV. 41). Only Belford sees that death is her refuge from the agony when 'the soul aspiring, the body sinking' tear her tender frame in pieces (1308).

Lovelace, who admits neither responsibility nor reality, persuades himself that the lady's ill health results from the vile arrest and implacableness of her friends (1123). Looking as usual to imperial comparisons, he argues that he is less culpable than Aeneas for whom Queen Dido killed herself, less to blame than 'our famous maiden queen' Elizabeth who cut off the head of a sister-queen. Anyone would gratify a ruling passion if he could, and therefore he is '*comparatively* a very innocent man'. He consults his own perverse inner light when he offers to marry and repair, for 'if by these, and other like reasonings, I have quieted my own conscience, a great end is answered. What have I to do with the world?' (1142–3). It would be a jest to die for what passed between them, for her triumph has been infinitely greater than her sufferings, and an occasion, he adds in a recurrence of the comet metaphor, for her to blaze out with a 'meridian lustre'. But the hectic quality of his reasonings conceals the most soul-harrowing woes (1309–10) when, suffering the torments of the damned, he rides restlessly between Uxbridge and London, forbidden yet longing to see her, and willing her not to die (letter 463).

Lovelace, the arrogant emperor who 'proudly, like Addison's Cato, delighted to give laws to my little senate' (1147), demands again that Belford give up confidential letters written by his general, king, emperor and prince (1237). But as soon as Belford shows them to Clarissa, they bar up the door of her heart as she used to do her chamber door against him (1209). Desperate to resume control, Lovelace seizes centre-stage by his claim that it is he who suffers, who 'can neither eat, drink, nor sleep; nor, what's still worse, love any woman in the world but her'. He even says that it is he who will die (1182). Frantically he spawns new plots. He will visit her disguised as a parson, 'petticoated out' as he had once before: 'I was thought to make a fine sleek appearance, my broad rose-bound beaver became me *mightily*, and I was much admired upon the whole by all who saw me', he says (1144). Love and death merge in him yet again when he arrives at the Smiths' dressed in 'a never worn suit, which I had intended for one of my wedding suits – and liked myself so well, that I began to think with thee that my outside was the best of me'. He had rehearsed as he went. 'I charged my eyes to languish and sparkle by turns: I talked to my knees, telling them how they must bend; and, in the language of a charming describer, acted my part in fancy, as well as spoke it to myself' (1209). But his audience is not at home.

In the savage foolery of frustration he pretends to be a justice of the peace with a search-warrant, until his violence betrays who he is. Abusively witty, high-handed, and sneering, he assumes the part of an aristocratic customer buying washballs, and threatens their servant with a penknife: 'I only wanted, said I, to take out two or three of this rascal's broad teeth, to put them into my servant's jaws.' He tyrannises, demands snuff and gloves, drives a customer away by telling her she is homely, and, pretending to a pretty genteel lady that he is a salesman, pushes gloves on to her footman's fingers until they burst. Lovelace concludes his performance by contemptuously 'flinging down a Portugal six-and-thirty' before a gathering won by his little saturnalia, who cry out, 'A pleasant gentleman, I warrant him!' By this play he plots to disabuse the good people of the notion they have of him, 'a perfect woman-eater' with claws and fangs – a policy, as he explains, to show them what a harmless, pleasant fellow he is. But even he is shaken when immediately afterwards the whore Sally grotesquely mimics Clarissa: 'the little beast threw herself about my neck, and there clung like a cat' (letter 416).

Belford reproves Lovelace for wantonly hunting the poor lady, who 'like a harmless deer that has already a barbed shaft in her breast, seeks only a refuge from thee in the shades of death' (1224). Clarissa, who flees Lovelace, and has been rowed about all day on the Thames to escape him (1246), yearns still for what might have been. 'O my dear, that it had been my lot (as I was not permitted to live single) to have met with a man by whom I could have acted generously and unreservedly!', she writes (1263). Her friendship with Anna has shown her capable of 'love as pure as the human heart ever boasted' (1342); her last act will be to kiss the miniature of her *'sweet and ever-amiable friend – companion – sister – lover!'* (1357). Even Belford, if divested of body, could be 'all light and all mind' in such an eternal friendship (1348), but Lovelace would be the ruin of her soul (1275).

By the analogy of this more than sisterly love which has bound them as by one mind (1163), Clarissa argues for marriage based on an intellectual friendship finer, as Belford explains, than the grosser fumes of sensuality. He grieves that such a mind as Clarissa's was 'vested in humanity to be snatched away from us so soon' (1132), and Lovelace too sees how her exalted head is hid among the stars (1184). Clarissa, like the sun in Shakespeare's Sonnet 33, cannot he says be obscured by slander:

> *Marry and repair, at any time*; this (wretch that I was!) was my plea to myself. To give her a lowering sensibility; to bring her down from among the stars which her beamy head was surrounded by, that my wife, so greatly above me, might not too much despise me – this was part of my reptile envy, owing to my *more* reptile apprehension of inferiority – Yet [she], from step to step, from distress to distress, to maintain her superiority; and, like the sun, to break out upon me with the greater refulgence for the clouds that I had contrived to cast about her . . .   (1344)

In a vision whose elaborate details recall a baroque church, Lovelace imagines Clarissa's intercession and his attempt to clasp her in his arms, when

> immediately the most angelic form I had ever beheld, vested all in transparent white, descended from a ceiling, which, opening, discovered a ceiling above that, stuck round with golden cherubs and glittering seraphs, all exulting: Welcome, welcome, welcome! and, encircling my charmer, ascended with her to the region of seraphims; and instantly, the opening ceiling closing, I lost sight of *her*, and of the *bright form* together, and found wrapped in my arms her azure robe (all stuck thick with stars of embossed silver), which I had caught hold of in hopes of detaining her; but was all that was left me of my beloved Miss Harlowe. And then (horrid to relate!) the floor sinking under *me*, as the ceiling had opened for *her*, I dropped into a hole more frightful than that of Elden and tumbling over and over down it, without view of a bottom, I awaked in a panic; and was as effectually disordered for half an hour, as if my dream had been a reality.
>   (1218)

The poet's bright star has become Mary, divine intermediary to all but Lovelace.[3]

Clarissa proceeds calmly to death as a 'lovely skeleton' (1231), in marked contrast to the rake Belton, whose Faustian friend Mowbray calls 'what's a clock?' as he dies (1228). In a trick worthy of Lovelace himself, Clarissa writes, 'I am setting out with all diligence for my father's house', but she means of course God's house, not Mr Harlowe's. Decoyed away to Berkshire, an over-joyed Lovelace revises his dream:

The ceiling opening is the reconciliation in view. The bright form, lifting her up through it to another ceiling stuck round with golden Cherubims and Seraphims, indicates the charming little boys and girls that will be the fruits of this happy reconciliation. The welcomes, thrice repeated, are those of her family, now no more to be deemed implacable.

But what, he asks nervously, is his tumbling over and over through the floor into a frightful hole, descending as she ascends? 'Ho! only this; it alludes to my disrelish to matrimony: which is a bottomless pit, a gulf, and I know not what' (1233–4).

Wilfully, he believes her falling away to be due to pregnancy, but Clarissa is in fact very ill. Morden's emissary at least foresees her death, when 'the flower of the world would be gone, and the family she belonged to would be no more than a common family' (1246). Her desire for peaceful death makes her use a metaphor that causes the furiously baffled Lovelace to believe Clarissa 'capable, as Gulliver in his abominable Yahoo story phrases it, of saying the *thing that is not*' (1271), but she is past all stratagem now. In a traditional image she talks of putting off her clinging, en-cumbering body 'as if it were an occurrence as familiar to her as dressing and undressing' (1276), and so angelic is she that Belford has not the least thought of her sex (1299). About to be divested of 'these *rags of mortality*', her intellect is clear and strong (1341), so what signifies this 'transitory eclipse?', writes Mrs Norton in Lovelacian imagery, 'you are brightened and purified, as I may say, by your sufferings!' (1328).

Not Lovelace but Clarissa is now the playwright, stage-manager and principal actor, and she breeds not a child but letters to end misreading. Her evidential story conveys a will of her own that has long been denied her (1191), together with the demonstration that Lovelace is the blackest of villains and she the brightest of innocents (1314). Quoting from Job 31:35–6, she reiterates her old desire for words to signify and convince: '*Oh that one would hear me! and that mine adversary had written a book! – Surely, I would take it upon my shoulders, and bind it to me as a crown! For I covered not my transgressions as Adam, by hiding mine iniquity in my bosom*' (1164). Her wish comes true when Belford, arguing truthfully in self-defence that 'thy let-ters are not the most guilty part of what she *knows* of thee', shows her Lovelace's 'strangely-communicative narrations' which will prove her innocent (1174–5). Belford promises to protect her memory and gain her the 'fair audit' she craves (1304) by means of her letters, that (on the principle of the critic Longinus) must move the reader when she is

writing of and in the midst of *present* distresses! How much more lively and affecting, for that reason, must her style be, than all that can be read in the dry, narrative, unanimated style of persons relating difficulties and dangers surmounted! The minds of such not labouring in suspense, not tortured by the pangs of uncertainty about events still hidden in the womb of fate; but on the contrary perfectly at ease; the relater unmoved by his own story, how then able to move the hearer or reader?   (1178)

In careful organisation of her own death, Clarissa has purchased a coffin upon which she reads and writes. Etched there to match inscriptions from Job and the Psalms are emblems of eternity and time, a crowned serpent, a winged hourglass, the head of a white lily snapped off short and just falling from the stalk. Her burial-dress is ordered, for Clarissa dies, she says, like the 'divine Socrates' for being innocent, not guilty (1305–7). Having 'meditated the spot, and the manner, and everything, as well of the minutest as of the highest consequence, that can attend the solemn moments', she will here end her life, and she begs her friends to stay away lest they make her want to live (1276–7). Morden sees Clarissa just before she dies:

One faded cheek rested upon the good woman's bosom, the kindly warmth of which had overspread it with a faint, but charming flush; the other paler, and hollow, as if already iced over by death. Her hands, white as the lily, with her meandering veins more transparently blue than ever I had seen . . .   (1351)

Still in ignorance of her approaching dissolution, and never more Faustian than in this, Lovelace refuses to accept eternal separation from a woman who is his alive or dead. 'Is not damnation likely to be the purchase to me, though a happy eternity will be hers?', he asks. Her death Belford announces with a terse obliquity equal to Lovelace's own after the rape, 'I have only to say at present – Thou wilt do well to take a tour to Paris; or wherever else thy destiny shall lead thee!!!' (1358–9). The narration then moves brilliantly back from the announcement of her death to the instant of it, then back again to the moment when her voice still speaks. Forgiving Lovelace, blessing them all, Clarissa calls to her true, her only bridegroom, 'come – Oh come – blessed Lord – JESUS!' (1362).

The last volume of *Clarissa* is profoundly disquieting, if we consider it as real. Death grants Clarissa powers she never had in life, and Anna despairingly restates the case against marriage as if death formed the only escape from women's inevitable fate. Mary Astell certainly thought so, when she wrote that a woman 'will freely leave him the quiet Dominion of this World, whose Thoughts and Expectations are plac'd on the next'. Only in heaven, says Astell, will there be a time 'when her Sex shall be no Bar to the best Employments', and her 'Soul shall shine as bright as the greatest Heroe's'; only there is the true consolation for the neglect, contempt and injuries which brutal power may cause her in this world (*Marriage*, p. 84). So too, it seems, for Clarissa.

Clarissa's grandfather's will began her troubled history; her own last will and testament closes it. The precise communication she always sought is supported at last by law, when through posthumously delivered letters, the funeral procession, the service, and the reading of her will, she enforces her desires as she never has before. Since she planned this whole sequence of events and reaction before her death, the result is exactly as she wished, her restoration to angel and pure mind. Everyone falters before her irresistible forethought, save Anna, who resists her injunction to marry, and Morden, who determines upon revenge. Gradually 'Providence' assumes control. The guilty meet bad ends, and Lovelace, threatened by madness and the law, drifts towards his fatal meeting with Morden.

Clarissa speaks from the dead with the authority of the dead, her eleven letters to family, friends, and Lovelace so far reinstating her as her family's queen that even James complies with her wish to be placed pointedly at her grandfather's feet (1381). If Lovelace, 'a man very uncontrollable, and as I am nobody's', insists upon viewing '*her dead* whom he ONCE before saw in a manner dead', he is to receive her note: 'Gay, cruel heart! behold here the remains of the once ruined, yet now happy, Clarissa Harlowe! See what thou thyself must quickly be – and REPENT – !' (1413).

Her hearse processes through the countryside, like Queen Eleanor's, evoking a respect never seen even at the funeral of princes. A microcosm to the world, Clarissa's body is a little space in which is included 'all human excellence' (1407–8). Her will restores her mother's usurped power (1423) and enables her own accusations and vindications unanswerably to be heard. 'Now at reading this, will you pity your late unhappy sister!', she has written, 'NOW will you forgive her faults, both supposed and real. And NOW will you afford to her *memory* that kind concern which you refused to her before!' (1373). James accuses Lovelace, Arabella

117

turns on James, and Mr Harlowe grotesquely reproaches both 'for the parts they had acted and put him upon acting'. Her final prayer drives them into solitary retirement, their unity against her splintered at last (1421–2).

Clarissa's wish that her sufferings will redound more to her honour than to her disgrace comes entirely, remarkably true. Now in her absence, others demand that her voice be heard more attentively than it ever was in life. Anna for instance writes,

You must everywhere insist upon it, that had it not been for the stupid persecutions of her relations, she never would have been in the power of this horrid profligate: and yet she was frank enough to acknowledge that were *person*, and *address*, and *alliance*, to be allowably the *principal* attractives, it would not have been difficult for her eye to mislead her heart.

(1467)

The extracts from her letters, avidly read, do indeed instantly convert the family to Clarissa's point of view (IV. 533).

Though a woman, Clarissa by means of her will distributes rich possessions and property. The passionate, powerful phrase 'I desire' constantly recurs as she itemises pictures, plate, cash, clothing, furniture, jewellery, books, portraits, needlework and mourning rings to be handed out like heaped coals of fire. Her will, plainly written to prevent the usual 'confusion and disagreement in families, and so much doubt and difficulty, for want of absolute clearness in the testament of departed persons', obviates all cavils about words since she has written coolly and in health. Her seven sheets of paper, signed, sealed, published and declared, make up this last will and testament (1412–20), but her whole story has always been what Richardson originally called it, *The Lady's Legacy*, signed, sealed, delivered and unarguable, or so he must have hoped.

Typically, James Harlowe attempts to take over her will even when she is dead. He and Arabella, 'true will-disputants', grasp at hundreds and lose thousands when Morden turns revolted from his heirs. Her cousin knows that if Clarissa had chosen an executor from within the family, her will would indeed have been no more regarded that if it had been the will of a dead king, of Louis XIV in particular; but where that monarch's will was indisputable only in life, Queen Clarissa's is only absolute in death (1421–2).

Death fixes Clarissa into a full-length portrait of a queen, an icon, the image of a perfect woman:

The desirable daughter; the obliging kinswoman; the affectionate sister (all envy now subsided!); the faithful, the warm friend; the affable, the kind, the benevolent mistress! – Not one fault remembered!   (1448)

What interests Richardson is how she became so. In a Conclusion expanded in later editions, he explains the making of Clarissa, both by a negative comparision with the whores Sally Martin and Polly Horton, and, positively, by an abstract of her accomplishments. Reiterating his Lockeian view that children are 'so many lumps of soft wax, fit to take any impression that the first accident gave them', he shows how Sally had been so spoilt by early education and experience that Lovelace could dexterously whip his net over her before she could cast hers over him. Similarly, Polly's uneducated mother had given her 'that sort of reading which is but an earlier debauchery for young minds, preparative to the grosser at riper years, to wit, romances and novels, songs and plays', so that

At fifteen she owned she was ready to fancy herself the heroine of every novel and of every comedy she read, so well did she enter into the *spirit* of her subject: she glowed to become the object of some hero's flame; and perfectly longed to begin an intrigue, and even to be *run away with* by some enterprising lover: yet had neither *confinement* nor *check* to apprehend from her indiscreet mother: which she thought absolutely necessary to constitute a Parthenissa!

Little wonder that 'like early fruit, she was soon ripened to the hand of the insidious gatherer' (IV. 540–4).

Clarissa's education was quite otherwise, as Anna tells us. An easy mistress of words, 'since the pen, next to the needle, of all employments, is the most proper, and best adapted to [women's] geniuses', she could challenge men of mere learning, like Brand:

stiffened and starched . . . into dry and indelectable affectation, *one sort* of these scholars assume a style as rough as frequently are their manners: they spangle over their productions with *metaphors*: they rumble into *bombast*: the *sublime*, with them, lying in *words* and not in *sentiment*, they fancy themselves most exalted when least understood; and down they sit, fully satisfied with their own performances, and call them MASCULINE.

Clarissa's natural, middle-class, Christian, auto-didactic and woman-educated superiority challenges those unoriginal souls who poke and scramble about in the classical pits, 'fit only to write *notes* and *comments* upon other people's *texts*; all their pride, that they know those beauties of two thousand years old in *another* tongue, which they can only *admire*, but not *imitate*, in their own'. And these, says Anna bitterly, 'must be learned men, and despisers of our *insipid* sex!' Clarissa challenges equally Lovelace's proud advantages of birth, gender, and education, and his '*wit*, that wicked misleader', which (as Locke had said) forfeits all title to judgment (IV. 495).

Richardson rushes to prevent the old canard that Clarissa, if clever, must be a '*learned slattern*': she disowns one friend learned in Virgil and Horace, who 'knew not how to put on her clothes with that necessary grace and propriety which should preserve to her the love of her husband', and another, who affecting to be thought as learned as men, could find no better way to assert her pretensions than by despising her own sex. Although Clarissa asserts that a woman's excellence in any tongue but English endangers her usefulness to the family, her own competence at Italian, French and some Latin bears out Anna's belief that her sex is inferior in nothing to the other but in want of opportunities, of which 'the narrow-minded mortals industriously seek to deprive us, lest we should surpass them . . . in what they chiefly value themselves upon'. Nor did her learning affect her own appearance, for

Long after *her* [hours perhaps of previous preparation having passed], down would come rustling and bustling the tawdry and awkward Bella, disordering more her native disorderliness at the sight of her serene sister, by her sullen envy, to see herself so much surpassed with such little pains, and in a sixth part of the time.

Clarissa's art concealed art, whether in dressing, reading, singing or speaking with 'genius and observation'. In painting too she was self-taught. Women, that is, may educate themselves through the use of their natural gifts as Richardson himself had done, unlike '*modern* ladies', whose time, 'in the short days they generally make, and in the inverted night and day, where they make them longer, is wholly spent in dress, visits, cards, plays, operas, and musical entertainments' (IV. 497–501).

Her benevolence to the poor shows women how to handle money, her choice of books shows them how to develop their minds, her tenacious memory demonstrates how to make fine observations without the need for foreign assistance (IV. 503–5). In a programme for all to follow, Clarissa – through early rising, the teaching of Mrs Norton, the help of divines and the assistance of her own genius – surpassed most of her age and sex, and most educated men:

Yet how do these poor boasters value themselves upon the advantages their education gives them! Who has not seen some one of them, just come from the university, disdainfully smile at a mistaken or ill-pronounced *word* from

a lady, when her *sense* has been clear, and her sentiments just; and when
he could not himself utter a single sentence fit to be repeated, but what
he borrowed from authors he had been obliged to study, as a painful
exercise to slow and creeping parts? (IV. 505–6)

Scorning the privilege of aristocratic men, middle-class Clarissa has
radically fashioned herself.

Anna is the first to disobey, for, believing that it was the whole
institution of marriage that brought the tragedy about, she cannot
bear to marry. Kept from seeing Clarissa because she is a woman,
she only now, when her friend is dead, may see her 'sweet companion! – my lovely monitress! – kissing her lips at every tender
invocation'. Is this where being a woman inevitably leads, 'is this
all! – is it all, of my CLARISSA's story!', she asks. Like the women
in *A Midsummer Night's Dream*, she loved the dear creature as never
woman loved another; 'we had but one heart, but one soul, between us: and now my better half is torn from me – *what shall I
do!*' (1402–4). Even Morden, who thinks the too fervent flame of
female friendship more properly absorbed by marriage, must
admit that Anna and Clarissa are exceptions because of their fine
minds:

Both had an *enlarged*, and even a *liberal* education: both had minds thirsting
after virtuous knowledge. Great readers both: great writers – (and *early
familiar writing* I take to be one of the greatest openers and improvers of
the mind that man or woman can be employed in). (1449–50)

Clarissa, who never found a man blessed with a mind like her own
(1422), urges her friend to marry Hickman, but her story tells
Anna that potentially, all men deceive. She hates the whole sex for
Lovelace's sake, she says, 'even men of unblamable characters;
whom at those times I cannot but look upon as persons I have not
yet *found out*' (1425).

Clarissa's recognition that married women have frequently promised to obey men they respect neither intellectually nor morally
is in fact unanswerable. Neither did she herself choose to restore
her reputation by marriage when identity and liberty would be lost.
She is no example to her friend in this. And when Clarissa advises
Anna to aim at that gentleness and meekness which are 'the peculiar
and indispensable characteristics of a real fine lady', except in cases
of honour or virtue (1455), she forgets how often she herself had
been warm in such a case. Anna only copies her friend when she
writes to Belford,

do you think I ought not to resolve upon a single life? – I, who have such an opinion of your sex, that I think there is not one man in an hundred whom a woman of sense and spirit can either *honour* or *obey*, though you make us promise *both*, in that solemn form of words which unites or rather *binds* us to you in marriage?

When I look round upon all the married people of my acquaintance, and see how *they* live, and what *they* bear, who live *best*, I am confirmed in my dislike to the state.

Men, she says, 'contrive to bring us up fools and idiots in order to make us bear the yoke you lay upon our shoulders; and that we may not despise you from our hearts (as we certainly should if we are brought up as you are) for your ignorance, as much as you often make us do (as it is) for your insolence'. So how can she marry at all? Could she live with a sordid or imperious wretch, she asks, and ought a man of a contrary character to be plagued with her? Hickman is more like a brother than a lover, nor did any man deserve her beloved friend. Well might she grieve that 'neither of our parents would let us live single'.

Foisting the loathsome Solmes on to Clarissa had turned her indifference to Lovelace into regard, and Anna too is trapped by Hickman's patience in the face of her dislike of all men, of him, and of matrimony. He has brought down her pride and made her accept his addresses. Finding it hard to recede, she vexes him in a hundred ways to make him hate her and decline his suit. Like Clarissa, she fears marriage, in which everything is

an impediment: every shadow a bugbear – Thus can I enumerate and swell perhaps only *imaginary* grievances: 'I must go whither he would have me go: visit whom he would have me visit: well as I love to write . . . it must be to whom he pleases.' And Mrs Hickman (who as Miss Howe cannot do wrong) would hardly ever be able to do right. Thus, the tables turned upon me, I am reminded of my broken-vowed obedience; Madamed up perhaps to matrimonial perfection, and all the wedded warfare practised comfortably over between us (for I shall not be passive under insolent treatment) till we become curses to each other, a byword to our neighbours and the jest of our own servants.

Anna asks why a free woman must become a dependent wife, why must she be 'teazed into a state where that *must* be necessarily the case' when now she can do as she pleases, and wishes only to be let alone to please herself:

And what, in effect, does my mother say? 'Anna Howe, you now do everything that pleases you: you now have nobody to control you: you go and you come: you dress and you undress; you rise and you go to rest: just as you think best: but you must be happier still, child!' –

As how, madam?

'Why, you must marry, my dear, and have none of these options; but in everything do as your husband commands you.'

Although Clarissa has died to avoid these 'imaginary grievances' – loss of freedom, forced obedience, and marriage warfare – she still presses Anna to marry, 'writing as from the dead' (letter 523). Morden believes that pregnancy will domesticate Anna (IV. 470), and Belford states confidently that if Hickman admits her superiority to half of his sex and to most of her own, she will make an excellent wife. The Conclusion relates that Anna has made Mr Hickman one of the happiest men in the world. They have two fine children, and except for her insistence on dispensing the poor fund as her prerogative, in every other case there is but one will between them, his or hers, as either speaks first, upon any subject (1491–2). The 'proof' of this astonishing claim will have to wait for *Grandison*, however.

After Clarissa's death, Lovelace's story is brilliantly resumed by his friend Mowbray. Echoing Lovelace's former cynicism towards Clarissa, he asks what great matters has she suffered 'that grief should kill her thus'. Lovelace, however, as 'mad as any man ever was in Bedlam', strikes the bearer of the fatal news, who calls it 'brutish to abuse a friend, and run mad for a woman'. As the woman-hater Lovelace would once have said himself, 'how love unmans, and softens, and enervates!' (1359–60). Mowbray's sneer is Lovelace's own. 'What a rout's here about a woman? For after all she was no more', he says (1382).

Lovelace sits 'grinning like a man in straw; curses and swears, and is confounded gloomy; and creeps into holes and corners like an old hedgehog hunted for his grease' (1360). Like the crazed kings, lovers and playwrights in Bedlam in the last print of Hogarth's *A Rake's Progress*, he reads with the air of a tragedian his plan to have the lady opened and embalmed, or sits silent in a corner when he has tired himself with his 'mock-majesty and with his argumentation (who so fond of *argufying* as he?) and teaching his shadow to make mouths against the wainscot'. Fighting against the fact of her death, he demands to preserve in a golden receptacle her heart, the passionate part of her 'to which I have such unquestionable pretensions, in which once I had so large a share'. He calls her 'Clarissa Lovelace', and claims defiantly, 'is she not mine? Whose else can she be? She has no father nor mother, no sister, no brother; no relations but me.' Whose was she living, he asks, and 'whose is she dead, but mine?' A Filmerian patriarch still, he argues

123

that since he is her 'husband', her will must now, next to his own will, 'be observed, for she is my wife; and shall be to all eternity. I will never have another.' He will control her memory and mind by securing her papers, and who dare call him to account (1382–5)?

But by Clarissa's death Lovelace's power is gone, and Belford, humouring him with scornful ease, suggests pacifying him with a lock of hair near to her colour (1386). Now Lovelace must endure loss of identity, when he says, 'I am still, I am still, most miserably absent from myself! Shall never, never, more be what I was!' He like Clarissa might be imprisoned and oppressed, 'the sport of enemies! the laughter of fools! and the hanging-sleeved, go-carted property of hired slaves; who were perhaps to find their account in manacling, and (abhorred thought!) in personally abusing me by blows and stripes!' He resists confinement even by doctors 'armed with gallipots, boluses, and cephalic draughts', and being a man of changes, abominates this 'cursed still-life', with nothing active in him or about him but hell's pain, 'the worm that never dies' (1428–31).

Desperately trying to recover his old Don Juanish self, he invites Belford to Italy, where Satan will give him 'a fine strapping *bona roba*, in the Chartres taste,[4] but well-limbed, clear-complexioned, and Turkish-eyed; thou the first man with her, or made to believe so, which is the same thing; how will thy frosty face shine upon such an object!' There again will a 'composition' be made 'between thee and the grand tempter' that will make him sure of Belford for ever (1432). Refusing as always to plead guilty, he marvels again that great men are praised and even deified by orators and poets for their butcheries and depradations, while he, 'a poor, single, harmless prowler; at least *comparatively* harmless; in order to satisfy my hunger, steal but one poor lamb; and every mouth is opened, every hand is lifted up against me' (1437). But Anna replies that only 'MAN! Vile, barbarous, plotting, destructive man!' destroys through wantonness and sport where animals destroy through hunger and necessity (IV. 501).

As soon as Lovelace hears that is he is to be '*manifested* against, though no prince', he wriggles and turns as of old. In a second mock trial before his family he blames Clarissa. Not wanting to be her prisoner for life, he says, he had stolen her bag of gold out of ignorance that 'the miser did actually set so romantic a value upon the treasure'. He brazenly accuses Clarissa of avarice, the Harlowes' presiding sin: 'Suppose this same miserly *A*, on awaking and searching for, and finding his treasure gone, takes it so much to heart, that he starves himself; Who but himself is to blame for that? – Would either equity, law, or conscience, hang *B* for a murder?' In any case, 'what honour is lost, where the *will* is not violated, and the person cannot help it?' Lovelace thus slickly tries to acquit himself, and against Lord M.'s insistence that if an unlawful act results in a capital crime, he is answerable for both, responds boldly again,

is death the *natural* consequence of a rape? . . . And if not the *natural* consequence, and a lady will destroy herself, whether by a lingering death as of grief; or by the dagger, as Lucretia did; is there more than one fault the *man's*? – Is not the other *hers*?

Having reduced the accusation to common theft, he argues for acquittal on the charge of murder. He had offered to purchase forgiveness through the acceptance of terms he first boggled at, 'but it would not do: the sweet miser would break her heart, and die; and how could I help it?' In a million cases, he declares, nine hundred and ninety-nine thousand have not ended as this has ended (1437–9). Finally he lashes out at Belford for judging him when he himself could have released the lady from the enchanted castle. Attacking Belford's appearance, and parrying with a shifting, quicksilver defence, Lovelace yet again gets free.

Lovelace's spirits revive with his quasi-legal triumph and the animating effects of abuse. 'He was glad, he said, to find himself alive; and his two friends clapping and rubbing their hands twenty times in an hour, declared that now once more he was all himself; the charmingest fellow in the world; and they would follow him to the furthest part of the globe.' They set out for Europe by way of Gad's Hill, where Prince Hal found Falstaff, that other emblem of vice, deception and good company, and they rejoice that 'there is no living without him, now he is once more himself' (1460–2). But 'something has been working strangely retributive', as Lovelace himself allows (1428). The deaths of Belton and Tomlinson convince him that fate spins thread for tragedies simply to give dismal themes to Belford (1436), but if providence is indeed at work, the principal in the affair will not be spared. Mrs Sinclair, the 'true mother' of Lovelace's mind (1433), is already in torments. In a squalidly Hogarthian scene she lies foaming, raving, roaring, and burning, a mountain of anguished flesh:

Behold her then, spreading the whole tumbled bed with her huge quaggy carcass: her mill-post arms held up, her broad hands clenched with violence; her big eyes goggling and flaming-red as we may suppose those of a salamander; her matted grizzly hair made irreverend by her wickedness (her clouted head-dress being half off) spread about her fat ears and brawny neck; her livid lips parched, and working violently; her broad chin in convulsive motion; her wide mouth by reason of the contraction of her forehead (which seemed to be half-lost in its own frightful furrows) splitting her face, as it were, into two parts; and her huge tongue hideously rolling in it; heaving, puffing as if for breath; her bellows-shaped and various-coloured breasts ascending by turns to her chin and descending out of sight with the violence of her gaspings.

Her 'daughters' are 'unpropped by stays, squalid, loose in attire, sluggish-haired, under-petticoated', with their eyes half opened, winking and pinking, mispatched, yawning, stretching, as if from the unworn-off effects of the midnight revel; all armed in succession with supplies of cordials', and

The other seven [whores] seemed to have been but just up, risen perhaps from their customers in the fore-house, and their nocturnal orgies, with faces, three or four of them, that had run, the paint lying in streaky seams not half blowzed off, discovering coarse wrinkled skins: the hair of some of them of divers colours; obliged to the blacklead comb where black was affected; the artificial jet, however, yielding apace to the natural brindle: that of others plaistered with oil and powder; the oil predominating: but every one's hanging about her ears and neck in broken curls, or ragged ends; and each at my entrance taken with one motion, stroking their matted locks with both hands under their coifs, mobs, or pinners, every one of which was awry. They were all slip shod; stockingless some: only underpetticoated all; their gowns, made to cover straddling hoops, hanging trollopy, and tangling about their heels; but hastily wrapped round them as soon as I came upstairs. And half of them (unpadded, shoulder-bent, pallid-lipped, feeble-jointed wretches) appearing from a blooming nineteen or twenty perhaps overnight, haggard well-worn strumpets of thirty-eight or forty.

Where Clarissa's death had been seemly and serene, Mrs Sinclair's makes Belford think himself already 'in one of the infernal mansions'. His attempt at spiritual counsel fails, and he flees from this brutish wolf, bull, and salamander to fresh air. Mrs Sinclair dies at last through hourly increasing tortures of body and mind such as Clarissa, by her determined dualism, had escaped (letter 499).

Meanwhile Morden is closing in. Belford, in a last act of loyalty, tries to avert a cool and deliberate act of revenge for an evil absolutely irretrievable by the plea that his friend would have repaired by marriage. 'Her will inviolate, [she] would have got over a *mere personal* injury', he says (1442). Clarissa also argues from the dead that duelling is both a usurpation of the Divine prerogative and an insult upon magistracy and good government, as in Shadwell's play (see p. 69). Life, she says, should not depend upon a private sword, and since a few months of misery have made her happy to all eternity, why demand a 'dreadful expiation'? (1444).

Against them both Morden cites Lovelace's wanton, premeditated mischief, his carrying of her to a vile brothel, and the base, unmanly acts used to effect his wicked purposes. Like Brutus swearing revenge after Lucretia's death, he calls Lovelace a monster, a man of defiance, whose name it would be a merit to blot out (1447). Lovelace responds with predictable quickness, linking as always love and death, 'that solemn act, were it even to be marriage or hanging, which must be done tomorrow, I had rather should be done to-day' (1476). He agrees to meet Morden at Trent.

Lovelace, who knows now that he has not adequately valued Clarissa's excellences because of the mean opinion of the sex which he has imbibed from early manhood, finds there is no match for her in all Europe. When, as he admits, he had no cause for policy or revenge since she never treated him as Miss Howe treated Hickman, nothing but his cursed devices have stood in the way of his happiness. After all his machinations to 'bring down so pure a mind to my own level', her everlasting happiness comforts him, an observation which looks, as he remarks, 'like the confession of a thief at the gallows'. With a Faustian reference to twelve o'clock, Lovelace goes willingly to the duel, where, passively suicidal like Clarissa, he will not kill Morden if he can help it (letter 535).

In the fatal duel, which is distanced by the narration of a French valet, Lovelace is hurt, carries on, and falls. 'Ah monsieur, you are a dead man!', exclaims Morden. Even as Lovelace acknowledges the power of luck and cursed fate, he insists still that he has freely chosen death: 'be ye all witnesses,' he says, 'that I have provoked my destiny, and acknowledge, that I fall by a man of honour'. Outrageous and delirious, he cries out, 'Take her away! take her away! but named nobody.' He calls upon Clarissa, and composing himself,

spoke inwardly so as not to be understood: at last, he distinctly pronounced these three words,

LET THIS EXPIATE!

(letter 537)

But does it? Allegorically speaking, Clarissa has been a comet to foretell disaster. An embodiment of goodness and innocence who

127

must fail in the contest with evil until Christ comes again to reign, she has nevertheless prepared for that day by her unmasking of Anti-Christ, the foul fiend, Satan, vice, the eternal embodiment of evil in carnal man; through her, avarice and the hierarchy of learning have been exposed. This, I think, is what Richardson meant to do, but since, like Spenser, he turned to realism to enlarge his allegory, we must ask how this one deed can in reality expiate the avarice, the tyranny, the deceptions, the rape, the misery and the death? Lucretia's death put an end to Roman tyrants, but Lovelace and Clarissa fall destroyed by the institutions that made them. Lovelace's last words proved as debatable as all the rest, and the tumult of readings and misreadings which burst forth even as he died drew Richardson into his last attempt, *The History of Sir Charles Grandison*.

7

To *Grandison* and after

The History of Sir Charles Grandison evolved, like Richardson's other
novels, out of rewriting its predecessor. The conviction that *Clarissa*
had failed pushed him to it, the evidence an ominous bulk of debate
which accompanied its writing and publication.[1] Perhaps only
Richardson's equals, like Johnson of the prodigious memory who
called it 'not only the first *novel*, but perhaps the first *work* in our
language', and Fielding, who marvelled at its 'wonderfull Art',[2]
possessed the necessary quickness to master and comprehend the
details of this huge book. Other readers criticised the tragic ending,
or in wild contradiction complained that Clarissa was too prudish,
too cold, too fond, and too obedient to her gloomy father's curse.
They attacked the Harlowes, objected to the book's length, and were
attracted to Lovelace rather than to Hickman. Such responses had
already forced Richardson to spell out Lovelace's villainy even in
manuscript,[3] until after two painful years of consultation and revision, he published *Clarissa*'s first two volumes in 1747. The Preface
pre-empts criticism and restates his purposes to caution parents
against the '*undue* Exertion of their natural Authority' over their
children in the marriage choice, and to warn children against preferring a man of pleasure to a man of probity 'upon that dangerous,
but too commonly received Notion, *That a Reformed Rake makes the
best Husband*'.[4] Far from deflecting criticism the Preface naturally
drew attention to it. Five months of revision and a contrariety of
comment preceded the publication of volumes three and four in
April 1748. Richardson's friend Aaron Hill criticised the defence
of Clarissa's death in the Postscript even before it was printed, and
in December 1748 when the last three volumes appeared, the whole
world could make the same complaint.

Lady Bradshaigh, writing pseudonymously as Mrs Belfour,
especially tried to fend off disaster. Because she loved Clarissa but
admired Lovelace, she longed to see them happy together, and even
after the rape implored him to recall the dreadful sentence by blot-
ting out but 'one night, and the villainous laudanum, and all may
be well again' (Eaves and Kimpel, p. 222). Although Richardson
replied that to marry Clarissa to Lovelace would merely repeat

129

Pamela's conclusion (Carroll, p. 92), his rebuke that he had other ends in view than 'the trite one of perfecting a private Happiness, by the Reformation of a Libertine' (Carroll, p. 103) did not silence Lady Bradshaigh, who pined after a happy ending for years. In 1755 her sister Lady Echlin's alternative ending in which Clarissa dies of fatigue and Lovelace reforms before dying[5] made Richardson burst out bitterly that she might as well have reformed all the Harlowes, sent Clarissa to live with her widowed mother, and packed Lovelace off to govern an American colony. Lady Echlin was a typically engaged, typically inadequate reader. Under-educated, inexperienced, unable to see beyond marriage as the highest good for women or to rise to his challenge of what women could suffer, be and do, she proved one of the 'careless or super-ficial Examiner[s]' that Richardson despaired of.[6] When the younger readers he had hoped to reach also pitied the handsome, rakish Lovelace, Richardson might well feel the desire to have his piece 'end happily (as 'tis called) will ever be the test of a wrong head, and a vain mind' (Eaves and Kimpel, p. 219). Handicapped by low expectations about women's spiritual lives, unwilling to con-front pain, complexity and death as Richardson (or Euripides, or Shakespeare) had done, shrewd but unsophisticated readers like Lady Bradshaigh and her sister denied *Clarissa* and tried to censor it. Such wretched misreading was far from being creative, and it brought Richardson down from the imaginative daring of *Clarissa* to the prevailing self-consciousness of *Grandison*.

After *Clarissa* Richardson rethought his whole endeavour. Hav-ing been 'willing to try whether, by an Accommodation to the light Taste of the Age a Religious Novel will do Good',[7] he had hoped in an age of general depravity to '*steal in*, as may be said, and in-vestigate the great doctrines of Christianity under the fashionable guise of an amusement' (Postscript, p. 350). *Clarissa* had been '*prin-cipally* suitable to the Years and Capacities of Persons under Twenty of the one Sex, and under Thirty of the other', and its sentiments had appeared 'in the humble Guise of a *Novel* only by way of Accommodation to the Manners and Taste of an Age overwhelmed with a Torrent of Luxury, and abandoned to Sound and sense-lessness' (Carroll, pp. 75, 117). But Richardson had set himself the impossibly paradoxical task of training *Clarissa*'s readers at the same time that he wrote for them. In the Preface and Postscript to the various editions he attempted to direct their wayward response, and in a pamphlet defended the 'warmth' of the fire scene. He added little abstracts to 'obviate as I went along, tho' covertly, such

Objections as I had heard' (Carroll, p. 125); he revised in manuscript, proof, and new editions. Over two hundred pages of alterations, many of which appeared as a separate volume for purchasers of the first edition, were added to 'the poor *ineffectual* History of Clarissa' (Carroll, p. 132) by the time the third appeared in 1751, and as late as the fourth edition in 1759, two years before his death, he was still anxiously modifying the text.[8]

Many revisions affect only the style, but significant revisions often blacken Lovelace and defend Clarissa in apparent response to the debates. Among the rarer deletions to the second edition Richardson struck out Lovelace's voluptuously baroque fantasy of Clarissa as Plenty with a 'Twin-Lovelace' at each breast, 'pressing with her fine fingers the generous flood into the purple mouths of each eager hunter by turns' (1st ed., IV. 260). Third edition revisions again defend Clarissa's wariness and filial deference, Lovelace becomes more vengeful and more prodigal in his plots, and the Isle of Wight plot, a genuine 'restoration' from manuscript, identifies Lovelace even more closely with Shadwell's vicious libertine (see p. 83). Two new letters, as Richardson freely announced in the Postscript, were inserted to improve Hickman 'by way of accommodation' to such ladies as loved spirit in a man. Lady Bradshaigh in 1761 sent Richardson her marked-up copy of *Clarissa*, but the limited revision to the 1759 fourth edition suggests that once Richardson was properly embarked on *Grandison* he counted on his new novel to supply his answers instead.

This sad tale of response and counter-response, indeed the whole history of Richardson criticism, confirms Locke's fear that consensus about meaning is fragile, and communication relative. Richardson himself had encouraged subjective reading when he urged his friends to identify with characters who offered provocative examples of dissent, while the very sophistication of his hiding behind the 'umbrage' of masked characters spinning fictions subverts any comfortable conviction about truth, legitimises every point of view, and allows for modes that challenge signification itself, that is, irony and satire. Lovelace's levity, his extravagant, attractive energy that derives from the over-doing of satire, and his witty, restless letters that promote him to an epistolary elite with the heroine, put all in doubt. And if even a Clarissa's perception proves imperfect in this world of echoes and mirrors, what hope is there for us? Her retreat to the unassailable simplicity of death leaves readers who replay this vast text floundering for direction in a book where nothing is sure, as in life itself.

Richardson did not want to write another book, but the *Clarissa* debates and the success of Fielding's *Tom Jones* in 1749 convinced him that he must. Johnson's *Rambler* No. 4, which warns against mixed characters (like Tom), supports exemplary ones (like Clarissa), and prescribes a moral role for fiction very much like Richardson's own, could well have confirmed his conception of *Grandison*, in which good and evil are much more clearly distinguished than before.[9]

The *Grandison* correspondence contains Richardson's most elaborate consultations yet.[10] To forestall trouble, he tested the good man on his friends in private letters and the letters of *Grandison*, while they for their part, emboldened by discussing *Clarissa*, seized so eagerly at the chance of sharing in the new creation that they prolonged the new book's composition for years. Above all, the fact that it was no sooner written than read meant that reconsideration or rewriting were made virtually impossible. Writing to the moment as much as his characters, Richardson could never think it out again.

While he attempted to repair in *Grandison* the difficulties of *Clarissa*, Richardson fought for 'approbation' on all fronts (Carroll, p. 182). The debates were intense: for instance Hester Mulso, later Mrs Chapone, reported by her brother to be 'voluminous' on the subject of parental authority, wrote a long first letter, Richardson's answer was thirteen close pages, Hester's reply seventeen and Richardson's thirty-nine. Colley Cibber swore that she would never be married.[11] Richardson must often have felt, as he wrote to young Miss Grainger, that like many of his readers she was 'not at all changed in your sentiments for all that has been answered, though convinced of the reasonableness of the answers. This is very discouraging in our correspondence' (Carroll, p. 153).

Grandison begins with elements that he knew had worked before. The arrival of Harriet Byron in London alerts several suitors, of whom the most importunate is Sir Hargrave Pollexfen. In response to her rejection he abducts her and attempts a forced marriage. Sir Charles Grandison rescues her and takes her home to his sisters, where though a hero and admiring, he unaccountably fails to propose. The cause is the lovely Italian Clementina della Porretta, whose English tutor he had become after saving her brother Jeronymo. Torn between duty and love, Clementina's mind is giving way. Sir Charles, having proposed a compromise that girls of the marriage should be educated as Catholics and boys as Protestants, prepares himself to accept whatever she decides, so that

Harriet can do nothing except hope, her time occupied meanwhile by the proposal of Lady D. on her son's behalf, and by Charlotte Grandison's marriage to Lord G. Sir Charles is also loved by his young and wealthy ward Emily Jervois, and by Olivia, a rich Italian heiress. Clementina having at last renounced him, he marries Harriet, a last-minute surprise being provided in the fair Italian's flight from parental persuasion to England. At the end she is still not married to their choice, the Count of Belvedere.

Many of these characters appear as 'proof' that Richardson was right in *Clarissa*. For example, to answer charges of prudishness in his heroine Richardson demonstrates his real commitment to matrimony in the marriages of Sir Charles and his sisters; warning devices like Sir Hargrave Pollexfen suggest that Clarissa was not 'over-nice' to reject Lovelace; Sir Charles' father Sir Thomas demonstrates the long-term consequences of rakish ways, and Richardson hints with a new harshness at Abelard's fate, castration, when Sir Hargrave expires and Jeronymo's groin injury fails to heal.

In response to misreadings of *Clarissa* Richardson simplifies his own complexities. He distinguishes his paragon from his devilish rakes, though prolonged pleading from Lady Bradshaigh for 'moderate rakery' (Carroll, p. 179) made him allow, in ludicrous capitulation, that Sir Charles could be 'a Rake in his address, and a Saint in his heart' (III. 93) – a man who, had he been a free liver, would have been a dangerous man (II. 272). The resulting character is stiff, awkward, and almost unable to move. Richardson next created a close copy of the derided suitor, ennobled him, and married him to the lively Charlotte Grandison to prove such a marriage could work. Most extraordinary of all, he calls attention to it. When Harriet calls her 'a very Miss Howe', Charlotte replies, 'to a *very* Mr. Hickman' (I. 229). Harriet and Sir Charles weigh in to support Lord G.'s sense of grievance, and we too feel more for a character much more visible than his former avatar.

Richardson then engrafted Hickman's goodness on to Lovelace's dash to create the good, the handsome, the admirable Sir Charles Grandison. Although he argues through Harriet, 'What is beauty in a man to me? You all know, that I never thought beauty a qualification in a man', for even if plain and hard-featured Sir Charles would be what is far more eligible in a man, 'very agreeable', Sir Charles is actually 'very fine', tall, slender, healthy and sun-tanned, with fine teeth. His beauty and majesty are fit to make him king, his manners easy, free and accessible. He has travelled to some purpose, his marriage would break hearts, he dresses fashionably and richly, he admires handsome women, he maintains a tasteful equipage (I. 181–2).

Like Lovelace, then, Sir Charles is handsome, amorous, and martial. But lest love be thought to dominate his life, he does not declare it, and though heroic in several duels, wins one by a jerk and a twist, another by talking his way out, and yet another by self-defence in foreign parts. Most notably, Richardson reacted to the debates by eliminating the energy, wit and deceptions of Lovelace along with their vehicle, his confidential letters. Sir Charles speaks little and writes less, his unrevealing record of the past doubly distanced when copied by Dr Bartlett and recopied by Harriet. Beside that eloquent soliloquist Lovelace, how could a man all public face and smothered private life have ever hoped to please? Richardson tried to humanise Sir Charles by family pride and passion, but neither this nor the agony of choosing between two women does the trick. Richardson created a blank where a character ought to be, and readers keen to 'carve' found nothing there to work on. The main imaginative problem is that Sir Charles is a man, and not therefore to be oppressed. Education, experience, money, power, and the law are all his, so that even Sir Thomas' fatherly unpleasantness is no burden to him. If he suffers in love we do not see it until late on. He has never been popular with readers, for everyone envies success, as Clarissa knew. The failures in the character, however, are proportionate to the ambition of Richardson's plan, as we shall see.

His new heroine Harriet Byron he designed to 'keep the middle course' between Pamela and Clarissa, and Clarissa and Miss Howe (Carroll, p. 179). Accomplished like Clarissa and satirical like Anna, she soon loses the latter part of herself except for rare flashes to Charlotte Grandison, and her patience is rewarded in the happy ending that so many readers of *Clarissa* had clamoured for. Her Clarissa aspect is transferred to Clementina the second heroine, with instant success. John Duncombe, for instance, relished 'the tender distress of your fair Italian', and wanted to know whether 'poor Clementina' was 'dead, or worse than dead'.[12] But the Richardson who had bravely murdered one woman dared not kill off another. Attentive to readers' objections that Clementina must neither die nor live single, he suggested only that she would marry.

In a replay of the filial obedience debate, Clementina is oppressed not by hateful Harlowes but by parents who love her and delegate their violence to the Catholic Church. Neither money nor power, those two great motivators of bad actions, matter in this reductionist version of *Clarissa*, nor, since Clementina has 'fallen' before we meet her, does her fight against passion. The great political theme of oppression and resistance developed in the first two books almost disappears. And since Sir Charles is neither her antagonist nor her tormentor but a sufferer as passive as she, Clementina looks more abstract than emotional when she sets love against her duty, country and religion. Lovelace's exhilarating evil tempted and destroyed Clarissa, but Clementina loves a man whose goodness is his only asset. Her mind, which breaks from thwarted love, not violation, may be prosaically treated by modern specialists, and when she returns, child-like, to the shelter of her home, her development into an adult is denied her. Being Italian, she has the real option of taking herself to the nunnery that Clarissa longed for, and if the Count of Belvedere is hardly visible as a character, by the same token he cannot be obnoxious to her. But marriage is destiny in *Grandison*, not celibacy or death. After the *Clarissa* debates which challenged him to produce a marriageable man, Richardson turns his attention from women to training men up for them, and, like Jane Austen, tells men what to be if they wish to marry heroines.

Grandison begins therefore in continuation of *Clarissa*, not out of its own inner necessities, and its composition may be closely traced from his correspondence. Encouraged into writing it by friends reluctant to see an end to *Clarissa*, Richardson read aloud to them brief, entertaining sketches of a young woman come to town, and before the story line became peremptory, invented a number of characters who would mostly disappear. Harriet Byron is abducted then rescued by the hero so perfunctorily that he had to concoct a reason why they should not immediately marry – that is, a second heroine, who nearly sank his book when Richardson could no more choose between them than Grandison could. Knowing polygamy to be impossible, Richardson fell back on the solution of a divided heart. Because Harriet's happy marriage, he knew from Pamela's example, would lose readers' sympathy, he tried a last trick to retain interest by inserting a frightening dream for Harriet and the threat of assassination for Sir Charles. But what about Clementina?

The illegal printing of the first six volumes by Irish pirates granted Richardson a breathing space of seven months in which to circulate manuscript and proofs, consider the comments that followed along with criticism of the first six printed volumes, and change his last volume accordingly.[13] The conclusion in which nothing is concluded for Harriet, Clementina, Olivia, Emily, or a reformed

Charlotte is the result. Many scenes seem to be inserted merely to answer criticism of early volumes, as Samuel Johnson realised when he remarked upon 'a trick of laying yourself open to objections, in the first part of your work, and crushing them in subsequent parts. A great deal that I had to say before I read the conversation in the latter part, is now taken from me'.[14]

Even after these changes at the last moment Richardson could not rest. In a Preface which recapitulated his life's work, he inserted an 'unlucky omission' to prove Sir Charles' patriotism, and added a Concluding Note to defend both the religious compromise with Clementina and Sir Charles' controversial perfection and ability at duels. He reiterated his position in an elaborate, directive Index. From private letters he chose for separate publication one to a lady who was solicitous for an additional volume, and another to a friend who had objected to the compromise (both printed in the O.E.N. edition), and finally he assembled from all three novels a collection of moral and instructive sentiments (1755). In the years remaining to him he would revise *Grandison* five times, often in response to correspondents.[15]

Richardson may have made difficulties into virtues when he said that his novels trained readers to be carvers, makers of moral choice. But when intervention rendered composition painful, the uncompromising courage that drove *Clarissa* through to its conclusion was leached away. Sick, exhausted and feeling his age, he had to realise yet again that all his remedies could have little effect. Lady Bradshaigh's comment in her *Grandison* (the seventh volume is now in the Huntington Library) remained unanswerable: 'I think this will be missed by some if omitted, as it has been in' (VII. 239).

Real life and fiction interact continuously in Richardson's last book. Begun almost as a diary of his daily correspondence, its continual deference to real life and real people means that the debate over *Clarissa* at first controls it and even the pink and yellow ribands of Lady Bradshaigh's maiden aunt enter it. But if the accents of the good man are indistinguishable from Richardson's, if Charlotte Grandison and her sister 'pull caps' like Lady Bradshaigh and her sister in their youth, if Miss Talbot and Miss Carter see their suggestion that he be not misled by false glory or false shame turn up in the novel (I. 183), his friends might well believe themselves 'Pigmalionesses' and demand the power he could not share. To forestall them by knowing their minds, Richardson involved his friends and let them think they could change the course of events. When his creation became so like theirs that they could believe in it, so real that the characters of one could be referred to by the characters of another, he thereby brought trouble on himself. *Grandison* collides with reality often enough to be buffeted out of its autonomy as a fiction, and all too often the golden images of poesy are supplanted by the leaden ones of history.

The contemporary time-scheme of *Grandison* allowed Richardson triumphantly to justify his abrupt ending by arguing to the 'Lady' that since *Grandison* finished in the present day, as indicated by a reference to the '45 Rebellion, it could not continue. But the Shandyan recognition that each real passing day added another day to the novel forced him to reconsider. Pestered for another volume, he invited contributors to whom he discovered he could not relinquish the pen. Just as he had reared up at Aaron Hill's alterations to *Clarissa* and ignored Lady Echlin's revised ending, now again Richardson reasserted dominion. If he could not do it, others should not, and he forced the project to lapse. Only death could wrest *Pamela, Clarissa* and *Sir Charles Grandison* from Richardson's hands, when on 4 July 1761 the novels passed to those later generations of readers whom he was right, after all, to trust.

8

Men, Women, and Italians:
The History of Sir Charles Grandison

Sir Charles Grandison, said Richardson, was the completion of his whole plan (Carroll, p. 235). This portrait of an exceptional man to match his exceptional woman inevitably took him away from Clarissa–comet to Sir Charles Sun–King, centre of an adoring universe, for if the curse of being special brought resistance and death upon Clarissa, this special man inherits the earth. Clarissa's descent from the models of Eve, whose aspirations after knowledge and free will gave birth to sin and death, of Elizabeth I, in whom a man's soul warring with a woman's body made her forfeit sexuality for royal power, and of Lucretia, who died to defeat tyranny, led her unswervingly to tragedy. No woman could change the world, but a special man just might. To a new kind of gentleman, benevolent, sensitive, conscious of duties as well as rights, social rather than individualistic, woman-like and Christ-like rather than man-like in the old pagan, heroic and patriarchal ways – to such a man, to Sir Charles Grandison in short, one might safely entrust male power. Modelling himself as he may on Adam, Christ, and Solomon, Sir Charles stands forth as an ideal king, and an ideal man for Britain.

By the end of his story Sir Charles, by a backwards progression, has returned to the restored world of the millennium in which marriage recovers its original dignity and felicity.[1] Here, as in the first, suppressed story of Genesis, he is Adam to two Eves, the 'fallen' Clementina della Porretta and the unfallen Harriet Byron, with whom to live in Paradise at Grandison Hall – or so at least Harriet explains when she says that Sir Charles would in Adam's place have politely refused the fruit and regretted Eve's lapse, but 'done *his own duty*, were it but for the sake of posterity, and left it to the Almighty, if such had been his pleasure, to have annihilated his first Eve, and given him a second' (II. 609).

Grandison Hall confirms Sir Charles as Adam. His house exhibits his mind, for from the windows, the gardens and lawn are 'as boundless as the mind of the owner, and as free and open as his countenance'.[2] Sir Charles' garden 'being bounded only by sunk fences, the eye is carried to views that have no bounds' (III. 272–3), and so too 'our general Sire', says Milton in *Paradise Lost*, had 'prospect large/Into his neather Empire neighbouring round' (IV. 144–5). The Grandison estate, with its stream, fish, vineyards, flowers and fruit, seems paradisal when everything flourishes that belongs to Sir Charles. The very servants live in paradise (III. 285). As in Milton's prelapsarian garden, a contented gardener with his busy wife works among trees laid out on the pattern of paradise: that is, a semicircle of fruit trees planted on a natural slope, 'all which in the season of blossoming, one row gradually lower than another, must make a charming variety of blooming sweets to the eye', sheltered by rows of pine, cedars and firs (III. 273), as in *Paradise Lost*:

> and over head up grew
> Insuperable highth of loftiest shade,
> Cedar, and Pine, and Firr, and branching Palm
> A Silvan Scene, and as the ranks ascend
> Shade above shade, a woodie Theatre
> Of stateliest view.
> . . . . a circling row
> Of goodliest Trees loaden with fairest Fruit,
> Blossoms and Fruits at once of golden hue
> Appeerd, with gay enameld colours mixt.   (IV. 137–49)

If this is Eden, Clementina's Italian garden is the opposite scene of Fall. Here in a fertile garden of alleys and winding walks Clementina meets her lover; here they sit and read *Paradise Lost* (II. 144). 'What happy times were those, when I was innocent, and learning English!', laments Clementina (II. 482), remembering how admiration turned into guilty awareness of love. She falls however alone, for Sir Charles' love is only 'brotherly'. The primal sin also is re-enacted in Clementina's garden when she dreams that Sir Charles lies dead and bleeding in the orange grove (II. 241), killed by a 'Cain', as Harriet dreams (III. 149). From this garden of Fall and sin, Sir Charles will prudently flee.

Sir Charles is second Adam as well as first when he follows traditional exhortations to imitate Christ. Although he is exemplary in virtue, his trial in worldly Italy balances sexual coolness with hints of suffering, for the Christ whom he copies is perhaps the ultimate expression of a theme dear to the eighteenth century, virtue in distress. In an attempt to counter attacks on the unreasonable miracles of the Old Testament, attention turned in the eighteenth century to the Revelation of the New, to God made man in tangible Christ. The image of Christ contains many features characteristic of the man of feeling[3] – sexual innocence, impotence in the face of worldly power, sensibility, empathy and charity. Christ's poverty and vulnerability, his wounds, his lack of traditional masculinity, his being too good for a wicked world, even the morbidity of the Crucifixion and the languor of the Deposition could serve as a model for many an eighteenth-century heroine or hero. Christ's image, mediated through the quietism of Richard Steele's idea, expressed in essays and plays, of the Christianised Hero, may have contributed to the fascination with virtue on trial and in distress. But such idealism is hard to reconcile with realism, as Richardson found, and Sir Charles' virtue even to chastity (II. 497) provoked ridicule from the practised rake Colley Cibber, who, said Richardson, bitterly,

undertook to draw [the good man], and to whom, at setting out, he gave a mistress, in order to shew the virtue of the hero in parting with her, when he had fixed upon a particular lady, to whom he made honourable addresses[.] A male-virgin said he – ha, ha, ha, hah! when I made my objections to the mistress, and she was another man's wife too, but ill used by her husband; and he laughed me quite out of countenance.

(Carroll, p. 171)

At home in his native land, however, Sir Charles is Christ come again to reign. In imitation of the Almighty (II. 307) he palliates the sins of Mrs Oldham his father's mistress in the same way as Christ did to the woman taken in adultery, attacking his rakish cousin Everard's zeal 'to punish a poor Magdalen, who, *tho'* faulty, was not so faulty as himself' (I. 355), and reminding the sisters who humiliate her, walking as stately and as upright as duchesses in a coronation procession (I. 367), that mercy is a virtue (I. 355).

Being a man, Sir Charles is God's representative on earth. Here Richardson is boldly attempting to say what it means to be a Christian in his own time, to show, as he wrote in the Concluding Note, 'by a series of facts in common life, what a degree of excellence may be attained and preserved amidst all the infection of fashionable vice and folly' (III. 466). Spenser, who wrote in his *Faerie Queene* of friendship and chastity, temperance and justice, holiness and courtesy, would have no difficulties in comprehending Sir Charles. Neither would Blake, who could easily see Christ walking upon England's mountains green, and found that *Grandison* had won his heart.[4] Richardson's vision of Christ as a realistic eighteenth-century gentleman is, however, unimaginable for most of us now. As he said himself, 'A fine task have I set myself! to draw a man that is to be above the common foibles of life; and yet to make a lover of him!' (Carroll, p. 186). Far better, surely, to leave God invisible and unknowable than to make this paragon walk the earth, a man in whom the passion of a Renaissance prince sits uneasily with pacifism, worldliness with saintliness, and ideal portraiture with the new realism that Richardson himself pioneered.

At once England's representative and its finest flower, Sir Charles is a model tourist and observer. He faces down six Pandours (I. 257), and releases Dr Bartlett from the Turks (I. 460), for seas are nothing to one who considers all nations as joined on the same continent, and if called, would undertake a journey to Constantinople or Pekin, with as little difficulty as some others would to the Land's-end (II. 30). He wishes that different nations would consider themselves as the creatures of one God, 'the Sovereign of a thousand worlds!' (III. 367), but until they do, friendship makes a 'bridge over the narrow seas; it will cut an easy passage thro' rocks and mountains, and make England and Italy one country' (III. 454).[5] He is nevertheless a patriot, and teaches the Italians English by means of Milton, who like himself 'had deservedly a name among them'. A firm supporter of the Union and the Hanovers, and known to be warm in the interest of his country, he retires when the Porrettas rejoice at news of the '45 (II. 122–4). He carefully praises both the fine women of Scotland (I. 236) and the merchants of Great Britain (I. 455), and even for Clementina will not renounce his Protestantism: their daughters are to be educated by their mother and their sons by him, and he proposes a stay of year and year about, or three months a year in his beloved country rather than perpetual exile from it (II. 130). His eventual home-coming makes Aunt Eleanor chuckle and mump for joy that her nephew will not go out of England for a wife (III. 22), but bigoted criticism of his internationalism forced Richardson to spell out, in an 'unlucky omission',

How could Sir Charles, so thorough an Englishman, have been happy with an Italian wife? His heart indeed, is generously open and benevolent to people of all countries: He is, as I have often heard you say, in the noblest sense, a Citizen of the World: But, see we not, that his long residence abroad, has only the more endeared to him the Religion, the Government, the Manners of England? (III. 263)

The tone may well be ironic when he writes to the lady importunate for a sequel that after the book ends Jeronymo will go to Bath, 'And do you think that those salutary springs will not, for the honour of our country, quite establish him?' (III. 468).

Sir Charles Grandison is British, and a king among men.[6] Saintly Charles I and rakish Charles II, autocratic Sun–King but constrained by British law, Sir Charles is glamorous as the pale, puffy Hanovers could never be. What a king he would make, says Harriet. 'Power could not corrupt such a mind as his' (I. 446), for he gives examples to princes (I. 456). Like the Great Mogul (I. 252), he flutters a whole bookful of adoring women, and thus fulfils Lovelace's wildest and most polygamous dreams. Incorruptible, powerful, merciful and just, Sir Charles over-rides even the wishes of the dead. He decides the most important choices of their lives when he arranges marriages for Caroline, Charlotte, Emily and the Danbys, deals punctiliously with his father's mistresses, banishes his uncle's, and procures for him a wife who is only too glad to have him. Unlike Lovelace he scorns the laws of honour and owns only 'the Laws of GOD and my Country' (I. 242). George Eliot may have noted approvingly[7] that this accomplished hero had 'the taste and strength of mind to dispense with a wig', but the youthful Sir Charles' fine curling auburn locks waving about his shoulders suggest rather Milton's comparison of a king to Samson, 'with those his illustrious and sunny locks the laws waving and curling about his godlike shoulders'.[8] A dispenser of truth and justice (I. 254), he is more penetrating than a sun-beam: he 'goes to the bottom of an affair at once, and wants but to hear both sides of a question to determine' (I. 361). There is 'no living within the blazing glory of this man!' writes Harriet in despair (I. 384).[9]

Richardson, who cannot resist imagining what a perfect man would be like in real life, typically makes Charlotte say peevishly to her brother, 'Nobody has the shadow of belief, that *you* could be wrong' (I. 401), and Harriet, observing that he treats women as 'perverse humoursome babies' (II. 272), complain of

A most *intolerable* superiority! – I wish he would do something wrong; something cruel: If he would but bear malice, would but stiffen his air by resentment, it would be something. As a MAN, cannot he be lordly, and assuming, and where he is so much regarded, I may say *feared*, nod his imperial significance to his vassals about him? (II. 89)

Sir Charles may be intolerable to the unregenerate, but the manner in which he exercises his God-given power makes him heroic in quite another way.

Unlike the male Harlowes, this Domestic King assists women. It is all very well for Harriet to argue that women have 'souls as well as men, and souls as capable of the noblest attainments' (I. 19) and should therefore be educated as she has been, when they actually are not. Many debates in *Grandison* therefore explore just what is possible for women. Like Clarissa, Harriet knows, for instance, that not all the 'lords of the *creation*' are wiser than all women (I. 47), an assertion proved in the first debate on learning and languages where she engages publicly with a pedant and a fop. Although it is a set-piece not integral to her character, and in spite of her victory being taken away from her in revisions to the seventh volume and the third edition,[10] the exchanges comically show how intelligent women threaten the pedant's belief that women are 'but domestic animals of a superior order', their importance for men heightened by their ignorance (I. 70). Sir Hargrave mocks his fear of a learned wife, but his own idea that possession of such a 'jewel' is worth boasting of when 'the woman is more a husband's than a man is a wife's' draws Harriet's challenge. 'Have all the men this prerogative-notion, Lucy?' she asks coolly (I. 82).

While it is inadvisable for women to be illiterate like Italian women, as if their husbands and fathers thought them only 'children of this world, and not heirs of a better hope, by the little care taken in improving their understanding', as Harriet says tartly (III. 361), classical learning can be dangerous, as the mannishness of Miss Barnevelt 'proves' (I. 62). The ideal compromise is presented in Miss Clements, ingenious and unaffected, who has not 'suffered her pen to run away with her needle; nor her reading to interfere with that housewifry which the best judges hold so indispensable in the character of a good woman'. Where talents exist, women should cultivate them, says Harriet,[11] and 'where no duty is neglected for the acquirement; where modesty, delicacy, and a teachable spirit, are preserved, as characteristics of the sex, it need not be thought a disgrace to be spposed to know something' (I. 102). But she agrees with Sir Charles that if women are ahead when young, men may 'ripen into a superiority', for men's intellects 'generally hold longer, are capable of higher perfection, and serve to nobler purposes' (I. 184).

If men are indeed superior, they have responsibilities to help others. Sir Charles argues that men should prove their superiority by their protection of women (II. 140), and although he is convinced that courage depends on education (III. 181), an extensive and important debate in volume VI, letter 55, about 'man's usurpation, and women's natural independency' which makes him slily remark, 'how I love my Country! ENGLAND is the *only* spot in the world, in which this argument *can* be properly debated!', explores all the main issues. Mrs Shirley pleads with men to assist women by not talking to them only of insipidities, and Sir Charles, recalling individual female prodigies, praises his sister. In general, though, he subscribes, as Charlotte says, to 'a natural inferiority in the faculties of us, poor women; a natural superiority in you, imperial men'.[12] Physical strength is decisive, for

Why has nature made a difference in the beauty, proportion, and symmetry, in the *persons* of the two Sexes? Why gave it delicacy, softness, grace, to that of the woman . . . strength, firmness, to men; a capacity to bear labour and fatigue; and courage, to protect the other? Why gave it a distinction, both in qualities and plumage to the different sexes of the feathered race? Why in the courage of the male and female animals? – The surly bull, the meek, the beneficent, cow, for one instance?

He allows that all human souls are equal, but adds the Cartesian view that the very 'design of the different machines in which they are inclosed, is to super-induce a temporary difference on their original equality'. In another world, he promises, 'when Sex ceases, inequality of Souls will cease; and women will certainly be on a foot with men, as to intellectuals, in Heaven'.[13]

If the battle is all to the bull, the cow has the last, subversive word. If, says Charlotte with a sarcasm very like Mary Astell's, a little knowledge is allowable to women, 'Will you have the goodness to point out to us what this compatible learning is, that we may not mistake – and so become excentric, as I may say, burst our orb, and do more mischief than ever we could do good?' In this novel, though, no comet challenges the ordering of the heavens, and Charlotte may well complain that women are only allowed 'in this temporary state, like tame doves, to go about house, and-so-forth'. But like Pamela after her marriage, she only whispers it.

Of course Sir Charles is patronising. He is a patron, and essential to women so long as they are physically and politically weak. In this book the man with power helps women without it, just as Darcy was to act on Elizabeth Bennet's behalf to save Lydia in *Pride and Prejudice*. Having shown in *Clarissa* a woman destroyed by the tyrannical misuse of authority, Richardson now offers the more practical solution of turning patriarchal power to good ends. If women seek men like Sir Charles, they will therefore get a better deal than they would otherwise, and if men copy him, they will be no longer Lovelaces, nor Solmeses, nor Harlowes, but Grandisons. All Richardson's anxious gratulation only proves, though, how difficult he found it to convey.

Given the cooperation of men, women can thus save themselves by education and by the marriage-choice. Sir Charles even says they can save the nation. Harriet perceives that

there are more bachelors now in England, by many thousands, than were a few years ago: And, probably, the numbers of them (and of single women, of course) will every year increase. The luxury of the age will account a good deal for this; and the turn our Sex take in *un*-domesticating themselves, for a good deal more. (I. 231)

Sir Charles thinks too that Englishmen are not what they were, for 'a wretched effeminacy seems to prevail among them. Marriage itself is every day more and more out of fashion; and even virtuous women give not the institution so much of their countenance, as to discourage by their contempt the free-livers' (II. 10). But if men will be good, they will be chosen by good women, and, as the rake Everard ruefully knows, Sir Charles 'may with more safety *steal an horse*, than I *look over the hedge*' (I. 429). Patriotic women should prefer good men, for 'it is more in the power of young ladies than they seem to imagine, to make fine men', as Richardson wrote to a friend (Carroll, p. 164). Within his book, it works. Charlotte agrees that if all men were like her brother, 'there would not be a single woman, and hardly a bad one, in the kingdom' (I. 291); Emily would happily marry a man formed by his example (III. 396); young women are right to marry when young men are so desirous to copy Sir Charles Grandison (III. 443). The fact that five ladies would let Sir Charles choose among them shows that policy if not principle would 'mend us men', says the old roué Lord W. (II. 43), but unfortunately, until it does, Kitty Holles and her friends 'never, never, can think of marrying, after we have seen Sir Charles Grandison, and his behaviour' (III. 239). Lucy Selby says tetchily of the rake Greville, 'to be sure the man is not a Sir Charles Grandison. Who *is?*' (III. 308), and Charlotte finds that her brother has made her think contemptuously of all other men (II. 320).

In *Grandison* Richardson assists women who do not want to be Clarissas by showing them that marriage, once restored from its corruptions, can work to their advantage. He knows that in the real world heiresses are pursued, clever women marry dull men, rakes will not reform, and the marriage market flourishes. Aristocracy rarely coincides with virtue, merchants like young Danby find women a drug on the market (I. 452), broken soldiers marry for money, and so do bankrupt aristocrats like Everard Grandison, who gains the £25,000 of a middle-class widow in exchange for a framed, glazed, genealogical table of the Grandisons (III. 348).

How then is a woman to find the friendship with security that she needs? If marriage had diminished Pamela and threatened Clarissa, here Richardson, a 'matrimony-promoter' as much as Sir Charles (II. 323), demonstrates that at least ideally it can expand women's lives.

Marriage, then, remains the best option for women, and a duty whenever it can be entered into with prudence, as Harriet's grandmother Mrs Shirley writes. As though Clarissa had never lived, she adds, 'What a mean, what a selfish mind must that person have, whether man or woman, who can resolve against entering into the state, because it has its cares, its fatigues, its inconveniencies!' (I. 304). Sir Charles too, a great friend to the married state 'especially with regard to our sex', as Harriet says (I. 290), is for having everybody marry (I. 428).

Single women such as Mrs Penelope Arby, 'surrounded with parrots and lap-dogs! – So spring-like at past fifty, with her pale pink Lustring, and back head', make young girls realise that 'a single woman is too generally an undefended, unsupported creature. Her early connexions, year by year, drop off; no new ones arise; and she remains solitary and unheeded, in a busy bustling world; perhaps soured to it by her unconnected state' (III. 397). But an unsupported state is better than an oppressed and miserable one (III. 401), and worthy young single women who have had no lovers, or having had one, two, or three, have not found a husband, may have rather had 'a miss than a loss, as men go' (I. 232). To ridicule old maids as Charlotte does is to play into men's hands by making them 'Lords of the Creation' (II. 662), for out of their fear of staying single, many a poor girl goes up the hill with a companion she would little care for when the state of a single woman is so peculiarly unprovided and helpless. Sir Charles responds with Mary Astell's solution, the Protestant Nunnery. Why did he not settle it a fortnight ago, 'and made poor me a Lady Abbess?', asks the married Charlotte fretfully (II. 355).

Richardson attacks romances for the same reasons that we now look askance at the Mills and Boons or Harlequins of popular fiction. As he saw, these images of women wooed in exotic surroundings by adoring lovers they scarcely know induce unrealistic, unhelpful expectations of women's lives. Equality between a love-object and her admirer is impossible, and a woman is encouraged to see love as the only relationship that matters. Richardson mocks romance when Sir Charles teases his sister out of her expectations of being placed 'upon the mossy bank of a purling stream, gliding thro' an enamelled mead' (II. 98), and he criticises romantic notions of fidelity to first love, or love at first sight. But Harriet understandably refuses to marry if she cannot win Sir Charles (I. 390), having no reason to endeavour to conquer a passion not ignobly founded (II. 158). Knowing herself to be a romancer, she nevertheless writes, 'he was my first Love; and I never will have any other', adding, 'is not the man Sir Charles Grandison?' (II. 542). Her mock-heroic dream, which recalls the romantic Biddy in Steele's *Tender Husband*, gains as much from romance as it loses:

when fancy is more propitious to me, then comes my rescuer, my deliverer: And he is sometimes a mighty prince (dreams then make me a perfect romancer) and I am a damsel in distress. The milk-white palfrey once came in. All the Marvelous takes place, and lions and tygers are slain, and armies routed, by the puissance of his single arm. (I. 285)

Harriet's romantic obstinacy is undoubtedly in a good cause, and yet Lady D. gently points out the consequence if it were not. The active life of marriage, she says, is far preferable to continuing obstinately in a single state 'to indulge a remediless sorrow'. How can Harriet, if Sir Charles marries Clementina, live happy 'in a friendship with two persons, when they are united by indissoluble ties, the very thought of whose union makes your cheek fade, and your health languish. Ah, my beloved Harriet! is not this a fairy-scheme?' (II. 546–7).

First love is 'first nonsense' (III. 306), a sentiment confirmed by Mrs Shirley. Her friend Mrs Eggleton[14] had talked her out of romantic notions which were fashionable in her youth but are no longer, when women are so 'greatly obliged to the authors of the Spectators'. To her hesitation at marrying a suitor who was no heroic Oroondates, Mrs Eggleton had promised that esteem, heightened by gratitude and enforced by duty, would soon ripen into love. But, Mrs Shirley had asked, what if one falls in love with another man after marriage, like the Princess of Cleves? That story was written with dangerous elegance, replies Mrs Eggleton, but the Princess deluded herself (III. 398–400). Lady G. concludes confidently, though hypothetically, that Harriet was indeed romantic, but 'Pho, pho, never fear but Harriet would have married before my Brother and Clementina had seen the face of their second boy – no *girls* shall he have, for fear they should be Romancers.' So too Clementina. 'Leave her sea-room, leave her land-room, and let her have time to consider; and she will be a Bride' (III. 406). Equally romantic is the notion of love at first sight, which is 'an indelicate paroxysm' in a man, but in a woman, 'who expects protection and instruction from a man, much more so' (II. 357). Having said this, Richardson moved quickly to insert in his seventh volume a hint that Sir Charles fell in love with Harriet in the fraction of time before she could fall for him (III. 284).

If marriage is a woman's only profession, the definition of love becomes not just a courtly quibble but a necessary protection and a promise. Milton's ideal of amorous, relaxed, cheerful, friendly love between unfallen Adam and Eve was obviously attractive to Richardson,[15] for Sir Charles, 'a Rake in his address, and a Saint in his heart', is pleasantly informal in company:

> a seat not being at hand, while the young Ladies were making a bustle to give him a place between them (tossing their hoops above their shoulders on one side) . . . he threw himself at the feet of my aunt and me, making the floor his seat.
>
> I don't know how it was; but I thought I never saw him look to more advantage.

From the floor he tells 'two or three very pretty humorous stories; so that nobody thought of helping him again to a chair, or wishing him in one' (III. 92–3). To the astonishment of his sisters he makes an ardent, polite lover (III. 111), and at the wedding feast waits gallantly on his new wife with a napkin over his arm (III. 233). Like Eve to Adam Harriet flings her fond arms about his neck, and 'hiding my glowing face in his bosom, called him, murmuringly, the most just, the most generous, of men' (III. 284). He is to her 'my friend, my Lover, my HUSBAND, every sweet word in one' (III. 305).

The prospect of marriage nevertheless makes her tremble when it means

> a change of condition for life! New attachments! A new course of life! Her name sunk, and lost! The property, person and will, of another, excellent as the man is; obliged to go to a new house; to be ingrafted into a new family; to leave her own, who so dearly love her; an *irrevocable* destiny!

Because women 'dressed out in ribbands, and gaudy trappings, and in Virgin-white, on our Wedding days, seem but like milk-white heifers led to sacrifice', it is imperative that they marry a man they can love (III. 235–6), a man who like Sir Charles recognises 'in the face of the sun, obligations that he had entered into at the altar' (III. 456). Sir Charles is in fact Mary Astell's ideal man. A woman, she says, should 'stay till she meet with one who has the Government of his own Passions, and has duly regulated his own Desires, since he is to have such an absolute Power over hers'. The sole object of love should be 'amiable Qualities, the Image of the Deity impress'd upon a generous and godlike Mind', which, 'in imitation of that glorious Pattern it endeavours to copy after, expands and diffuses it self to its utmost Capacity in doing Good' (*Marriage*, pp. 38–9). Love, says Harriet's grandmother, is a natural passion (I. 309), but the friendship that Sir Charles offers out of respect for mind as well as body (II. 301), being disinterested, and more intellectual than personal, is nobler than love. Without friendship love is a 'prostituted name! made to cover all acts of violence, indiscretion, folly, in both sexes!' (I. 269), so that, she concludes,

Mild, sedate convenience, is better than a stark staring-mad passion. The wall-climbers, the hedge and ditch-leapers, the river-forders, the window-droppers, always find reason to think so. Who ever hears of darts, flames, Cupids, Venus's, Adonis's, and such-like nonsense, in matrimony? – Passion is transitory; but discretion, which never boils over, gives durable happiness. (III. 30)

Richardson's last novel therefore explores, through several different women, the profession that most women share.

The first, Harriet Byron, comes to town to seek her fortune in marriage. She is tested by love, and rewarded by the friendship she desires. Richardson clearly enjoyed sketching this sprightly, satirical woman, who copes with pedants and fops and suitors pestering her for love simply because they admire her. Spirited enough to resist Sir Hargrave and his corrupt clergyman, she manages, though muffled, gagged and blind-folded, to call out to her deliverer (I. 166). Her 'trial' is simply to wait, like Fanny Price's hard role of passivity, suffering and endurance, until she gains a husband, money, and a home. When, as a woman, she may not volunteer her love, she gives it another name. 'We were to be popt off with your gratitude, truly!', says Charlotte (II. 414–15). Hers is a 'wedded heart' (II. 289) allowably entangled in a hopeless passion, for 'if we women love an handsome man, for the sake of our eye, we must be poor creatures indeed, if we love not good men, for the sake of our hearts' (I. 212). Where Pamela and Clarissa were abducted and assaulted, Harriet suffers 'trial' by rival. She is sustained by an important interview in which Sir Charles expresses the hope for a more tender friendship than that of sister (II. 301), but the distressing scenes in Italy keep her in a suspense which destroys her health. He, holding himself in readiness to answer Clementina's call, is 'a man *divided in myself*, not knowing what I *can* do, hardly sometimes what I *ought* to do', fettered, he says, where Miss Byron and the lady abroad are free (II. 383–4). Unlike

Clarissa, Harriet is fortunate in having none but comforters about her (II. 541), and champions too. As Mr Selby says indignantly,

Oh! the poor Harriet! a flower of the world! She deserved not to be made a second woman, to the stateliest minx in Italy: But this is my comfort, she is superior to them both. Upon my soul, madam, she is. The man, were he a king, that could prefer another woman to our Harriet, does not deserve her.   (II. 538)

Her last 'trial' is the acceptance of his second-placed love. Sir Charles may explain that 'had I never known Clementina I could have loved [Harriet], and *only* her', but since the fair Italian did in fact gain his affection, he is a rejected man. Harriet's relatives urge her not to think of such notions as divided or second-placed love (III. 10–19), and Greville's vulgar description of Sir Charles as 'another woman's *leavings*' (III. 32) must push her towards acceptance. The surprise revelation that before he went to Italy he told Dr Bartlett 'that I should be much more happy in marriage with the Lady of Selby-house, were she to be induced to honour me with her hand, than it was possible I could be with Lady Clementina' (III. 55), allays her fears, and if Clementina was his first love, Sir Charles' love for Harriet is still a decent '*Widower-Love*'. In a sentence whose halting clauses betray Richardson's unease, the hero declares 'a passion, that would have been, but for one obstacle, which is now removed, as fervent as man ever knew' (III. 57). Sensing still that she is the invader of another's rights, Harriet represents powerfully her anxieties about sexuality, pregnancy and rejection when she dreams she is married, not married, rejected, hiding in holes and corners, dragged out of a subterraneous cavern, turned into an angel of light. A dear little baby is put in her arms, perhaps Lucy's, perhaps Emily's, perhaps Clementina's. As Milton knew, marriage guarantees nothing when it depends on the continuance of love, and if he 'cannot love the poor creature who kneels before you, *that* shall be a cause sufficient with me for a divorce: I desire not to fasten myself on the man who cannot love me' (III. 148).[16] At this delicate crisis in the novel Richardson characteristically subverts his own seriousness by Charlotte's laughter:

Ass and two bundles of hay, Harriet. But my brother is a nobler animal: He won't starve. But I think, in my conscience, he should have you both. There might be a law made, that the case should not be brought into precedent till two such women should be found, and such a man; and all three in the like situation.   (III. 195)

Clementina's arrival in England gives Sir Charles a chance to confirm his choice. 'My Harriet is another Clementina! You are another Harriet!', he says cautiously (III. 343), but signs himself to Harriet 'Wholly yours' (III. 332). Harriet helps herself and him by her instant friendship with Clementina, although as Charlotte shrewdly remarks, Harriet is romantically a 'little tinctured with Heroism' in her sympathy (III. 439), indeed they are 'Heroines both, I suppose; and they are mirrors to each other; each admiring herself in the other. No wonder they are engaged insensibly by a vanity, which carries with it, to each, so generous an appearance; for, all the while, Harriet thinks she is only admiring Clementina; Clementina, that she's applauding Harriet' (III. 418).

Harriet thus forces Sir Charles to declare his preference. Her last flash of independence is in resisting his demand for an early wedding. He, momentarily like Lovelace, has committed a 'pretty piece of deceit' when he has her sign a doubled-down paper to grant his wishes. If he is a plotter, 'thank God you are not a bad man', says Harriet (III. 107). The 'law' though is on his side when he refers her to the arbitration of three family judges who force an earlier day upon her (III. 131). But it has been worth the waiting, as Harriet, repeating the lesson of *Clarissa*, knows. 'What a victim,' she writes, 'must that woman look upon herself to be, who is compelled, or even *over-persuaded*, to give her hand to a man who has no share in her heart?' (II. 347). What she gains from Sir Charles is entry into public life, for if he is 'the best of brothers, friends, landlords, masters, and the bravest and best of men' (I. 303), she is a fellow-heart 'admiring and longing to promote and share in such glorious philanthropy' (I. 389). A princess in everyone's eye (III. 79), she enjoys, when in church, feeling her face glow 'on the whispering that went round. I thought I read in every eye, admiration of him, even through the sticks of some of the Ladies fans' (III. 84). Her wedding is elaborate, her possession of Grandison Hall triumphal, her portrait will be hung among his ancestors, she will bear his children. 'What a happy lot is mine!', she says, rejoicing (III. 287). She has insisted upon her own preference and choice being freely granted, and although Charlotte called her a simpleton for refusing 'a man, an Earl too! in the bloom of his years, 12,000 good pounds a year!' (I. 274), the world is not exactly lost for love when Sir Charles is richer, better, and more benevolent than he.

Harriet marries the perfect man with the full approbation of her relations. The tragedy of *Clarissa* goes rather to the wife of the Harlowesque tyrant Sir Thomas Grandison, a woman for whom a

crown of righteousness is laid up in heaven (I. 318). His two
daughters submit to a tyrant father much more complexly and
realistically portrayed than the absent Mr Harlowe, a father whose
tyranny derives from resentment of their youthful sexuality, their
capacity to supplant him, and the way they make his own wenching
look foolish. Because he 'has the notion riveted in him, which is
common to men of antient families, that daughters are but incum-
brances, and that the son is to be everything', he will give each
of them no more than £5,000 (I. 315). 'Snubbing, chiding, and
studying to find fault with them', he prohibits their correspondence
with their brother. Charlotte, who 'never had any notion of obeying
unreasonable commands', disobeys (I. 321). Scenes of him exercis-
ing his power are, however, defused by their pastness, his interven-
ing death, the league of sympathy between the sisters, and the
humour that allows Charlotte to control them, so that these 'trials'
are never so severe as Clarissa's. Sir Thomas resists the older sister's
marriage because it reminds him of his age, complaining, 'I have
nothing to do but to allot you the fortunes that your lovers, as they
are called, will tell you are necessary to their affairs, and then to
lie me down and die. Your fellows then, with you, will dance over
my grave; and I shall be no more remembred, than if I had never
been – except by your brother' (I. 338):

Both his daughters would now be set a romancing, he supposed. They were,
till now, modest young creatures, he said. Young women should not too
soon be set to look out of themselves for happiness – He had known many
quiet and orderly girls set a madding by the notice of men. He did not
know what business young fellows had to find out qualifications in other
mens daughters, that the parents of those daughters had not given
themselves leisure to discover. A daughter of *his*, he hoped, had not encouraged these discoveries. It was to him but as *yesterday*, when they were
crowing in the arms of their nurses; and now, he supposed, they would
be set a crowing after wedlock. (I. 324)

Early marriages are inconvenient to him, 'a man's children treading
upon his heels, and *shouldering him* with their shoulders: In short,
my Lord, I have an aversion to be called a grandfather, before I
am a *grey* father.' He does not wish to divide his money with his
daughters when he needs it for himself and his son (I. 326), and
he means to make as good a bargain for them, and with them, as
he can (I. 329). With a nasty relish he plans to sell his daughters:

Why, Caroline, you *shall* have a husband, I tell you. I will hasten with
you to the London market. Will you be offer'd at Ranelagh market first?
the concert or breakfasting? – Or shall I shew you at the opera,

or at the play? Ha, ha, hah! – Hold up your head, my amorous girl! You shall stick some of your mother's jewels in your hair, and in your bosom, to draw the eyes of fellows. You must strike at once, while your face is new; or you will be mingled with the herd of women, who prostitute their faces at every polite place. (I. 340–1)

To Lord L.'s objection that as female fortune-hunters sent out purely to save their father's pocket (I. 332), they will find themselves among 'the flocks of single women which croud to Ranelagh and Vaux-hall markets, dressed out to be *cheapened*, not *purchased*' by parents anxious to dispose of these drugs on the market (II. 553), he threatens to disown and beggar them and throw them out of their home. He fears that 'when my ashes are mingled with those of your mother, then may you keep open house in it, and trample under foot the ashes of both', and believes their father's authority is grievous to them: 'They want to shake it off. They find themselves women-grown. They want husbands' (I. 344). But death ends his power to hurt, and the absolute power which Sir Charles inherits he does not abuse.

Unlike the avaricious Harlowes, Sir Charles divides his mother's jewels between his sisters, grants them £10,000 each as a dower (I. 382), and shames his miserly uncle Lord W. into liberality towards his discarded mistress. He protects his ward Emily Jervois' money along with her person, who although young, possessed of £50,000, and theoretically vulnerable to every address, proves prey only to her abandoned mother, 'a termagant, a swearer, a drinker, unchaste' (I. 385). In confrontations with Mrs Jervois and her soldier friends, Major O'Hara and Salmonet, Sir Charles stands Emily's champion where Clarissa had had none. For this young woman, who loves her tutor–guardian as Vanessa loved Swift's Cadenus (I. 231), Richardson in an admission of defeat creates Beauchamp, a man he openly calls 'a second Sir Charles Grandison' (I. 440). Once her former love is redefined as filial reverence and gratitude, she can begin to consider the man so remarkably like Sir Charles.

Olivia warns by contrast against wealthy women who are too soon made their own mistresses. Spoilt, passionate, not averse (being Italian) to drawing a poniard upon Sir Charles (II. 380), she tempts Sir Charles as Potiphar's wife tempted Joseph (Carroll, p. 278). She is humbled and rebuked for her forwardness. What an uncontrollable man she would have been, what a sovereign, says Sir Charles. 'Look into the characters of absolute princes, and see whose, of all those who have sullied royalty, by the violence of their wills, you would have wished to copy.' She promptly surrenders to this 'Prince of a man', for what prince, king, emperor, is so truly great as he (II. 642–5)?

One problem remains: what if the woman is cleverer than her husband? In a world where there are not enough Sir Charles's to go round, Charlotte Grandison, like Jane Austen's Charlotte Lucas, is not granted a hero, and like her settles for comfort rather than joy (II. 264). Her brother laughs unfeelingly that she waits for a man in the clouds (II. 97), but, as she complains, she cannot both save the nation and live in a real world:

What can a woman do, who is addressed by a man of talents inferior to her own? Must she throw away her talents? Must she hide her light under a bushel, purely to do credit to the man? She cannot pick and choose, as men can. She has only her negative; and, if she is desirous to oblige her friends, not always *that*. Yet it is said, Women must not encourage Fops and Fools. They must encourage Men of Sense only. And it is *well* said. But what will they do, if their lot be cast only among Foplings? If the Men of Sense do not offer themselves? And pray, may I not ask, If the taste of the age, among the Men, is not Dress, Equipage, and Foppery? Is the cultivation of the mind any part of their study? The men, in short, are sunk, my dear; and the Women but barely swim. (I. 230)

Sir Charles' solution is simple: 'if you cannot have a man of whose understanding you have an higher opinion than of your own, you should think of one who is likely to allow to yours a superiority' (II. 99). But what about the force of custom? If women are supposed to stand in awe of their husbands, she says sharply, 'is marriage a state of servitude or of freedom to a woman?' (I. 299).

Charlotte is pressed to marry by a brother who loves her, who claims that she is entirely mistress of her own conduct and actions. He will not, says Sir Charles, lay a load upon her free will (I. 402). A previous entanglement, however, proves how much she needs help, when, galled by her father's tyranny, she had 'girlishly wished for Liberty – MATRIMONY and LIBERTY – Girlish connexion! as I have since thought', and ominously surrendered to Captain Anderson the power of father, guardian, and brother all together (I. 406–8).

Her successful suitor Lord G. is, after the *Clarissa* debates, more sympathetically developed than Hickman, even if his character as traveller, connoisseur in antiquities, 'and in those parts of *nice* Knowlege, as I, a woman, call it, with which the Royal Society here, and the learned and polite of other nations, entertain themselves', provokes Charlotte's ridicule (I. 229). She, who still seeks (wrongly) a manly man, thinks slightingly of one with an effeminate shell and china taste. If she marries a fool, she plans to be sovereign ever after. 'What a duce shall a woman marry a man of talents not superior to her own, and forget to reward herself for her condescension?', she says (II. 321). Even on the way to be married she admits she despises him, and she whispers in levity during the service (II. 340–1).

Charlotte lays down conditions for matrimony that are very like Millamant's provisoes in Congreve's *The Way of the World*, Act IV. Millamant refuses to give up her will, pleasure, and liberty, nor will she be called fond names. She will wear what she wants to, write to whomever she likes without interrogation or wry faces, come to dinner when she pleases, and dine in her dressing-room when she is out of humour. Her closet must be inviolate. She must be sole empress of her tea-table, which must never be approached without leave. Wherever she is, Mirabell must always knock before he comes in. 'These articles subscribed, if I continue to endure you a little longer, I may by degrees dwindle into a wife', she says. All these articles are acted out in scenes of Charlotte's marriage, for instance when she demands not to be interrupted in her closet (II. 392), rebukes Lord G. for bolting in with too little ceremony (II. 328), refuses to be a doll or a toy, and resents that he dresses his baby, herself, as a fashion doll (II. 434–47). In these ways she shapes her marriage to protect herself.

Her tormenting of her husband, however, is more like Mrs Sullen's in Farquhar's *The Beaux' Stratagem*. Because Lord G., that unthreatening Solmes, is 'always squatting upon one's cloaths, in defiance of hoop, or distance' (II. 434), she drives him out of the house by pinning an apron on him, and plays the harpsichord to show her own harmoniousness until he dashes his hat down upon it and demolishes it (II. 502). Like Mrs Sullen, too, she applies the language of warfare to her private relationship, as in her 'one struggle for my dying liberty, my dear! – The success of one pitched battle will determine which is to be the general, which the subaltern, for the rest of the campaign. To *dare* to be sullen already!' (II. 359–60). Rebelling against his majesty, she is imperial when he is imperious, and resents it as an insolent act of prerogative when he contracts for a house and makes her 'his chattels, a piece of furniture only, to be removed as any other piece of furniture, or picture, or cabinet, at his pleasure'. She ends cuttingly, 'My Lord, to be sure, has dominion over his bird. He can choose her cage. She has nothing to do, but sit and sing in it' (II. 499–504).

But Charlotte soon finds that Lord G. has more wit, more humour, more good sense and more learning than she ever imagined. She is pregnant, and in a few months' time will be grave as a cat (II. 543–5). From the exercise of real cruelty, when she pretends his mouth is fly-blown from gaping (III. 261), Richardson pulls her back in the revised seventh volume, but not before all the important questions about maistrie, power, and finally courtesy, have been raised. Childbirth makes her solemn, and she wraps her jewels up in cotton, like other women, 'with sighs that perhaps they have worn them for the last time, and doubtful whom they may next adorn' (III. 358). The fine girl she bears is a disappointment to Lord G.'s family, but everyone is confident that she will be 'matronized now. The *mother* must make her a *wife*' (III. 388). In her own words Charlotte stands as 'an example of true conjugal felicity, and an encouragement for girls who venture into the married state, without that prodigious quantity of violent passion, which some hare-brained creatures think an essential of Love', proved when Lord G. breaks in enchanted on a scene of her nursing her child. 'I bowed my face on the smiling infant, who crowed to the pressure of my lip', writes Charlotte, who realises that his submission will ruin her. 'What shall I do – for my Roguery?' (III. 402–3). As Harriet writes, 'Such a Setting-out in matrimony; who would have expected Charlotte to make such a wife, mother, nurse!' (III. 460), but the scenes are pleasantly done.

Three realistic women and a melodramatic Olivia, three practical solutions and an unfinished story. Harriet is locked into a waiting game with the option of a marriage of convenience, Emily is fobbed off with a clone, Charlotte after her entanglement falls back on her brother's choice, and Olivia simply disappears. The Englishwomen at least belong firmly in a mid-eighteenth-century, realistic England, but the most complex woman in the book, the Italian Clementina, is as allegorical and as literary as Clarissa.

Clementina's preference, like hers, is for the spiritual life, and yet in Sir Charles appear such perfections of mind as well as of body that he seems to fulfil all her needs. A Magdalen in love with this god-like, virginal, perfect and unapproachable 'Christ', she is ravaged by her dualism into a madness whose manifestation in her rambling, fragmentary letters inevitably recalls Clarissa. She suppresses her love like Viola (II. 153) because she cannot love a heretic, and she suffers in symbolic martyrdom when bled, crying to Sir Charles, 'do *you* wish to see me wounded? – To see my heart bleeding at my arm, I warrant' (II. 193). Her claim that she goes on God's errand to save a soul when she seeks out Sir Charles (II. 203) is as blatant a self-deception as Harriet's cry of 'gratitude', and when her parents deceive her by their insistence that they do not persuade her, she has to ask Sir Charles to sign a legalistic statement in order to find out truth (II. 207). Sir Charles too calls her love by other names, asking, 'Was not the future happiness of the man she esteemed, the constant, I may say, the *only* object of her cares?' (II. 487). Faced with the paradox of their loving cruelty she becomes mad, raving, and gloomy, and is threatened with the 'Strait Waistcoat' by her cousin Laurana, her next inheritor. Informed that she has free will, she must whisper rebelliously that 'we poor women are not suffered to go any-whither; while men – ' (II. 461).

Told to decide Sir Charles' destiny while knowing what her family want, Clementina admits her love, and in an episode that would be copied by Charlotte Brontë in chapter 32 of *Jane Eyre*, talks of him for one quarter of an hour by her English watch (II. 521). Although the marriage agreement is drawn up to protect Sir Charles' Protestantism (II. 530–2), she uses her free will once she is granted it:

I have *reason* in my request, Camilla, said she. I must not be contradicted, or expostulated with: My head will not bear opposition, at this time. Is it a slight thing for such a poor creature as I have been, and am, to be put out of her course? Am I not to have a meeting with the Chevalier Grandison, on the most important act of my life? My mamma tells me, that I am to be now the mistress of my own will; Don't *you*, Camilla, seek to controul me.   (II. 557)

Allowed to act, Clementina does as her family wants. In a letter to bind them as spoken words never could, she rejects Sir Charles, her tutor, her brother, and her friend, in fear that he will convert her and take her from her country. Suppressing the demands of the body, she begs to be 'God's child, the spouse of my Redeemer only' (II. 564–6).

Now, however, Grandison is the family's choice, and she must be persuaded all over again. In helpless capitulation she says that 'if you will not, if you cannot, set me free; I will obey my friends, and make you as happy as I can', only to have him turn the decision back on her once more (II. 573–4). The contest in generosity is prolonged, but at last she stands firm: she cannot marry a heretic, a man allied to perdition (II. 597).[17] Sir Charles encourages her to reject a man as steady in his own faith as she is in hers, urging her against the veil because in marriage she can serve God better than if she sequestered herself from a world that wants her example (II. 616–19). It is all very reasonable, but Clementina feels the pain:

> She clapt her hands together – He is gone! – O stay, stay, Chevalier
> – And *will* you go? –
> I was in too much emotion to wish to be seen – She hastened after me
> to the stairs – O stay, stay! I have not said half I had to say –
> I returned, and, taking her hand, bowed upon it, to conceal my sen-
> sibility – What further commands, with a faltering voice, has Lady
> Clementina for her Grandison?
> I don't know – But will you, must you, *will* you go?
> I go; I stay; I have no will but yours, madam.   (II. 637)

She writes a proclamation of her renunciation, witnessed as if it were true (III. 165), but the woman who has loved Sir Charles Grandison can never be happy with any other man. The '*more* than compulsion' (III. 60) has started all over again, this time to make her wife to the Count of Belvedere.

This erotic, sympathetic woman often resembles another passionate pupil to a 'father, brother, husband, friend', Pope's Eloisa,[18] who poring over Abelard's letters remembers,

> Thou knows't how guiltless first I met thy flame,
> When Love approach'd me under Friendship's name:
> My fancy form'd thee of Angelick kind,
> Some emanation of th'all beauteous Mind.

Eloisa's idolatrous spirituality recurs in Clementina, together with her black melancholy and the probability of her keeping forbidden fires alight even in a convent, for if Clementina takes the veil, Sir Charles fears that ill will and slander will follow her into the most sacred retirements (III. 428). To avoid profaning a sacrament, that is, marriage against inclination, against justice, against conscience (III. 340–1), she flees to England where she wins Harriet's sup-port. 'Why, taking advantage of her Sex, is such a person to be controuled, and treated as if she were not to have a will; when she has an understanding, perhaps, superior to that of either of her *wilful* brothers?', writes Harriet in friendly indignation (III. 353). Clemen-tina, Clarissa-like, blames herself. She signs the six articles that Sir Charles draws up, and in exchange for an end to compulsion, staying single, and the liberty to choose her own way of life and attendants, promises to forgo the veil (III. 375).

A court of young women debates the matter under the guidance of Mrs Shirley. Kitty picks up the nagging worry of the novel, 'can the woman be happy in a second choice, whose first was Sir Charles Grandison?', to which Mrs Shirley returns the impossible solution, that 'as there is but *one* Sir Charles Grandison in the world, were his scheme of Protestant Nunneries put in execution, all the rest of womankind, who had seen him with distinction, might retire into cloisters' (III. 396). Clementina is pushed towards the Count by a combination of Olivia's hint that she pursues a married man, Harriet's cold, caught on a walk together, her family's wishing eyes and sighing hearts, and her madness being said not to be hereditary (III. 434). So thoroughly beaten that she sees her family's cruel treatment as indulgence (III. 451), Clementina asks only for a year's consideration, and with breath hard-fetched invites her suitor to stay on (III. 449, 441).

As though he had never been part of the problem, Sir Charles imports English specialists to treat the symptoms, merely, of her madness. His attitude is advanced, his toleration of her sensibility, religion and culture Lockeian, and on Clementina's behalf he combats family tyranny, religious oppression, confinement, and torture. But Richardson is honest enough to see that this does not solve the cause of her distress. Half-heartedly he produces the Count of Belvedere: if Sir Charles was Apollo (II. 51), this man is perhaps Apollo Belvedere. Father Marescotti thinks that she will domesticate herself (II. 219), but Richardson dared only hint that she might marry, and claimed in the Conclusion that out of complaisance to his readers he left to them the decision of this important article (III. 468). Meanwhile a little temple marks the special triple friendship, and as Harriet says in relief, 'every thing that *can* be adjusted, is' (III. 455–6). Richardson's readers would not, however, be so satisfied.

Sir Charles is not, like Abelard, thwarted in his potency, but a certain cold rectitude in his dealings with Clementina, together with his known chastity and irresistibility to women,[19] make them not dissimilar. Castration is 'very proper punishment, I ween, for all Libertines', says Charlotte (II. 431), but it is Sir Charles who, though no rake, is virtuous even to chastity because of being a Joseph and a Christ. Richardson tried to brazen out the incompatibility in his models by making Charlotte plead, 'Don't let the Ladies around you, nor the Gentlemen neither, hear this grace supposed to be my brother's. Nobody about us shall for *me*. I would not have my brother made the jest of one Sex, and the aversion of the other; and be thought so singular a young man' (II. 497).[20] But Sir Charles' lack of sexual feeling could well have resulted from

Richardson's commitment, imaginatively, to Abelard and Eloisa's tale.

Clementina is in fact powerful beyond immediate explanation, so much so that she appealed to readers much more than Harriet. Even Richardson found as he wrote that 'she rises upon me', and did not know 'what to do with her, or to fetch up Harriet again, and make her the principal Female character' (Carroll, pp. 194–5). Her attractiveness derives from the spirituality that she shares with Clarissa, as well as from her name, popular among Jacobites after the marriage of James Stuart to Maria Clementina Sobieski in 1719. The proposed compromise about the education of Sir Charles' children by Clementina, which copies that of Charles I and Henrietta Maria (II. 219), inevitably recalls the revolution that followed. England, Richardson seems to be saying, should not marry Catholicism.

Clementina is also striking because of the mythological, literary and Biblical sources that make up her character.[21] As well as being an Eloisa, she is a sacrificial victim who calls herself Iphigenia when blooded (II. 194), and who confronts her oppressors like Lucretia. She reads *Hamlet* (II. 155), and her Ophelia-like struggle between love and duty ends in madness; she carries flowers (II. 524) and attempts suicide by water (II. 246). All these prototypes had appeared in Clarissa, whom she resembles in her madness and her belief that she cannot live long (II. 631). Most obviously, though, she is the woman from the Song of Solomon.

Emotional, impressionistic the Song may be, but many people have read it as realistic. In it a woman loves a man who for his good name is loved by upright men and by virgins. She praises him, though she herself is 'black', and her mother's children are angry with her. They sit together in a fruitful garden, and she is sick of love. Suddenly the lover is gone. She seeks this man 'whom my soul loveth' in the streets of the city until she finds him. 'I held him, and would not let him go, until I had brought him into my mother's house, and into the chamber of her that conceived me.' He calls her 'my sister, my spouse', speaking of her as a fruitful and spiced enclosed garden, chaste as a spring shut up, 'a fountain sealed . . . a fountain of gardens, a well of living waters, and streams from Lebanon'. Again the lover disappears, and again she seeks him. 'My beloved had withdrawn himself; and was gone: my soul failed when he spake: I sought him but I could not find him: I called him, but he gave me no answer.' She is punished by watchmen who 'smote me, they wounded me; the keepers of the walls took away my veil from me. I charge you . . . if ye find my beloved, that ye tell him, that I am sick of love.' She praises the lover as her 'beloved, her friend'. To him she is 'my dove, my undefiled . . . the only one of her mother . . . the choice one of her that bare her'. She invites him into the vineyards, wishing that 'thou wert as my brother, that sucked the breasts of my mother! When I should find thee without, I would kiss thee; yea, I should not be despised. I would lead thee, and bring thee into my mother's house, who would instruct me.' She leans on her beloved as they come up from the wilderness, and since her love is stronger than death, many waters cannot quench it, neither can the floods drown it. The Song ends in indecision, with the woman again calling to her beloved.

Clementina's story paraphrases all these events. Since she too is sick of love for a man that everyone admires, her 'brother' and her friend, she identifies herself openly with the woman of the Canticles when she copies out lines that apply to Sir Charles and herself (II. 247). She loses him several times and restlessly wanders about to find the one whom 'my Soul loveth' (II. 565), she praises him, she leans on him in the garden (II. 632), she meets him in her mother's house. Persecuted, confined and wounded by her brothers and relatives, she blames herself for her pride in loving him, sees herself as despised (II. 207), and acquiesces in her punishments. The loved only daughter of her mother, she knows love but chooses chastity, just as Lucretia was pure though ravished. Deprived of the wish to take the veil, she seeks Sir Charles in England, then flees to her mother in shame for what she has done. Her fidelity figured in her embroidery of Noah's Ark and the rising deluge (III. 158), she ends the book still loving, still yearning.

Allegorically, Clementina's *hortus conclusus* with its fruits, spices and oranges, where the lovers meet,[22] is an emblem of the Church yearning for union with the Redeemer. The mysticism of this innocent visionary, Clementina (II. 296), her *contemptus mundi*, her enthusiasm, martyrdom and sainthood (III. 351), her constant preference for a union of souls to a temporal union, her desire to be the spouse of her Redeemer only – all these appear in her letter renouncing Sir Charles (II. 564–7). Her appeal, 'I am in the midst of briars and thorns – Lend me, lend me, your extricating hand; and conduct me into the smooth and pleasant path, in which you at first found me walking with undoubting feet' (II. 612). resembles the emblem of grace rescuing the spouse from the wilderness. The heat of her home, Italy, reads allegorically as the heat of passion that made the woman of the Canticle black, for commentaries on the Song explained that the woman had been burned by the sun for tending a vineyard not her own, just as Clementina is punished for loving a foreigner. The sun stands for justice, and here the allegory extends to Sir Charles, the just man from whose eye a dazzling sun-beam seems to play (III. 213). He is just, he is wise, he is 'a Prince of the Almighty's creation' (II. 236), he is the sun of the New Covenant. By such a reading Sir Charles is the Redeemer with whom the Spouse, Mary or Eve, longs to unite her soul. Solomon espouses someone else in the Song, and Clementina too encourages her Solomon to find another bride (II. 617).

When Richardson introduces a second heroine so richly charged with erotic and religious significances she nearly sinks his book. He is simply engaged with her as he is not with Harriet. To redress this dangerous imbalance he recalls Sir Charles to Harriet in the same way, when she dreams that Italy was 'a dreary wild, covered with snow, and pinched with frost: England, on the contrary, was a country glorious to the eye; gilded with a sun not too fervid; the air perfumed with odours, wafted by the most balmy Zephyrs from orange-trees, citrons, myrtles, and jasmines' (III. 149). This means that Clementina's love is a desert, a waste-land, while hers is the garden of the Spouse, temperate, fruitful, stirred by spiced winds, a very English Eden. Not Clementina but Harriet is now the Spouse appropriate for the Solomon, the Christ, the god-like man who is Sir Charles Grandison.

In *Clarissa* Richardson had managed to combine the powerfully allegorical and the realistic, the eternal and the quotidian. In *Grandison*, like so much else, they are separated out. The raised aspect of Clementina, mistress of the Psalmist, is hard to reconcile with the sublunary world of England to which she comes, while the heroic and exemplary aspects of Sir Charles prove too high for his mundane life. This hero unhappily bestrides two worlds, as Richardson's division of his characters into 'Men, Women, and Italians' would suggest.

Johnson was not wrong, however, when he told Richardson that he had above all other men the art of improving on himself.[23] The generosity, ambition, tolerance and inventiveness of *Grandison* communicate a vision of an ideal world, where, if power and hierarchy must still remain entrenched, reasonable men turn their privilege to good purposes, and women ask for and receive friendship and trust, in marriage.

Occasions for all to be great occur in such a world. Heroism is no longer defined as martial barbarism but as something domestic and copiable. By examples from a whole range of his society, merchants, aristocrats, pedants, fops, women to fifty from fifteen, he shows how heroism may be achieved. Emily is heroic to give up Sir Charles (III. 323), Lucy Selby is heroic to conquer a first love (III. 437), Clementina's sacrifice wins her a martyr's palm (III. 351). When Sir Charles, instead of accepting a challenge, chooses 'the true heroism' of Christianity which is meekness, moderation, and humility (I. 263), he appears to Harriet in a 'much more shining light than an hero would have done, returning in a triumphal car covered with laurels, and dragging captive princes at its wheels'. How much more glorious a character is that of ' *The Friend of Mankind* than that of *The Conqueror of Nations!*' (II. 70); what is the 'boasted character of most of those who are called HEROES, to the unostentatious merit of a TRULY GOOD MAN?', writes Harriet (III. 462). In answer to the general depravity of his times Richardson proposes simply, optimistically, a change of heart. Blake, the heir to many seventeenth-century ideas, would have recognised this paradise within, this change in men's thinking that is the true mark of the millennium. It is not merely fortuitous that Sir Charles brings about the conversion of at least one Jew (I. 254), nor that his home, Colnebrook, is the site of a famous Digger colony,[24] for in this book Blake's arbitrary Nobodaddy, who stalked the pages of *Clarissa*, is transformed into a gentle man. George Eliot, at least, was satisfied, and thought the morality perfect.[25]

When Sir Charles returns to England and to Harriet, Aunt Eleanor dreams of 'the music of the spheres, heaven, and joy, and festivity' (II. 655), for as Charlotte perceives, the other characters are mere 'Satellites to the Planets', Sir Charles and Harriet (III. 224). In the spacious firmament of Addison's great hymn, the planets revolve likewise about their benevolent and impartial sun:

> In Reason's ear they all rejoice,
> And utter forth a glorious Voice,
> For ever singing as they shine,
> 'The hand that made us is Divine'.

In *Night Thoughts*, Richardson's favourite poem by his friend Edward Young, these planets reciprocally afford an emblem of millennial love (IX. 703). So too in *Grandison* he provided a vision which was indeed the completion of his whole plan, an ordered universe revolving about Sir Charles.

Samuel Richardson had told of Pamela, who by the force of

reasonable words rose from among the dispossessed to become moon to her husband's sun, and of Clarissa, comet on a disastrous path, whose brief life exposed the temptations of Anti-Christ. Now he ended his career with Sir Charles, a man who by sheer force of example holds in paradisal harmony his house, his country and his brave new world. In all fairness he could not have been asked to do more.

Notes

Introduction

1. My understanding of millennial ideas has been drawn largely from Norman Cohn, *The Pursuit of the Millennium* (1970), Charles Webster, *The Great Instauration: Science, Medicine, and Reform, 1626–1660* (1975), Christopher Hill, *Antichrist in Seventeenth-Century England* (1971), and *The World Turned Upside Down: Radical Ideas during the English Revolution* (1972). Milton's prose and poetry are also of course indispensable sources. For Richardson's sympathy with Bacon, the greatest of the Moderns, see my 'Learning and Genius in *Sir Charles Grandison*', in *Studies in the Eighteenth Century*, 4, ed. R. F. Brissenden and J. C. Eade (Canberra, 1979), 167–91. John Locke he praised in the continuation to *Pamela* (IV. 110–11).

2. Mary Astell's constant theme is also the recovery of marriage and knowledge from their present corruptions, by means of reasonable words. Her treatise on marriage ends with a vision of millennial love, as does, incidentally, Judy Chicago's account of *The Dinner Party: A Symbol of our Heritage* (New York, 1979). A great deal of feminist theory is implicitly millenarian.

   Although Richardson could have encountered Astell through his friend Mrs Chapone (Florence M. Smith, *Mary Astell*, Columbia University Press, 1916, p. 165), he may well have read her work earlier than that. He did not correspond with Chapone until 1750 (Eaves and Kimpel, p. 351), and, as A. H. Upham long ago pointed out, the personal similarities of Clarissa to Astell are striking, even to the coffin which the dying Astell wrote upon. See 'Mary Astell as a Parallel for Richardson's Clarissa', *Modern Language Notes*, 28 (1913), 103–5.

3. Ian Donaldson's *The Rapes of Lucretia: A Myth and its Transformations* (Oxford, 1982) is essential reading for a sympathetic understanding of Richardson.

4. See my introduction to John Duncombe's *The Feminiad* (1754), Augustan Reprint Society No. 207 (1981). Ellen Moers, in the *New York Review of Books* (10 February 1972), 27–31, first called Richardson a women's liberator. Rae Blanchard's 'Richard Steele and the Status of Women', *Studies in Philology*, 26 (July, 1929), 325–55, and Dorothy Gardiner's remarkable *English Girlhood at School: A Study of Women's Education through Twelve Centuries* (Oxford, 1929) are particularly full and helpful on the matter.

5. *Some Reflections upon Marriage*, 4th edition (1730), repr. New York (1970), p. 106.

6. Janet Todd, in *Women's Friendship in Literature* (New York, 1980) provides a modern feminist reading of Richardson; Florian Stuber studies Mr Harlowe in his 'On Fathers and Authority in *Clarissa*', *Studies in English Literature*, 25, 3 (1985), 557–74, and Morris Golden compares the politics of *Clarissa* to the real world in 'Public Context and Imagining Self in *Clarissa*', *ibid.*, 575–98.

7. Samuel Richardson, *'Clarissa': Preface, Hints of Prefaces, and Postscript*, ed. R. F. Brissenden, Augustan Reprint Society No. 103 (1964), p. 14. See also Eaves and Kimpel, p. 556.

8. *cf.* Mary Astell, *A Serious Proposal to the Ladies for the Advancement of the True and Greatest Interest*, 4th edition (1701), repr. New York (1970), p. 38.

9. In MS the letter reads 'Carvers', that is people who choose for themselves, not 'Carpers'.

10. John Preston, in *The Created Self: The Reader's Role in Eighteenth-Century Fiction* (1970), also discusses how Richardson 'created' his readers.

11. See Eaves and Kimpel, p. 535. For a more extensive discussion of the relationship between the two men, see my 'Samuel Johnson, Samuel Richardson, and the Dial-Plate', *British Journal for Eighteenth-Century Studies*, in press.

12. See Anna Seward, *Variety: A Collection of Essays* (1788), p. 215.

13. Carroll, pp. 141, 157, 316.

14. *The Letters of Samuel Johnson*, ed. R. W. Chapman (Oxford, 1952), letter 49.2.

1 *Pamela*

1. Richard Steele, to whom Richardson may well be indebted for much of his thinking about ideal relationships, attacked the double standard of frailty for men and women. Women's dishonour is proclaimed, he says, while 'he who did the wrong sees no difference in the reception he meets with' (*Guardian* No. 45, quoted in Blanchard, 'Richard Steele and the Status of Women', p. 349).

2. See also Katharine Rogers, 'Sensitive Feminism versus Conventional Sympathy: Richardson and Fielding on Women', *Novel*, 9 (1976), 256–70, and *Feminism in Eighteenth-Century England* (Illinois, 1982). Antony J. Hassall, in 'Women in Richardson and Fielding', *Novel*, 14.2 (1981), 168–74, defends Fielding against her charges of chauvinism.

3. *Clarissa*, p. 83, and *Grandison*, III. 9.

4. *cf.* Astell, 'Men are possessed of all Places of Power, Trust and Profit, they make Laws and exercise the Magistracy . . . which by the strongest Logick in the World, gives them the best Title to every Thing they please to claim as their Prerogative' (*Marriage*, p. 123).

5. Although written before the Glorious Revolution of 1688, Locke's two treatises have usually been read as a justification for it. I have used Peter Laslett's edition (Cambridge University Press, 1960, reprinted Mentor Books, New York, 1965), based on Locke's annotated copy, but

the differences from the book commonly read in the eighteenth century are not significant for my purposes. Richardson's friend Hester Mulso Chapone, for instance, knew the *Two Treatises* well enough to quote from them on the limits of a daughter's obedience. See Rogers' book, *op. cit.*, p. 81.

6. *cf.* Astell, who also argues that the subordination of women was a prediction not a command, and that the service a woman is obliged to pay any man 'is only a Business by the Bye, just as it may be any Man's Business and Duty to keep Hogs' (*Marriage*, pp. 108, 99).

7. See Laslett, p. 83.

8. *Poems upon Several Occasions*, 2 vols. (1748, 1751), II. 67, 10.

9. Ed. J. W. Gough (Oxford, 1976), p. 129.

10. *The Rapes of Lucretia*, pp. 59–61.

11. *cf.* the Countess of Winchilsea writing of women poets, 'like State Pris'ners, Pen and Ink deny'd' (*The Poems of Anne Countess of Winchilsea*, ed. Myra Reynolds (Chicago, 1903), p. 45).

12. *cf.* Steele's *Tender Husband*, 'tho' our Amours can't furnish out a Romance, they'll make a very pretty Novel' (IV. ii).

13. See Laslett, p. 130.

14. *Marriage*, p. 107. Rogers says that Astell was one of the few people to apply Locke's libertarian teaching to the family (*op. cit.*, p. 74). Richardson was of course another.

15. Mark Kinkead-Weekes has pointed out that she is tempted for forty days and forty nights. See his introduction to the Everyman edition, repr. in *Samuel Richardson: A Collection of Critical Essays*, ed. John Carroll (New Jersey, 1969), pp. 20–7.

16. D. C. Muecke comments on the fairy-tale aspects of *Pamela* in 'Beauty and Mr. B.', *Studies in English Literature*, 7 (1967), 467–74.

17. Quoted in Bernard Kreissman, *Pamela–Shamela: A Study of the Criticisms, Burlesques, Parodies, and Adaptations of Richardson's 'Pamela'* (Nebraska, 1960), p. 24.

18. II. 111, *Marriage*, p. 128.

19. See Gough's introduction, p. xxxvii.

20. *cf.* Astell, who argues that only a queen would not have to obey her footman if she were married to him (*Marriage*, p. 97).

21. See William Shenstone, quoted in A. D. McKillop, *Samuel Richardson: Printer and Novelist* (North Carolina, 1936, repr. 1960), p. 82. Ellen Moers remarks that talented women read *Pamela* as 'Writing Rewarded' in her *New York Review of Books* article.

2 From *Pamela* to *Clarissa*

1. See Peter Sabor, 'The Cooke-Everyman Edition of *Pamela*', *The Library*, 5th series, 32.4 (1977), 360–6.

2. See Eaves and Kimpel, chapter 7, for the reaction to *Pamela* and Richardson's consequent revisions.

3. *Correspondence of Samuel Richardson* (1804), I. lxxvii. See also Carroll, p. 45.
4. See also Owen Jenkins, 'Richardson's *Pamela* and Fielding's "Vile Forgeries" ', *Philological Quarterly*, 44 (1965), 200–10.
5. R. F. Brissenden's edition, p. 3. Peter Sabor charts Richardson's growing doubts about his first novel in 'Samuel Richardson's Correspondence and his Final Revision of *Pamela*', *Transactions of the Samuel Johnson Society of the Northwest*, 12 (1981), 114–31.
6. This is close to Astell, *Marriage*, pp. 61, 124, 7, for instance.
7. Donald Ball, '*Pamela II*: A Primary Link in Richardson's Development as a Novelist', *Modern Philology*, 65 (1967–8), 334–42, makes some of the same points as I do.
8. See Frederick W. Hilles, 'The Plan of *Clarissa*', in Carroll's collection of essays, pp. 80–91.

3   The extraordinary woman

1. See *Grandison*, III. 480, and Bathsua Makin, 'A Learned Woman is thought to be a Comet, that bodes Mischief, when ever it appears', *An Essay to Revive the Ancient Education of Gentlewomen* (1675), Augustan Reprint Society No. 202 (1980), ed. Paula L. Barbour, p. 3. Johnson's *Dictionary* cites 'eccentric' as a new usage. After Halley, with the help of Newton's law of gravity, had calculated the orbit of the famous comet, due again in 1758, the word came to be applied to unusual, that is, intellectual or outspoken women. The word seems rapidly to have become pejorative. Sometimes Halley's comet has been brighter even than the moon.
2. *cf.* Robert Herrick's 'Knock at a Starre with my exalted Head', in 'The bad season makes the Poet sad'. Page numbers belong to the modern-ised first edition, ed. Angus Ross (Viking and Penguin, 1985), with occasional volume and page references to the third edition text of the Everyman edition.
3. Christopher Hill's 'Clarissa Harlowe and her Times', reprinted in Carroll's collection of essays, is essential reading on this aspect of the novel. See also Robert D. Moynihan, 'Clarissa and the Enlightened Woman as Heroine', *Journal of the History of Ideas*, 26.1 (1975), 159–66.
4. Richardson uses the name 'Filmer' for a minor character, p. 406.
5. Ian Donaldson also discusses the various meanings of 'will' in *The Rapes of Lucretia*, pp. 68–73.
6. *cf.* Astell, 'he may call himself her Slave a few Days, but it is only in order to make her his for the rest of his Life'; and, a woman makes a man 'the greatest Compliment in the World when she condescends to take him *for Better for Worse*. She puts her self intirely in his Power, leaves all that is dear to her, her Friends and Family, to espouse his Interests and follow his Fortune, and makes it her Business and Duty to please him!' What a brute must a man be, she adds, who betrays that trust (*Marriage*, pp. 30, 49–50).

7. *cf.* Millamant, who says, 'an illiterate man's my aversion', and 'Ah! to marry an ignorant that can hardly read or write!' (William Congreve, *The Way of the World*, Act III). Emma is equally scathing about Mr Martin, but quite wrong, in Jane Austen's *Emma*.

8. *cf.* Lady Wishfort's 'inhumanly savage; exceeding the barbarity of a Muscovite husband', in *The Way of the World*, Act V.

9. For Richardson's knowledge of this scene in *Romeo and Juliet* see Carroll, p. 104.

10. See Jean H. Hagstrum, *Sex and Sensibility: Ideal and Erotic Love from Milton to Mozart* (Chicago, 1980), for a valuable discussion of *eros* and *agape*.

4 King Lovelace

1. See John Carroll, 'Richardson at Work: Revisions, Allusions, and Quotations in *Clarissa*', *Studies in the Eighteenth Century*, 2, ed. R. F. Brissenden (Canberra, 1970), pp. 53–71, and 'Lovelace as Tragic Hero', *University of Toronto Quarterly*, 42.1 (1972), 14–25; Gillian Beer, 'Richardson, Milton, and the Status of Evil', *Review of English Studies*, n.s. 19 (1968), 261–70; and Yvonne Noble, '*Clarissa*: Paradise Irredeemably Lost', *Studies on Voltaire and the Eighteenth Century*, 154 (1976), 1529–45.

2. At the end of his life, Lovelace the poet lodged in the obscene holes and garrets where Belford declares all rakes will be reduced to ending their days (III. 483). See *Dictionary of National Biography*.

3. Mrs Bracegirdle excited incredulous surprise for her resistance to such assailants of her virtue as Lord Lovelace and Congreve, who wrote of her mixed kindness and coldness rather as Lovelace writes of Clarissa. When she politely but firmly returned the daily messages of Lord Lovelace, her virtue was rewarded by a purse of 800 guineas.

   Many of her roles could have contributed to Richardson's conception of Clarissa. Congreve created Millamant for her, for instance, and she also played the child in Otway's *The Orphan*, Iphigenia, Portia in *The Merchant of Venice*, Desdemona, Cordelia, Ophelia, Portia in *Julius Caesar*, Lavinia in Rowe's *Fair Penitent*, Statira in Lee's *The Rival Queens, or Alexander the Great*, and Isabella, the virginal woman whom Angelo tries to seduce, in *Measure for Measure*. See Margaret Anne Doody, *A Natural Passion: A Study of the Novels of Samuel Richardson* (Oxford, 1974), pp. 108–20, 145–7, McKillop, pp. 149–52, and John Dussinger, 'Richardson's Tragic Muse', *Philological Quarterly*, 46.i (1967), 18–33, for possible dramatic influences.

   The darling of the theatre, Mrs Bracegirdle made her last appearance in 1709, just when Richardson was an impressionable young theatregoer and apprentice. For further information see Philip H. Highfill Jr., Kalman A. Burnim, and Edward A. Langhans, *A Biographical Dictionary of Actors, Actresses, Musicians, Dancers, Managers, and Other Stage Personnel in London, 1660–1800* (Carbondale and Edwardsville, 1973–), vol. 2.

4. See *The Complete Works of Thomas Shadwell*, ed. Montague Summers, 5 vols. (1927).
5. An image from Aphra Behn's *The False Count: or, A New Way to Play an old Game* (1682), IV. ii.
6. 'Jew' was revised to 'Turk'. See Angus Ross's note, p. 1518.
7. Astell says very similar things about 'the low concerns of an Animal Life', in *Serious Proposal*, p. 158. Belford here sounds very like another reformed rake, John Donne, who also wrote of the difficult relation between mind and body. In *The Extasie* he used the example of modest violets – like those on Clarissa's dress – to explain how chastity and propagation might be reconciled. Richardson may well have known something of the poet, whose statue stood in its shroud in St Paul's near his home.
8. See Jean Gagen, *The New Woman: Her Emergence in English Drama (1600–1730)* (New York, 1954), chapter 11.
9. Oddly enough, Lovelace here echoes the famous arguments of Heloise against marriage, just as later he will imagine Clarissa rising up to heaven in the way that Heloise imagines Abelard abandoning her. See D. W. Robertson, *Abelard and Heloise* (New York, 1972), pp. 53, 198.
10. Lovelace mentions Mandeville's *The Fable of the Bees, or, Private Vices Public Benefits* (1714, enlarged 1723, Part II, 1729), p. 847; *cf.* Astell on the 'Engines' and 'Mine' of the obsequious man, in *Marriage*, p. 82. Margaret Anne Doody links him to the villain–heroes of Restoration tragedy in *A Natural Passion*, chapter 5, and Ian Donaldson remarks on his persistent self-Romanising compared with Clarissa's Christianity, in *The Rapes of Lucretia*, pp. 75–6.
11. In his own person Richardson said similar things about the dangers of militarism in classical times, without using them to legitimise tyranny as Lovelace does here. See my 'Learning and Genius in *Sir Charles Grandison*'.
12. Here Richardson, a successful apprentice himself, probably remembered the last two prints of Hogarth's series, *Industry and Idleness* (1747), which show the idle apprentice jolting off to the gallows in a cart, and the industrious one snug in his Lord Mayor's coach. This swarming scene in black and white is very similar to his friend's engravings.
13. Plenty and her twins appear in a fresco at Versailles, for instance. See also the twins at the end of Milton's *Comus*.
14. *cf.* Astell's question, to whom do women owe subjection when they have lost their master, 'Do we then fall as Strays, to the first who finds us?' (*Marriage*, p. 124).
15. *cf.* the sadistic cruelty of Ben Jonson's emblem for Avaritia and Luxuria, Sir Epicure Mammon, who fantasises about eating 'the swelling unctuous paps / Of a fat pregnant sow, newly cut off, / Dress'd with an exquisite and poignant sauce', in *The Alchemist*, II. i. Richardson's detail of boys putting out the eyes of birds with burning knitting

needles, Hogarth images in his first stage of cruelty but not in the preliminary sketch. Who then was inspired by whom in 1751, when Hogarth published his revised engravings, and Richardson his revised third edition?

16. Marijke Rudnik-Smalbraak particularly explores this recurrent image.
17. 'Bashful' is an adjective that Richardson used of himself (Carroll, p. 231).
18. Clarissa is called Gloriana on pp. 418, 542, 554, 672, for instance.
19. John Carroll, in 'Richardson at Work', points out that for *Clarissa* Richardson chose printing ornaments of Europa and the bull.
20. From Horace's *Odes*, IV. 2.

5 Death and the maiden

1. Donaldson remarks that Lucretia suffered dishonour, but Tarquin damnation, in *The Rapes of Lucretia*, pp. 52–3.
2. See Rita Goldberg, *Sex and Enlightenment: Women in Richardson and Diderot* (Cambridge, 1984), pp. 118–19.
3. Kinkead-Weekes' reading of the fragments is particularly fine, in *Samuel Richardson: Dramatic Novelist* (London, 1973), chapter 7.
4. See Angus Ross's note to letter 260.
5. Margaret Anne Doody's book reproduces a contemporary print, and mentions Hogarth's *South Sea Bubble*.
6. *cf.* the Roman hero Marcus Atilius Regulus, a consul whose Carthaginian captors put him to death in a chest lined with nails. See Donaldson, *The Rapes of Lucretia*, p. 139.
7. Astell argues similarly that if Cato chose death to escape the insults of a triumphant conqueror, 'can it be thought that an ignorant weak Woman should have Patience to bear a continual Outrage and Insolence all the Days of her Life?' (*Marriage*, p. 63).
8. Donaldson says that this commonplace of Greek and Roman thought was often used by Christian writers (*The Rapes of Lucretia*, p. 33).

6 Clarissa's will

1. *cf.* Astell's sardonic question as to how a 'refractory Woman' can possibly

believe him Wise and Good, who by a thousand Demonstrations convinces her, and all the World, of the contrary? Did the bare Name of Husband confer Sense on a Man, and the meer being in Authority infallibly qualify him for Government, much might be done. But since a wise Man and a Husband are not Terms convertible, and how loth soever one is to own it, Matter of Fact won't allow us to deny, that the Head many times stands in need of the Inferior's Brains to manage it, she must beg leave to be excus'd from such high Thoughts of her Sovereign, and if she submits to his Power, it is not so much Reason as Necessity that compels her. (*Marriage*, p. 61)

2. See B. C. Southam, 'Jane Austen and *Clarissa*', *Notes and Queries*, n.s. 10 (1963), 191–2.
3. *cf.* the 'Azure Robe' that like a celestial canopy is 'pounc't with Stars', in Robert Herrick's poem, 'Julia's Petticoat'.
4. Colonel Charteris was a well-known rake. See Angus Ross's note, p. 1525.

7 To *Grandison* and after

1. See Eaves and Kimpel, chapter 10.
2. See Eaves and Kimpel, pp. 338, 295.
3. See Eaves and Kimpel, 'The Composition of *Clarissa* and its Revision before Publication', *PMLA*, 83 (1968), 416–28.
4. See *Samuel Richardson, 'Clarissa': Preface, Hints of Prefaces, and Postscript*.
5. Edited with an introduction by Dimiter Daphinoff (Bern, 1982).
6. *Hints of Prefaces*, p. 13.
7. *Hints of Prefaces*, pp. 3–4. See also Carroll, p. 92.
8. Mark Kinkead-Weekes believes that Richardson was responding to criticism in his revisions, in '*Clarissa* Restored?', *Review of English Studies*, n.s. 10 (1959), 156–71, an argument which Shirley van Marter qualifies at least as far as the majority of them is concerned, in 'Richardson's Revisions of *Clarissa* in the Second Edition', *Studies in Bibliography*, 26 (1973), 107–32, and 'Richardson's Revisions of *Clarissa* in the Third and Fourth Editions', *SB*, 28 (1975), 119–52.
9. See however Michael Neill's 'Heroic Heads and Humble Tails: Sex, Politics, and the Restoration Comic Rake', *The Eighteenth Century: Theory and Interpretation*, 24.2 (1983), 115–39, which indicates that in the drama the process of separation had already begun.
10. For a full account, see my unpublished PhD thesis, '*Sir Charles Grandison* and the Little Senate: The relation between Samuel Richardson's correspondence and his last novel' (University of London, 1968).
11. *The Letters to Gilbert White . . . from . . . John Mulso*, ed. Rashleigh Holt-White (1907), letter 25.
12. See the introduction to *Grandison*, p. ix.
13. For a detailed account of the affair see my article 'The Reviser Observed: The Last Volume of *Sir Charles Grandison*', *Studies in Bibliography*, 29 (1976), 1–31.
14. *The Letters of Samuel Johnson*, ed. R. W. Chapman (Oxford, 1952), letter 51.1.
15. See the note on the text in the O.E.N. *Grandison*.

8   Men, Women, and Italians: *The History of Sir Charles Grandison*

1. Mary Astell's discussion of marriage also ends with a millennial vision of the wolf lying down with the lamb, from Isaiah xi.6.
2. Grandison Hall may be modelled on Dryden's great house in Northamptonshire, Canons Ashby. It is a tempting but unproven theory that Richardson wrote part of *Grandison* there, as the National Trust guidebook says. Some similarities do appear to exist.
3. See R. S. Crane, 'Suggestions towards a Genealogy of the "Man of Feeling" ', *English Literary History*, 1 (1934), 205–30, and John Dussinger, 'Richardson's "Christian Vocation" ', *Papers on Language and Literature*, 3 (1967), 3–19.
4. See Geoffrey Keynes, *A Bibliography of William Blake* (New York, 1921), p. 64.
5. Richardson's own international connections as printer and author were wide. See for instance his letter to Alexis Claude Clairaut (Carroll, pp. 236–8).
6. As Margaret Anne Doody points out, Viscount Grandison was a leading Royalist (*A Natural Passion*, p. 249), and 'grandisonus' means 'high-sounding'.
7. *The Mill on the Floss*, I. iv; *Grandison* I. 359.
8. *The Reason of Church Government*, in *Milton's Prose*, ed. M. W. Wallace (London, 1959), p. 142.
9. For other references to Sir Charles as the sun, see III. 132, 213, 227.
10. See my 'Learning and Genius in *Sir Charles Grandison*'.
11. *cf.* Astell, 'since GOD has given Women as well as Men intelligent Souls, why should they be forbidden to improve them?' (*Serious Proposal*, p. 18).
12. Astell remarks that every man is not superior to every woman, in *Marriage*, p. 97.
13. Steele thought similarly that the difference in men's and women's souls was the result of differing bodies, education, and employment. See Blanchard, p. 331, and *Tatler* No. 172. Boswell, however, thought the idea of sexual equality in heaven 'too ambitious', in *Life of Johnson*, ed. R. W. Chapman and J. D. Fleeman (Oxford, 1970), p. 944.
14. The name Mrs Eggleton probably came from a well-known actress. See Eaves and Kimpel, p. 47.
15. See Jean H. Hagstrum, *Sex and Sensibility: Ideal and Erotic Love from Milton to Mozart*.
16. *cf.* Farquhar's *The Beaux' Stratagem*, III. iii.

    SULLEN One flesh! rather two carcasses joined unnaturally together.
    MRS SULLEN Or rather a living soul coupled to a dead body.
17. Milton argued in his divorce tracts that marriage to an idolatrous heretic was a legitimate cause for separation.
18. For a parlour discussion of Abelard and Eloisa see Carroll, p. 327.
19. See D. W. Robertson, *Abelard and Heloise* (New York, 1972).

20. Richardson seems here to remember Wycherley's Horner, in *The Country Wife*, whose feigning of impotence is received in just this way.
21. This section is reprinted by generous permission of the editor, from ' "As if they had been living friends": *Sir Charles Grandison* into *Mansfield Park*', *Bulletin of Research in the Humanities*, 83.iii (Autumn, 1980), 360–405.
22. Here I draw upon Stanley Stewart's *The Enclosed Garden: The Tradition and the Image in Seventeenth-century Poetry* (Madison, 1966).
23. *Letters of Samuel Johnson*, No. 49.2.
24. See Hill, *The World Upside Down*, p. 101.
25. *The George Eliot Letters*, ed. Gordon S. Haight (New Haven, 1954–5), I. 240.

Further Reading

Pamela (1740–1), *Clarissa* (1747–8) and *Sir Charles Grandison* (1753–4) were frequently reprinted and often revised, sometimes extensively: see William Merritt Sale, *Samuel Richardson: A Bibliographical Record of his Literary Career with Historical Notes* (1936, repr. Hampden, Connecticut, 1969). Several abridgements of *Clarissa* exist.

Until recently the standard edition has been the Shakespeare Head edition of 1929–31, now superseded by the first edition of *Pamela* ed. T. C. Duncan Eaves and Ben D. Kimpel (Boston, 1971) and the 1801 edition ed. Peter Sabor and Margaret Anne Doody (Middlesex and New York, 1980), the first edition of *Clarissa* ed. Angus Ross (Harmondsworth and New York, 1985), and the first edition of *Sir Charles Grandison* ed. Jocelyn Harris (London, New York, and Toronto, 1972, repr. 1986).

Anna Laetitia Barbauld's edition of *The Correspondence of Samuel Richardson*, 6 vols. (London, 1804) is still the fullest, but John Carroll's *Selected Letters of Samuel Richardson* (Oxford, 1964) prints most of the important letters, with notes and commentary.

Alan Dugald McKillop's pioneering biographical and critical account, *Samuel Richardson: Printer and Novelist* (North Carolina, 1936, repr. 1960) is complemented by William Merritt Sale's *Samuel Richardson: Master Printer* (Ithaca, New York, 1950). T. C. Duncan Eaves' and Ben D. Kimpel's *Samuel Richardson: A Biography* (Oxford, 1971), being comprehensive, is indispensable.

Richard Gordon Hannaford's *Samuel Richardson: An Annotated Bibliography of Critical Studies* (New York and London, 1980) charts swings of opinion up to 1974. John Carroll provides useful outlines of criticism to the early seventies in *The English Novel: Select Critical Guides*, ed. A. E. Dyson (London, 1974) and *Samuel Richardson: A Collection of Critical Essays* (New Jersey, 1969), Mark Kinkead-Weekes tackles some of the wilder approaches in his *Samuel Richardson: Dramatic Novelist* (London, 1973), and Rita Goldberg examines recent criticism in *Sex and Enlightenment: Women in Richardson and Diderot* (Cambridge, 1984).

Kinkead-Weekes' close reading, and Margaret Anne Doody's establishment of literary, theological and artistic contexts in *A Natural Passion: A Study of the Novels of Samuel Richardson* (Oxford, 1974), were both pioneering in their generous celebration of Richardson's achievements. Ian Watt in *The Rise of the Novel: Studies in Defoe, Richardson, and Fielding* (London, 1957, repr. 1963) demonstrates his realism; Robert Adams Day in *Told in Letters: Epistolary Fiction before Richardson* (Ann Arbor, 1966), and John J. Richetti in *Popular Fiction before Richardson: Narrative Patterns 1700–1739* (Oxford, 1969) provide valuable background information. Donald L. Ball's *Samuel Richardson's Theory of Fiction* (The Hague, 1971) and Elizabeth Bergen Brophy's *Samuel Richardson: The Triumph of Craft* (Knoxville, Tennessee, 1974) show the consciousness of Richardson's artistry, Ira Konigsberg's *Samuel Richardson and the Dramatic Novel* (Lexington, 1968) his use of drama. Morris Golden's *Richardson's Characters* (Ann Arbor, 1963) and Cynthia Griffin Wolff's *Samuel Richardson and the Eighteenth-Century Puritan Character* (Hampden, Connecticut, 1972) explore the books psychologically, the latter within a context explained by Levin L. Schücking in *Die Familie in Puritanismus* (Leipzig, 1929) trans. Brian Battershaw (New York, 1970).

More recently, Marijke Rudnik-Smalbraak focusses on imagery and themes in *Samuel Richardson: Minute Particulars within the Large Design* (Leiden, 1983), and James Louis Fortuna discusses Richardson's ideas in *'The Unsearchable Wisdom of God'; A Study of Providence in Richardson's 'Pamela'* (Gainsville, 1980). R. F. Brissenden's *Virtue in Distress: Studies in the Novel of Sentiment from Richardson to Sade* (London, 1974), Ian Donaldson's *The Rapes of Lucretia: A Myth and its Transformations* (Oxford, 1982), and Jean H. Hagstrum's *Sex and Sensibility: Ideal and Erotic Love from Milton to Mozart* (Chicago, 1980) show the power of controlling myths and ideologies in Richardson's work; Ruth Perry in *Women, Letters, and the Novel* (New York, 1980) and Katharine Rogers in *Feminism in Eighteenth-Century England* (Illinois, 1982) show how significant women readers and women's issues were to Richardson's novels. In *Women's Friendship in Literature* (New York, 1980), Janet Todd surveys Richardson from a modern feminist point of view. Rita Goldberg meditates upon Clarissa's rape in her *Sex and Enlightenment: Women in Richardson and Diderot*; Carol Houlihan Flynn's *Samuel Richardson: A Man of Letters* (New Jersey, 1982) examines disjunctions between moralist and artist; Christina Marsden Gillis explores spatial design in *The Paradox of Privacy: Epistolary Form in Clarissa* (Gainsville, 1984); William Beatty Warner's *Reading 'Clarissa': The Struggles of Interpretation* (New Haven, 1979) applies Derridean analysis to a wilderness of competing texts; and Terry Castle, in *Clarissa's Ciphers: Meaning and Disruption in Richardson's 'Clarissa'* (Ithaca and London, 1982) perceives a text as much violated as its heroine. *Clarissa* was not, though, quite the virgin territory that Terry Eagleton thought it was in *The Rape of Clarissa: Writing, Sexuality and Class Struggle in Samuel Richardson* (Oxford, 1982), because sex, property and class had already been anatomised in that marvellous novel by Samuel Richardson himself.

Index

INDEX

For EU product safety concerns, contact us at Calle de José Abascal, 56–1°,
28003 Madrid, Spain or eugpsr@cambridge.org.

www.ingramcontent.com/pod-product-compliance
Ingram Content Group UK Ltd.
Pitfield, Milton Keynes, MK11 3LW, UK
UKHW012344130625
459647UK00009B/506

9780521315425